MODERN
LANGUAGE
CLASSROOM
TECHNIQUES
A HANDBOOK

MODERN LANGUAGE CLASSROOM TECHNIQUES
A HANDBOOK

EDWARD DAVID ALLEN
The Ohio State University

REBECCA M. VALETTE
Boston College

HARCOURT BRACE JOVANOVICH, INC.
New York / Chicago / San Francisco / Atlanta

ISBN: 0-15-561820-2

Library of Congress Catalog Number: 72-182321

Printed in the United States of America

PREFACE

The success of a foreign language course depends not only on the quality of the basic program but also on the flexibility with which the teacher uses that program. The aim of this handbook is to show the teacher ways of implementing and supplementing existing materials. The suggested teaching procedures may be used with large classes, small groups, and individual students. They may also be used with any method, inasmuch as a special effort has been made to include a variety of teaching approaches.

The emphasis is on teacher-made materials, although many of the techniques suggested may also be implemented with commercial programs, films, slides, and transparencies.

Part One of the handbook presents an overview of the language class. Ways of preparing supplementary materials are briefly reviewed. A variety of procedures for classroom management is suggested.

Part Two focuses on specific techniques for teaching the language itself, its sound system, its grammar, and its vocabulary. For the sake of simplicity we have used traditional grammar terminology. The actual techniques, however, cover a broad range of methods and approaches. All teachers will be able to discover many ideas for varying their instruction, no matter what their teaching situation or basic materials.

Part Three of the handbook presents ways of developing the skills of listening, speaking, reading, and writing. The aim of these procedures is to build up the student's ability to use the language as a vehicle for meaningful communication.

The final section of the handbook, Part Four, offers some suggestions for teaching culture, both daily life patterns and general civilization.

The Appendix contains sample lesson plans that show how several different procedures and techniques may be woven into a single class period.

This handbook does not treat the preparation of performance objectives and the use of learning contracts to individualize instruction.** However, teachers planning to adopt performance contracts will discover in this handbook many ways of varying classroom activities and of thereby avoiding the main danger of a poorly planned individualized program: student boredom.

In preparing this handbook, the authors have received the encouragement and assistance of a great many people. Special thanks go to Alfred N. Smith, Utah State University, who contributed several valuable techniques to this handbook. As materials were being written the following native speakers gave generously of their time and talents to assure the accuracy of the examples given in foreign languages: Jean-Paul Valette, Werner Haas, Thérèse Bonin, Joe Wipf, Jacob Voelker, and Esteban Egea. We are grateful to Virginia Allen for her inspiring ideas and to Renée S. Disick for her practical suggestions. We should also like to express our appreciation to Lorraine Strasheim, who read the manuscript with a critical eye, and to Albert Richards, our editor.

Finally, we wish to express our thanks to our many students and colleagues throughout the country who, although not mentioned by name, have helped us in the formulation of our ideas and to whom this handbook is gratefully dedicated.

E. D. A.
R. M. V.

** For suggestions in these areas see Rebecca M. Valette and Renée S. Disick, *Modern Language Performance Objectives and Individualization: A Handbook* (New York: Harcourt Brace Jovanovich Inc., 1972).

CONTENTS

PREFACE   v

PART ONE   THE LANGUAGE CLASS—AN OVERVIEW

ONE   THE TEACHER AND THE COURSE   3

1. The teacher   3
2. Scheduling   6
3. Team teaching   8
4. Individualized instruction   9
5. The basic program and supplementary materials   11

TWO   PREPARING SUPPLEMENTARY MATERIALS   12

1. Dittoes   12
2. Posters and charts   13
3. Cue cards   13
4. Transparencies for the overhead projector   13
5. Flannel board   15
6. Magnetic board   15
7. Pocket charts   16
8. Hints for nonartists   16
9. Making recordings   16
10. Audio-visual equipment   17

THREE IN THE CLASSROOM 19

1. Lesson planning 19
2. Individual and group instruction 22
3. Recorded speech 26
4. Music and games 31
5. Homework 32
6. Testing 36
7. Classroom management 38

PART TWO PRESENTING THE LANGUAGE

FOUR TEACHING THE SOUND SYSTEM 43

1. General considerations 44
2. Initial presentation 44
3. Developing listening discrimination 51
4. Pronunciation practice 53
5. Sound-symbol correspondences 55
6. Remedial work 60

FIVE TEACHING GRAMMAR: GENERAL PROCEDURES 64

1. General considerations 65
2. Supplementing the textbook 65
3. Presenting rules: a deductive approach 68
4. Presenting rules: an inductive approach 73
5. Pattern drills 80
6. Question-answer techniques 84
7. Written exercises 86
8. Remedial work 88

SIX TEACHING GRAMMAR: TECHNIQUES ARRANGED BY GRAMMATICAL CATEGORIES 90

1. Noun phrases 90
2. Verb forms 96
3. Complements 101
4. Basic sentence patterns 107

SEVEN TEACHING VOCABULARY 113

1. General considerations 114
2. Techniques of presentation 114
3. Improving students' retention 118
4. Cognates 121
5. Vocabulary building 126
6. Problem areas 131

PART THREE   DEVELOPING THE SKILLS

EIGHT   LISTENING COMPREHENSION   137

1. General considerations   137
2. Understanding individual words   138
3. Identifying and understanding sentences   140
4. Hearing structure signals   146
5. Listening to unfamiliar material   149
6. Understanding short oral passages   151
7. Understanding colloquial speech   156

NINE   SPEAKING   160

1. General considerations   160
2. Initial presentation: dialogue technique   161
3. Initial presentation: separate sentences   168
4. Practicing sentence patterns   172
5. Guided conversation   177
6. Free conversation   183

TEN   READING   189

1. General comprehension   189
2. Initial steps   190
3. Guided reading techniques   194
4. Reading longer selections   202
5. Literature in the classroom   207

ELEVEN   WRITING   216

1. General considerations   217
2. Copying   217
3. Writing from dictation   223
4. Practicing sentence patterns   227
5. Guided composition   232
6. Writing letters   236
7. Free composition   238

PART FOUR   BEYOND LANGUAGE

TWELVE   TEACHING CULTURE   245

1. General considerations   245
2. Evidence of the foreign culture to be found in
   the United States   246
3. Learning about the foreign culture   250
4. Analyzing and understanding the foreign culture   263
5. Contacting representatives of the foreign culture   269
6. Travel abroad   270

APPENDIX: SAMPLE LESSON PLANS   275
   INDEX   303

PART ONE
THE LANGUAGE
CLASS—
AN OVERVIEW

CHAPTER ONE
THE TEACHER
AND THE COURSE

The success or failure of a foreign language course may be evaluated by the progress of the students in language acquisition and cultural understanding and in the development of a positive attitude toward foreign language learning. One simple, direct measure is provided by enrollment figures: What percentage of students are continuing with language study? The students themselves, with their aptitudes and their weaknesses, form the given or the point of departure for the evaluation. The key question is, Did the course succeed or fail with respect to the students enrolled in it? and not, Would the course have been more successful had more able students been enrolled?

The success of a course depends on several factors, the most important of which is the teacher. The scheduling of classes, the outward form of the instruction, and the basic program being used are of secondary importance.

1.1   THE TEACHER

The teacher is the key figure in the language course. He alone sets the tone for the learning activities. If he is using a classical audio-lingual approach, he is an orchestra leader directing the apprentices in his charge. If he is using a highly programmed approach, he may simply survey student activity and answer occasional questions. In either of these cases, as well as in the classroom situations falling between these two extremes, the teacher plays a prime role in effecting his students' progress or lack thereof.

1.1.1 *The Teacher's Language Proficiency*

It is, of course, desirable that all language teachers be fluent speakers of the language they are teaching. At the same time, however, it is evident that the great majority of language teachers whose native language is English do not possess near-native fluency in the second language.

The professional teacher continually strives to improve his competence in the second language. He tries to get abroad at least once every five years, perhaps taking advantage of the low-cost charter flights of the professional organizations (such as MLA, ACTFL, the AATs). He tries to get to foreign films, possibly seeing them two or three times, once for entertainment and subsequently as a means of increasing his audio-lingual skills. He subscribes to at least one foreign periodical to keep abreast of current developments in the country whose language he is teaching. If possible, he listens regularly to radio broadcasts in the foreign language, on shortwave or (in many parts of the country) on local stations. He may even invite (and pay) a willing native speaker residing in his community to visit his language classes from time to time to note any mistakes he makes.

Yet, how effective can the native American hope to be as a foreign language teacher? The answer is that he may be highly effective.

First, his own continuing role as a student of the language he is teaching is sensed by his students. They will respond warmly to a person who doesn't pretend to "know it all," but who is truly committed to the learning process.

Second, a recent study has failed to find any definite correlation between teacher language proficiency and student language achievement at the elementary levels.[1] Although there may be many explanations for this lack of significant correlation, it seems plausible that a dynamic language teacher of average-to-low language proficiency who uses tape recordings and a variety of techniques in the classroom might well be more effective than the very fluent teacher who is less responsive to the needs of the students and lacks imagination in his teaching methods.

Although techniques in themselves cannot compensate for very poor language proficiency, they definitely enhance the effectiveness of the teacher in the classroom.

[1] See Philip D. Smith, Jr., *A Comparison of the Cognitive and Audiolingual Approaches to Foreign Language Instruction: the Pennsylvania Foreign Language Project* (Philadelphia: Center for Curriculum Development, 1970).

1.1.2 *Attitude of the Teacher*

The attitude of the teacher also influences a student's success. A study among elementary-school students seems to indicate that a teacher's expectancies are self-fulfilling.[1] In other words, if a teacher assumes that half of his class is incapable of mastering the German /y/, then many of his students will never learn the sound. If another teacher is confident that all of his students can produce the /y/, they all eventually find they can say it. If the teacher feels that modern languages are just for the bright student and that the slower ones will be unable to keep up, then many of his students will drop out at the end of the semester or the end of the year. *you won't have a job*

A positive attitude on the part of the teacher is essential to success. The many techniques suggested in this handbook will work only if the teacher himself is convinced that his students are capable of learning another language.

1.1.3 *Teaching for Mastery*

The pace of the class may be governed by three things, either singly or in combination: the book or program, the syllabus, and the ability of the students. For some teachers the book is the decisive factor: the First-Year Book, as the title indicates, must be covered in one year, no more, no less. In some school systems teachers are expected to adhere rigidly to a prescribed syllabus, which again makes no allowances for individual differences among classes and students.

Ideally, the pace of a language class, particularly at the beginning and intermediate levels, should be determined by the rate at which the students master the material. High attrition rates in foreign languages are an indication that most classes are paced too fast for the average student. Teaching for mastery means organizing instruction so that all students are given the opportunity to learn what is being taught. *give all opportunities*

Teaching for mastery also implies the creative use of a variety of teaching procedures. Since different students learn in different ways, the introduction of a new technique frequently helps a student overcome a learning problem. If a teacher expects his entire class to master the usage of the subjunctive, then he must utilize techniques to help the eye-minded as well as the ear-minded students, to help those who need explanation as well as those who learn best by developing their own generalizations, and to help those who are hesitant to express themselves and thus run the risk of looking foolish as well as those who are eager to try to express themselves and are unmindful of errors.

---

[1] See Robert Rosenthal and Lenore F. Jacobsen, *Pygmalion in the Classroom* (New York: Holt, Rinehart and Winston, Inc., 1968).

1.2 SCHEDULING

School schedules determine the basic arrangement of teaching time. However, no matter which of the following systems is being applied at a particular school, the actual foreign language class is ultimately as flexible or as rigid as the teacher makes it.[1]

1.2.1 *Setting up Time Blocks*

1.2.1a TRADITIONAL SCHEDULING

The day is broken up into periods of forty or fifty minutes in length. Each class meets a certain number of periods a week (usually five) in the same classroom with the same teacher. Sometimes one or two half-hour periods per week are scheduled in a language laboratory.

The teacher may treat the period as one long period for full-class activity, or he may alternate full-class activity with small-group work or individualized instruction. While he may cut the period up into smaller time segments, however, he can rarely arrange for activities lasting more than one period.

1.2.1b MODULAR SCHEDULING

The day is divided into modular units or "mods" of twenty minutes each. A French class, for example, might meet for two consecutive mods on Monday, three consecutive mods on Tuesday, two mods on Wednesday, one at 8:30 and the other at 2:30, not at all on Thursday, and two consecutive mods on Friday. Small-group activities, such as a conversation group or several interest groups, could meet during a single mod period. A film might be shown during the longer Tuesday class.

Unfortunately, it has happened that schools have adopted modular scheduling but that the teachers have failed to differentiate among the time combinations available to them. In other words, teachers have not adapted their techniques to the flexibility offered by the varied class periods.

1.2.1c FLEXIBLE SCHEDULING

Under flexible scheduling, time blocks can be moved as well as increased. For example, on Monday of the first week the German class might have a time block or mod of twenty minutes at 8:30. On Monday of the second week, this same class might meet for three mods at 1:00.

---

[1] For a more complete treatment of this subject, see Jermaine D. Arendt, *New Scheduling Patterns and the Foreign Language Teacher*, ERIC Focus Report No. 18 (1970). Available from MLA/ACTFL Materials Center, 62 Fifth Avenue, New York, N.Y. 10011, for twenty-five cents.

Flexible scheduling allows the teacher to request specific time arrangements to coincide with the week's lesson plan. A long time sequence could be requested, for example, to show a full-length foreign language film. However, since such a system calls for a complex computer program and considerable advance planning on the part of each teacher, the flexible scheduling arrangement often degenerates into the modular scheduling described in the previous section. An effective flexible scheduling arrangement does, however, make it possible to offer a greater variety of learning activities than the straight modular system does.

1.2.1d OPEN SCHEDULING

Open scheduling allows each student to plan his day's activities. This system cannot be implemented unless all courses are fully programmed with special sets of material for every level. The Spanish IV student, for example, can decide at what time he wishes to take Spanish and then go to the appropriate carrel, laboratory booth, or working table.

1.2.2   Back-to-Back Scheduling

With any of the time arrangements mentioned, it is possible to schedule classes *back-to-back*, that is, at the same time. Back-to-back scheduling can contribute to the increase of flexibility in several ways.

1.2.2a TRACKS OR STREAMS

If a school offers two or more tracks of a given language course, such as Spanish I, it is advisable to schedule these tracks at the same hour. Then if a student in the faster track or stream falls behind for any reason, he may be transferred to the slower track without any shift in his schedule. Similarly, if a student in the slower track begins to spurt ahead of the others, he may be transferred into the faster track.[1]

1.2.2b BETWEEN-CLASS EXCHANGES: SAME LEVEL

Back-to-back scheduling facilitates between-class exchanges. (The informal grouping of two or more classes is called informal team teaching. See section 1.3.) One first-year class may prepare a skit for another first-year class. Then for part of a period on the day chosen the two classes can be merged without raising any scheduling problems. Exchanges can be more frequent than this. For example, if both classes are progressing at similar rates, both might use the same set of tests. As a follow-through, one teacher might take those students from both classes who passed the test into one classroom while the other teacher would meet with the rest, who needed remedial work,

[1] See Michael Hernick and Dora Kennedy, "Multi-level Grouping of Students in the Modern Foreign Language Program," in *Foreign Language Annals*, Vol. 2, No. 2 (December 1968), pp. 200–204.

in the other classroom. The extent and variety of this between-class cooperation is limited only by the imagination of the cooperating teachers.

1.2.2c BETWEEN-CLASS EXCHANGES: DIFFERENT LEVELS

Classes of different levels may also benefit from back-to-back scheduling.
The faster students of the upper class might be excused at certain times to
help tutor students or guide small group conversation or pattern drill practice
in the lower class. Students in the upper class who have consistent difficulty
with a confusing point of vocabulary or grammar might prepare a presentation on this problem area and give it at the appropriate time in the lower
class. The teacher of the upper class might even wish to send those students
who, for example, are unsure of the partitive to the lower class on the day
that teacher is presenting the partitive to his students. The lower class, on the
other hand, might prepare short skits or dialogues for the upper class.

1.2.2d DOUBLE REGISTRATION

Double registration allows the gifted student to advance more rapidly than
his classmates without requiring additional time from the teacher. If Spanish II
and French I are offered at the same time, a gifted Spanish II student might
attend Spanish class three times a week and French class twice a week. Such
a student would do the work and receive credit for both courses.

1.3 TEAM TEACHING

In formal team teaching, two or more persons work with the same group of
students and share the responsibilities. The classroom teacher may also work
with the assistance of a student teacher, a teacher aide, or a native intern.[1]
Members of a department may work together in preparing course materials.

Each foreign language teacher or teacher aide has his own special contribution to make to the program. The beginning teacher can learn much from an
experienced and highly trained colleague. The older teacher can profit from
some of the new ideas brought in by the beginner.

1.3.1 *Three Classes and Three Teachers*

When three similar classes are scheduled back-to-back, the three teachers can
teach the combined classes as a team. This method is particularly effective if
one of the classrooms is large enough to hold fifty or sixty students. For
example, let us assume that three Spanish II classes of twenty-five students

---

[1] An intern is usually a salaried, beginning teacher who holds a bachelor's degree and is
in a supervised teacher-training program in order to earn certification.

each are scheduled at the same hour. On one or two days a week, fifty of the students meet in the large room with one of the teachers to view a film strip or see a grammar demonstration. At the same time, ten students are practicing conversation with the second teacher in the second classroom, while fifteen students are doing remedial work with the third teacher, whose talents are especially suited to this activity. It is also possible to have students in the larger group work independently. The smaller groups may be used for conversation practice, discussions, or even oral testing.

Since the grouping changes frequently, team teaching allows teachers to vary techniques and approaches to meet the needs of the students. Class size may be varied at will. Such a system does, however, require considerable planning on the part of the teachers concerned. It is most easily introduced in a programmed or partially programmed course.

1.3.2 *Grouping within One Class*

Frequently the teacher may receive assistance in teaching a single class. A student teacher may be working with one group of students in one part of the room while the head teacher is working with a second group. A teacher aide may be administering a speaking test to a third group of students in the language laboratory. In such cases the head teacher plans the lesson in consultation with his helpers.

1.3.3 *Informal Cooperation*

Teachers within a department can pool their resources on an informal level. A native speaker in a department may review his colleagues' recombined reading materials, correct stylistic errors, and record supplementary listening exercises. In exchange, the American teachers might prepare visuals or type Ditto masters which they would share with the native speaker. A teacher who has developed a cultural unit with slides and a work sheet for one class might be willing to present the same unit to a colleague's class. The teacher of an intermediate class might let a group of students rehearse an elementary dialogue and present it to a beginning class. The teacher who has been abroad might have brochures and realia to share with those who have not.

By pooling and exchanging talents, materials, and ideas, a foreign language department can develop a strong, articulated program.

1.4 INDIVIDUALIZED INSTRUCTION

In some schools foreign language instruction has been individualized. Individual pacing plans allow each student to progress through the prescribed material at his own rate. Individual instructional plans allow different students to engage in different kinds of activities. In both cases, however, some provision is made for whole-class or group activities. Not only does group work provide communication practice in the language, but the students themselves benefit psychologically from it.

1.4.1 *Programmed Material*

Programmed material makes use of some sort of "teaching machine." This may be simply a book with a grid which covers the correct responses for each frame, or a book plus tape, or a complex piece of hardware with audiostimulus and looping or branching facilities. Programmed materials are most suited for the teaching of reading and writing, grammar, and vocabulary. Programs in phonetics are also available. Communication and self-expression, however, require at least two people.

Students may work on programmed materials in large rooms with little supervision. Teachers are free to meet with small groups of students to practice language skills. Students who work through the program more quickly than others may be assigned special projects according to interest groups: developing a skit, preparing a display, reading sports magazines in the foreign language, and so on.

1.4.2 *Individual Student Contracts*

A *student contract* is a printed statement which describes a certain desired student behavior (an example for French: rewrite a given paragraph in the past tense, using the imperfect and the *passé composé* as appropriate), suggests activities the student may engage in to prepare himself for this behavior (presentations, exercises), and presents a sample test. When the student feels prepared, he takes a test covering the behavior. If he fails it, he is assigned additional activities to prepare him to take it again. One lesson may be divided into several contracts. In the above example previous contracts might have had the student review the forms of the imperfect, review the forms of the *passé composé*, and review how to distinguish between specific events and states of being or existing conditions. Other contracts might stress the oral production of these forms, making use of recorded materials and necessitating a spoken test.

Although the preparation of student contracts, learning packets, and tests to accompany the basic program requires a substantial investment of a teacher's time, those who have experimented with this type of teaching technique are enthusiastic. If the school is equipped with a media center, such a system may be readily implemented, but it is quite possible to use student contracts in a conventional classroom by rearranging desks to allow for different types of activities.[1]

---

[1] Sample teacher-made contracts are to be found in Rebecca M. Valette and Renée S. Disick, *Modern Language Performance Objectives and Individualization: A Handbook* (New York: Harcourt Brace Jovanovich, Inc., 1972).

1.5 THE BASIC PROGRAM AND SUPPLEMENTARY MATERIALS

Although teachers generally have a say in the selection of materials, a teacher, especially a new teacher, sometimes finds himself in the position of being handed a program and told to teach it. For this teacher, the program defines the course. The grammar and the vocabulary content of the lessons and their sequencing will determine the content and the sequencing of the teacher's lessons, unless he plans to write his own text via the Ditto machine.

The manner in which the content is presented to the students, however, is left to the determination of the teacher. It is possible to take an out-of-print traditional book of the 1930's and with the aid of homemade visuals teach a course stressing conversation and an inductive approach to grammar. It is possible to take an audio-lingual textbook, teach the vocabulary and sentence patterns first, and reserve the dialogue itself for comprehension practice at the end of the lesson. It is possible to take a review grammar and prepare individual learning packets so that students can work at their own pace. In other words, through a judicious choice of techniques and classroom procedures, the creative teacher can go beyond the structure of the assigned program.

Supplementary materials are usually available in all schools, even though they are sometimes difficult to find. Old readers may furnish selections which may be mimeographed or put on transparencies. Tapes from a previous textbook series, now no longer used, may provide additional material for listening comprehension. Old workbooks may have suitable grammar exercises for review work. Wall charts and maps can be used for speaking and writing cues. Preview materials from publishers might have new ideas for presentations of vocabulary and structure. Unused foreign language magazines may be cut up for visuals. Short English films, especially films taken in the country under study, could be shown, replacing the English sound track with the teacher's narration in the foreign language.

Effective teaching does not mean waiting for the ideal materials to be made available. It means investigating materials presently available and using them to their fullest extent.

CHAPTER TWO
PREPARING
SUPPLEMENTARY
MATERIALS

Many of the teaching techniques described in the latter part of this handbook utilize supplementary materials which have been prepared by the teacher. These materials, visual aids for the most part, can usually be made very rapidly. This chapter gives brief guidelines for the construction of various types of materials and the use of standard classroom teaching equipment.

2.1   DITTOS

The most widely used supplementary materials in foreign language teaching are undoubtedly sheets prepared on a spirit duplicating machine such as the Ditto.

Masters may be prepared with a typewriter, ball-point pen, or pencil. Errors are easily corrected by scraping the back of the master sheet and then writing in the new form. Clear corrections may be obtained by shifting the top sheet so that an unused portion of the purple backing sheet is directly below the space where the correction is being entered.

The master may also be prepared through a photostatic process using a Thermofax or similar machine and a typed or printed master. For example, the teacher might wish to have the entire class read a German newspaper article. He would cut out the article, edit it if necessary, perhaps type a few questions, and make a Xerox copy of the new page. The Xerox print would be used to prepare a Ditto master which would in turn provide copies for the entire class. If the materials to be used are copyrighted, the teacher should first request written permission from the publisher.

2.2   POSTERS AND CHARTS

Posters and charts are usually made of tag board, available from any arts and crafts supply store. This heavy cardboard can be supported on the ledge of the chalkboard or propped on a desk. It comes in a variety of bright colors.

Lines should be broad enough and words large enough to be easily visible from the back of the room. The indelible felt marker, such as the Magic Marker, is the best writing tool available. The darker colors are the most visible.

2.3   CUE CARDS

use color coding too

Cue cards can be used by both the teacher and the students. They range in size from 3×5 to $8\frac{1}{2} \times 11$—occasionally somewhat larger.

Ordinary 3×5 index cards may be used for single digit numbers and simple line drawings. The 4×6 are more suitable for longer numbers or words. Larger cards, perhaps of heavyweight construction paper or manila paper, may be used to mount magazine pictures.

Again, the teacher must be sure that the cards are easily visible from the back of the room. Letters and digits must be large and legible. Felt pens are the most convenient writing tools.

Cue cards which are to be distributed to the students should be marked on both sides. For example, the teacher may have distributed index cards with letters symbolizing Spanish cities (M—Madrid, T—Toledo, B—Barcelona, and so on). He might ask Joe in Spanish to hold up his card and then ask another student to tell where Joe lives. All students should be able to read the letter on the card.

2.4   TRANSPARENCIES FOR THE OVERHEAD PROJECTOR

Overhead transparencies are thin acetate sheets which can be bought at most school supply stores for approximately five cents apiece.[1]

---

[1] See also James J. Wrenn, *The Overhead Projector*, ERIC Focus Report No. 19 (1970). Available from MLA/ACTFL Materials Center, 62 Fifth Avenue, New York, N.Y. 10011, for twenty-five cents.

2.4.1 *Making Transparencies*

To write or draw pictures on a transparency you may use a grease pencil or, better yet, a water-soluble Vis-a-Vis pencil (broad or narrow tip). The narrow tip is more appropriate for writing. You can erase the transparencies with a paper tissue and reuse them as often as desired.

If you plan to use transparencies more than once, it is wise to use indelible felt pens. The colors show up brightly on the screen and do not fade with age. Cardboard frames, while not necessary, make the transparencies easier to handle and more convenient to file. These cost approximately ten cents apiece.

Transparencies may also be made from a written or printed master using a Thermofax or other duplicating machine. It is essential that the master be on white (or light colored) paper and that the black lines contain carbon. This means that you can use a dark lead pencil, india ink, a typewriter, or a Xerox copy, but you cannot use a ball-point pen or a purple Ditto sheet. If a typewriter is used, it is advisable to use primer (large) or pica type; elite type is very hard to read, even in a small classroom.

2.4.2 *Using Transparencies in the Classroom*

The overhead projector is a versatile machine which lends itself to a variety of presentations.

2.4.2a THE OVERHEAD AS A CHALKBOARD

It is possible to write directly on the transparency over a lighted projector. The overhead has an advantage over the chalkboard in that the teacher maintains eye contact with the students while writing. A typed quiz may be made into a transparency. When the class is finished, the teacher may fill in the blanks or indicate the correct answers with a grease pencil. He may use the transparency again with a subsequent class after having wiped off the correct answers. (The typed questions are permanent and will not be erased.)

2.4.2b THE OVERHEAD AS A POSTER

A drawing on the overhead may be used as a large poster. Instead of using a pointer, the teacher points to appropriate symbols or pictures with a pencil or a long, thin stick (such as a long Tinker Toy stick sharpened in a pencil sharpener). Here again the teacher can maintain eye contact with the students while cuing their responses with the overhead.

2.4.2c MASKING TECHNIQUE

A sheet of ordinary paper may be used to mask any part of the transparency. The teacher, however, can still read what is under the paper. For example, he might first expose a question, keeping the answer covered, and then slide down the mask to reveal the answer. In a two-column presentation, the right-hand column might be covered until the students have first read the left-hand column.

2.4.2d OVERLAY TECHNIQUE

Since acetate is transparent, it is possible to place two or more sheets on top of each other, building more complex drawings or sentences. It is conversely possible to begin with several sheets and remove them one by one to arrive at a simpler drawing or sentence.

For example, the basic transparency might have a table set for dinner with four chairs. The first overlay would put two people in the chairs and food on the table. The next overlay would add two guests. If the negative pattern in French were being presented, the basic transparency might have several sentences in the present tense, with the words appropriately spaced so that the overlay would contain the *ne* or *n'* and *pas* so that they would appear before and after the verb.

2.4.2e PUZZLE TECHNIQUE

Acetate transparencies may be cut into smaller pieces. It is possible in this way to shift words or phrases. In teaching word order in German, for example, you might prepare pieces which read as follows: *Ich weiß, daß / er / hat / Geld / sie / ist / nett.* First you would arrange on the overhead *er hat Geld.* Ask the students to identify the verb, and circle *hat*, using a grease pencil. Then put *Ich weiß, daß* at the front of the sentence and move the verb to the end. After removing that sentence, you would put *sie ist nett* on the overhead. Have students find the verb. Add the piece *Ich weiß, daß* and ask students where *ist* will go.

2.5 FLANNEL BOARD

The teacher can make an inexpensive flannel board by getting a piece of plywood, heavy cardboard, or artist's canvas and tacking or taping a piece of dark flannel to it. Pictures or cutouts can be displayed on the flannel board if you glue a small piece of flocking paper, sandpaper, or flannel to the back of the picture or cutout. Cutouts may also be made out of Pellon (a material used in sewing, available in any yard goods department) or from desk blotters. Words may be written on the Pellon or the blotters with felt pens.

2.6 MAGNETIC BOARD

Many of the newer chalkboards are magnetized and can be used as magnetic boards. Commercial magnetic boards are also available. One can be made by cutting a piece of light-weight sheet metal to a size of 24″ × 24″. Masking tape can be used to bind the sharp edges. The shop teacher may be able to help you with this project.

Magazine pictures and light-weight cue cards are held to the board by magnets. The order of the pictures or cards can easily be varied.

2.7 POCKET CHARTS

Pocket charts are available commercially; most elementary classrooms will have one. A pocket chart may be made very simply by taping the bottom and side edges of four or five narrow strips of oaktag to a larger sheet of oaktag which has been mounted on heavy cardboard or tacked to a bulletin board. These strips form pockets in which flash cards, cue cards, or pictures can be inserted.

2.8 HINTS FOR NONARTISTS

The teacher need not be an artist to make visuals. Simple line drawings are often even more effective than detailed sketches, because the main function of the drawing is to elicit speech, not to distract the eye.

Students remember symbols very easily, once their significance has been explained in English. The teacher might say that an inverted V represents a roof. Then he could quickly designate the following buildings:

church school bank train station bakery

The students may help generate simple drawings to cue vocabulary items.

Sometimes students themselves are willing to make posters and other visuals. Perhaps a lettering class in art could be persuaded, with the consent of the teacher, to prepare charts of grammar generalizations. Perhaps a colleague in another department likes making posters or charts; in exchange for his efforts the language teacher would render him another service. Any teacher who has an idea for an effective visual can usually get help in executing it.

2.9 MAKING RECORDINGS

Commercial recordings accompany almost all of the available foreign language programs. At some point, however, the teacher usually finds it desirable to prepare supplementary recordings.

2.9.1 *Editing Available Materials*

Often the available recordings do not completely meet the needs of the class. By using two tape recorders, or a record player and a tape recorder, the teacher can edit an appropriate lesson tape for the language laboratory or classroom. He may wish, for example, to use two review exercises from a previous lesson and three exercises of the current lesson. He may even want the students to go through one of the exercises twice. On a new tape the teacher duplicates the commercial recordings in the desired sequence. Using a microphone, he may add his own instructions between exercises.

2.9.2 *Bringing Radio Broadcasts to the Classroom*

In most parts of the country it is possible to receive foreign language radio broadcasts. Some of these originate in the larger cities or in regions where there are strong ethnic minorities. Others originate in Canada and Mexico. Some are especially prepared for language students and are broadcast on FM stations at regular times. The widest selection of broadcasts is available on short wave, which may be heard most clearly at night.

If the teacher has a tape recorder or a cassette recorder, he can tape these broadcasts and bring them into the classroom. Even beginning German students who are aware of the current news headlines will be able to grasp parts of the previous night's newscast transmitted from Cologne via short wave.[1]

2.9.3 *Recording Tests and Homemade Exercises*

If the teacher plans to record original materials, several steps must be followed.

A script must be prepared in advance. If the teacher does not possess native fluency, it is advisable to have a colleague read over the script and make necessary changes. If the script is a multiple-choice listening test, a colleague should read each item to look for possible ambiguities of interpretation.

Ample time must be allowed for the recording session; it usually takes two and a half to three hours to record an hour of tape. If two voices are required, as in a rejoinder-type item or exercise, the teacher should invite a colleague, or an available native informant, to assist in the recording. The making of a recording usually takes longer than one anticipates. Moreover, it is advisable to listen to the entire recording at the end of the session so that, if necessary, parts can be rerecorded at once.

2.10 AUDIO-VISUAL EQUIPMENT

Most schools have a variety of audio-visual equipment, which they encourage their teachers to use.

---

[1] See also Robert J. Nelson, *Using Radio to Develop and Maintain Competence in a Foreign Language*, ERIC Focus Report No. 11 (1969). Available from MLA/ACTFL Materials Center, 62 Fifth Avenue, New York, N.Y. 10011, for twenty-five cents.

2.10.1 *Scheduling Audio-Visual Equipment*

Although some language departments have their own audio-visual equipment, in many schools it is necessary to schedule the use of the equipment in advance. Sometimes the red tape seems interminable, but the persistent teacher soon discovers how to obtain the equipment he wishes to use with his classes. If a teacher uses a piece of equipment several times a week, or every day, most schools eventually allow that piece of equipment to remain in his classroom.

2.10.2 *Preparing to Meet Problems*

Sometimes the carefully scheduled piece of equipment arrives on time but then cannot be used because some component was not delivered. If the classroom has two-prong outlets, and most of the school's equipment has three-prong plugs, then it is wise to keep a three-prong adapter in the desk. If the classroom has an electrical outlet only at the back of the room and the teacher likes to have the overhead projector at the front of the room, then it is wise for him to have his own extension cord. If the tape recorder is occasionally delivered without the take-up reel, it is not an expensive matter to have an empty reel on hand. If the projector screen is not delivered, a well-known substitute is a light-colored classroom wall.

2.10.3 *Enlisting the Help of Students*

The teacher who is uncomfortable with complex mechanical equipment can usually find a student who can run the piece of equipment he wishes to use. If the basic program depends on films or film strips, the teacher may let students take turns running the projector. The responsibility of running a machine which the teacher finds complicated often increases the self-confidence of a student who is having difficulty learning the second language. It may also be possible to allow such a student to be excused from study hall to run the projector for another language class. The double exposure to the same lesson might provide the necessary extra practice to help that student improve his language competence.

CHAPTER THREE
IN THE
CLASSROOM

Time is the element most precious to language teachers: much more time than is available in schools is needed to learn a foreign language well. It is estimated that two and a half weeks of living with a French family are the equivalent of one whole year's instruction in a high school French class.

The teacher's primary concern in preparing the lesson and in carrying out class activities is to maximize the amount of learning that takes place, to involve the greatest number of students, and to reduce the amount of time devoted to matters not directly related to the business of acquiring language competence.

3.1 LESSON PLANNING

Careful planning is essential to successful teaching. The teacher must determine the educational aims of the lesson and then select activities that will contribute to the realization of those aims. These activities will vary from class to class according to the needs and abilities of the students concerned.[1]

[1] Sample lesson plans for an elementary, an intermediate, and an advanced class are to be found in the Appendix.

3.1.1   *Setting Lesson Objectives*

Lesson objectives should be stated in terms of student behavior, that is, in terms of what the student will be able to do as a result of instruction. It is for the student, after all, that the teacher has been hired and the basic program selected. It may be the teacher's aim to cover a particular unit by a given date, but the lesson objectives must specify the end result in student behavior: for example, the student will be able to answer yes / no questions using the present tense of the *-re* verbs plus the irregular verbs *prendre* and *mettre*.

3.1.1a   PERFORMANCE OBJECTIVES

Lesson objectives worded in terms of student behavior are called *performance objectives*, or instructional objectives, or behavorial objectives. It is not within the scope of this handbook to describe in detail the preparation and classification of performance objectives.[1]

Briefly, a formal performance objective contains four parts: the purpose of the behavior, the description of the behavior, the conditions under which it is to occur, and the criterion by which it is to be evaluated. A sample item is often included:

(1) Purpose: To demonstrate awareness of number markers in spoken French.

(2) Desired behavior: The student will indicate whether the direct objects (preceded by *le, la, l',* or *les*) in a series of spoken sentences are singular or plural.

(3) Conditions: He will hear fifteen sentences read aloud by the teacher at classroom conversational speed. Each sentence will be read only once.

(4) Criterion: The student must identify at least fourteen sentences of the following type correctly:

> Teacher: Je cherche les livres.
> Student: Plural.

The objective described might be one of several objectives for a particular lesson.

3.1.1b   ANALYZING THE AIMS OF THE LESSON IN TERMS OF PERFORMANCE OBJECTIVES

In determining the performance objectives of a lesson, the teacher must ask himself the following questions: What are the essential features of this

---

[1] For more information see Rebecca M. Valette and Renée S. Disick, *Modern Language Performance Objectives and Individualization: A Handbook* (New York: Harcourt Brace Jovanovich, Inc., 1972).

unit? What must *all* students get out of this unit if they are to continue with the next unit? (The concern here is for *minimum* performance to be required of every student in the class.) The teacher of an audio-lingual program might decide that the aural comprehension of the basic dialogue lines, presented in random order, is absolutely essential and insist that the students be able to select the English equivalents of such recorded sentences with complete accuracy. The teacher of a German class might decide that the students should be able to complete in writing at least nineteen out of twenty sentences with the appropriate form of *haben,* but that he will tolerate ten mistakes on a thirty-item test of vocabulary.

The teacher, in other words, decides in advance which features of the unit he intends to stress in his classes and what degree of proficiency he wants the students to develop with respect to each of those features.

3.1.2 *Planning Lesson Activities*

Once the objectives have been determined, the teacher selects appropriate lesson activities which will help him attain his aims.

The general nature of the activities will be determined by the objectives themselves. If the students are expected to hear the differences between subjunctive and indicative forms of verbs, for instance, the teacher must provide various types of listening practice.

The specific nature of the activities will correspond to the needs of the students and be determined by their age, their background, their interests, and their abilities. To a lesser extent, the physical classroom setup and the length of the class period must be taken into consideration.

3.1.2a INTEREST LEVEL

Young seventh graders might enjoy constructing a Spanish house or making relief maps. Twelfth graders might prefer debating current problems, such as pollution.

All students seem to be interested in developing closer contact with the foreign culture through foreign guest speakers, pen pals, short-wave radio, or films.

3.1.2b VARIETY *at least 5 different activities*

In order to hold the interest of most students it is necessary to provide a large number of varied activities. (The sample lesson plans in the Appendix contain seven activities for a forty-minute class period and nine for one of fifty minutes.) Although the numbers are arbitrary, the teacher should strive for a minimum of five activities per standard class period.

Often the teacher thinks his activities are varied, but in the minds of his students, there is only one activity repeated over and over again. If, for example, the lesson is on the future tense, a varied lesson might illustrate use of the future tense in a demonstration on the overhead projector, a dictation, a game, and a song.

Variety in the use of equipment and materials is also vitally important: for example, one day, the overhead projector might be used; the next day, the felt board; and the following day, the film strip projector. If one medium, such as the film strip projector, is used for all lessons, the class can become very dull.

3.1.2c   TIMING

All activities do not necessarily have to last the same amount of time. In general, intensive drills, such as pattern practice, should be done for only a few minutes at a stretch. Otherwise, the students are likely to become listless and cease to attach any meaning to what they are saying. An activity that requires physical movement, such as "Simon Says" or a physical response exercise, makes time pass quickly. In these cases it is advisable to know when to stop the activity, despite the students' protests to the contrary. It is better to end an activity when interest is high and then introduce it again, perhaps in a varied form at another class meeting, than to let it continue until interest begins to wane.

3.1.3   *Modifying the Lesson Plan in the Classroom*

It is sometimes necessary to abridge the lesson plan in the course of the lesson. Sometimes an activity takes longer than anticipated, or perhaps a fire drill cuts into the available class time. In such cases, it is usually wiser to eliminate one of the subsequent activities altogether than to try to rush through the entire lesson plan.

If an activity fails to interest the class, even though the teacher has spent a great deal of time planning it, it is best to drop it as quickly as possible and try something else. Often lack of interest is a sign that the class is not ready for the activity and that additional preparation is necessary.

3.2   INDIVIDUAL AND GROUP INSTRUCTION

Any classroom with movable furniture lends itself to a variety of instructional groupings ranging from the full class to individualized activities. Even a very large class may with ingenuity be broken down into small groups.

In a classroom where furniture is screwed to the floor, grouping may at first glance seem impossible. However, the combined ingenuity of teacher and students can devise viable solutions, such as having four Spanish conversation groups sit on Mexican blankets in the different corners of the room.

3.2.1   *Whole-Class Instruction*

In whole-class instruction the entire class is engaged in the same activity. Most frequently this activity is led by the teacher, who is giving instructions, modelling sentences, using the overhead, asking questions, leading drill, giving a talk on culture, and so on. The larger the class size, the more difficult it is for the teacher consistently to maintain the interest and participation of all the students.

Certain techniques help improve the effectiveness of whole-class instruction.

3.2.1a   ALTERNATING RESPONSE PATTERNS

In the early stages of a language course much repetition and guided response are necessary. The teacher can maintain an element of newness in the classwork by introducing unpredictable response patterns. Nothing is more boring to students than knowing that the teacher will call on each one individually, row after row. Even if the teacher randomly calls on one student after another, the rhythm may become monotonous; it can be broken by occasionally eliciting a response from the whole class, or a specific row, or only the girls, and so on.

3.2.1b   QUESTIONING TECHNIQUE

In questioning students, or in presenting the stimulus of any type of oral work, the teacher should always give the question or stimulus *before* calling out the name of the student. This way all students mentally prepare the correct response, aware that their turn may come next. If the name is called before the question is asked, many other students stop paying attention.

3.2.1c   MOVING THE CENTER OF VISUAL ATTENTION

A stationary object quickly loses its power to attract attention. The teacher seated at his desk at the front of the room is ineffective as a center of attention. Almost as ineffective is a teacher who remains standing at the front of the room during the entire class hour. The effective teacher must move around the classroom.

Visual and aural aids also contribute to varying the center of attention. The students' eyes go from the teacher to the wall map and pointer, from the teacher to the image on the screen, from the teacher to the flannel board, from the teacher to the tape recorder. Having students come to the front of the room to hold visuals brings additional people into the center of attention. Having students talk about cue cards that their classmates are holding up encourages the students to look around the room.

3.2.1d   SPEAKING UP

In any whole-class instruction it is necessary that all students hear what is being said. Not only must the teacher speak so that all can hear him, but he is responsible for making sure that students speak up clearly. Often a gesture, such as a cupped hand behind the ear, is sufficient to remind a student that he is speaking too softly.

3.2.1e   MAINTAINING THE PACE

The pace of the class should not be allowed to drag. If one student hesitates in responding, the teacher should quickly call on another student and then ask the first student the same question once more. Although students should not feel pressured or rushed, they should learn to respond quickly. A slowing of pace is almost always an indication that the teacher has moved through the material too quickly and that the students have not had the chance to assimilate it.

Transition from one activity to the next should be smooth. The teacher quickly loses the attention of a large class if he allows long moments of silence while he looks for his place in the textbook or shuffles through the material on his desk to uncover the appropriate visual.

3.2.2   *Half-Class Instruction*

The class can be divided in half for debates and contests. Each group prepares for an activity which will later involve the other group. Unless the class is small, however, the half-class groups are often still too large to be assigned projects or conversation practice.

3.2.3   *Ability Grouping*

The typical foreign language class is composed of students who have a wide range of abilities, needs, and interests. This is especially obvious by the time they reach their second year of study. Provision must be made for all students: those who are eager to advance quickly as well as those who enjoy language study, but require a slower pace. Ability grouping, however, can engender negative feelings, especially if one group is consistently identified, even though not in so many words, as the "dumb" group. Often it is advisable to alternate pure ability grouping with other types of grouping. Ability grouping is most workable if students are divided into three sections.

3.2.3a   THREE GROUPS WORKING ON ONE SKILL

The teacher has the entire class prepare a short reading lesson. Group A (the most talented) writes a composition without the teacher's assistance.

Group B (average) answers oral questions asked by the teacher. Group C (less talented) does a written completion exercise and a true / false drill on the reading.

3.2.3b SPECIFIC SKILLS GROUPS

The teacher sets up groups to work on specific skills: listening, speaking, pronunciation, grammar, reading, and writing. A student who reads fluently might have great difficulty with pronunciation, so he joins that special group.

3.2.4 *Interest Groups*

Interest groups are most effectively used with third and fourth level classes. The students have acquired basic linguistic notions and may be encouraged to use the foreign language to develop specific interests. Groups may use foreign periodicals to research topics such as aviation, clothing, politics, or pollution. Groups may also decide to write to foreign businesses for sample products, or to particular localities for travel brochures. Students dramatically inclined might like to prepare a short play. Another group might want to make a home movie with a foreign language sound track. One day a week or part of one day a week might be devoted to such interest-group activities.

3.2.5 *Small Conversation Groups*

At the second or third level most students can express themselves orally on a certain number of topics. In a whole-class conversation that lasts twenty minutes, for example, each student is allowed to talk for less than a minute. If the class is divided into groups of four, then each student can talk for about five minutes. Students quickly become adjusted to the hum of conversation around them.

Small conversation groups need initial guidance. The teacher might appoint a group leader and give him a list of lead questions. More advanced classes might read a controversial article and prepare questions they want to discuss.

The teacher circulates around the classroom, helping those who have trouble getting started, answering queries, and generally assuming the role of silent eavesdropper. The teacher might make note of errors and take them up in a subsequent lesson.

3.2.6 *Working in Pairs*

Even first-year language students can work profitably in pairs, especially on oral drills. If a teacher carries out an intensive drill for five minutes, calling on individual students, each student in a class of thirty will be speaking for only about five seconds, and the teacher will be speaking for two and a half minutes. If the drills plus correct responses are distributed to the students, or if the textbook already has the correct responses, then pairs of students can take turns playing the teacher: one holds the text and reads the cue, and the other answers. The end result is that each student is able to speak for two and a half minutes—almost thirty times as much as he would have in a whole-class drill. Moreover, he has not been able to daydream, as he might have done in the language lab, since he has been actively involved in the entire drill.

It is true that some students will make pronunciation mistakes as they read aloud, but the only way to learn the language is by practicing, and working in pairs does keep students speaking. The alert teacher will catch many of the mistakes as he walks around the classroom and can correct errors later, in private. He is also available to answer questions that students were too embarrassed to ask in front of the whole class.

3.2.7 *Independent Activities*

Independent activities at present usually revolve around the skills of reading and writing. Workbooks obviously lend themselves to independent work. Reading programs may be established to let the student work on his own. Some programmed materials are available in foreign languages. Contract teaching is also designed to let the student advance at his own pace.

The introduction of low-priced cassettes will make possible a greater variety of simultaneous activities in the classroom (see section 1.4.2).

3.2.8 *Mixed Grouping*

Not all students in a classroom must necessarily be engaged in the same type of activity. Half the class might be working on independent activities while the teacher reviews a grammar point with those students who need remedial help. One group may be listening over headsets while the rest of the class is working in pairs.

3.3 RECORDED SPEECH

Over the past fifteen years the use of recorded speech in foreign language instruction has become widespread. Bringing a variety of native voices into the classroom is a feat that can now be accomplished by the teacher in the most remote school district, thanks to the broad availability of commercial tapes and records.

3.3.1 *The Role of the Recording*

Foreign language recordings may fill one of several roles in the instructional program.

3.3.1a TO PROVIDE A MODEL FOR IMITATION

This is one of the original roles of recordings in language instruction. The students imitate the basic sentences and basic dialogues which have been recorded with or without pauses. If the teacher has not himself acquired a near-native accent, the recording allows him to present accurate models to his students in spite of his own personal deficiencies. The recording also lends itself to identical repetitions of material with no change in tone, pitch, or intonation.

3.3.1b TO PROVIDE CUES FOR ORAL DRILL

The advent of pattern drills paralleled the commercialization of tape recorders and language laboratories. The tape cues a drill and after a pause for the student's answer provides him with the appropriate response, thus reinforcing his right answer or allowing him to correct his mistake without delay.

3.3.1c TO PROVIDE SPEECH SAMPLES

The recording allows the teacher to capture a speech sample and bring it to the classroom so that the students may listen to it in a variety of ways. They can hear the entire recording, they can replay sections of it, and they can even replay parts of sentences. The recorded speech samples may be *contrived*, that is, they may be dialogues or readings written to accompany a set of instructional materials and especially recorded at a desired conversational speed. Recorded speech may be simply *controlled*, that is, a specific authentic speech sample, such as an interview broadcast, may be selected for its pedagogical value, edited, and made available to the students.

3.3.1d TO GIVE INSTRUCTIONS

The recorded voice may take the role of the teacher in giving instruction. Pronunciation tapes, for example, frequently not only provide models for imitation and exercises for practice but also tell the student what to listen for in discrimination drills and what factors to take into consideration in producing certain sounds or sound patterns.

3.3.1e TO TEST

Recordings can provide the stimulus for classroom tests. The student may write from taped dictation; he may indicate his comprehension of recorded passages by marking a multiple-choice answer sheet; he may check off boxes on a grid to show his ability to discriminate sounds and structural patterns, or he may respond orally to recorded cues. The consistency of the recording increases the reliability of a test that is to be administered more than once.

3.3.1.f FOR ENJOYMENT

Short recordings may be played simply for the enjoyment of the students. These may take a wide variety of forms: popular songs, student-prepared skits, radio commercials, mystery voices (a recording by a classmate or by a well-known public figure), announcements of language club activities, etc. Such recordings may be used in the classroom at the beginning or end of the hour. They may also be used between exercises on cassettes or laboratory tapes.

3.3.2 *Physical Installations*

Speech recordings may be used in the foreign language classroom, in a special room designed for that purpose, such as a learning center or listening booth in a library, or at home.

3.3.2a THE CLASSROOM

The simplest way to use recordings in the classroom is to play a tape reel, cassette, or record to the entire class. The students listen to the recording and the teacher leads the learning activities.

In an electronic classroom the teacher's desk becomes a console and the students hear the recording via headsets. Generally the teacher is also able to monitor individual students.

Groups of students or individuals may also work with recordings independently of the rest of the class if a program source and headsets are available. The program source may consist of individual cassette players or of a tape recorder or record player to which are connected several headsets.

3.3.2b THE STATIONARY LANGUAGE LABORATORY

Many schools are equipped with language laboratories located in a separate classroom. Classes are generally scheduled for the laboratory in advance, usually for two half-hour periods per week. In the simplest installation, the teacher plays a tape from the console, and all the students listen and respond to it. Although most laboratories were designed so that the teacher could individualize instruction by playing one tape for one group and another tape for another group, in practice the unavailability of appropriate commercial tapes differentiated by ability group within a given lesson and the lack of released time for the local preparation of such tapes have limited the activities of the language laboratory. Its possibilities are seldom fully exploited.

In several school districts schools are installing media centers. These centers generally contain individual learning carrels where students can work with their own cassettes and pace their own instruction.

3.3.2c AT HOME

Record albums accompanying many textbooks allow the student to practice basic sentences and drills at home. In the future the wider availability of cassette recorders will probably allow the teacher to assign homework with cassettes and correlated workbooks.

3.3.3 *The Nature of Student Participation*

For the recording to be effective as a teaching instrument, it must encourage student participation.

3.3.3a STUDENT RESPONSE

Student response to the recording as it is being played may take one of four forms:

(1) No outward response: The students listen but are not required to show any outward evidence of comprehension as the recording is being played. Perhaps the students will later be required to summarize or answer questions about what they have heard.

(2) Oral response: The students listen and speak. They may either be imitating the model on the tape or responding to instructions or cues.

(3) Written response: The students listen and indicate a response in writing, which may take the form of words (as in a dictation), symbols (as in a multiple-choice exercise), or drawing (as in an assignment that requires completing a scene or tracing an itinerary on a map).

(4) Physical response: The students may go through motions suggested on the tape. In the language laboratory this might consist of opening a workbook to the proper page. In a classroom this might include total physical response, such as standing, walking, or making an appropriate gesture.

3.3.3b VISUAL SUPPORT

Some recordings have no visual support whatever. The student is expected to put away books, pencils, paper, and simply concentrate on what he hears. This type of listening activity works well with the ear-minded student but often is less effective with the eye-minded student.

In the classroom or language laboratory visual support may be provided by the teacher in the form of a projection of pictures or diagrams using the overhead or slides. The visuals serve to reinforce the meaning of what is being said over the tape.

The textbook, workbook, or a printed Ditto sheet may be used to provide visual support in the form of words. Many students at first like to read what they hear and say, and then allow themselves to be weaned away from the support.

3.3.3c DEGREE OF STUDENT CONTROL

The use of the recordings is controlled either by the teacher or by the student. In using a broadcast, where the tape is played from the console or in the classroom, the teacher controls what is being listened to. Even if the students record their voices for fifteen minutes and then listen to their recordings for the second fifteen minutes, the teacher alone is controlling the pace of instruction. However, if the students can stop their own recordings and listen to parts over again, they are participating in the control of the lesson.

Students exercise the highest degree of control when they pace themselves. This can be done with a language laboratory run on the library system (usually unavailable in the secondary schools), or in the classroom with either a tape recorder and earphone jacks (with students running the controls), or with cassettes and cassette players. Homework discs also allow students to control their pace.

3.3.3d INCREASING THE EFFECTIVENESS OF THE LANGUAGE LABORATORY

Much of the negative feeling about the language laboratory can be traced to three sources: the lack of student participation, the absence of visual support for those who need it, and the rigidity of the teacher's control of laboratory activities.

The laboratory can become effective only if the students are actively involved in the scheduled activity. Otherwise students tend to fall asleep, respond unthinkingly, pass notes to their neighbors, or fiddle with the equipment.

The best solution is to use only tape programs which are correlated with lively workbooks. The alternate solution is to develop homemade visuals to use with recorded drills and exercises. For example, the teacher may be at the front of the laboratory with an overhead projector and screen visible to all the students. If a drill calls for pronoun substitution, he will use a transparency containing drawings for each pronoun (see section 6.3.1). As the cue is spoken on the tape, he will point to the appropriate symbol. Although he cannot hear the students' responses, he can watch their eye and mouth movements and check on their performance indirectly.

If the school has a language laboratory which cannot be scheduled on the library system, either because only broadcast equipment is available or because there is a lack of funds and personnel, then the students will have to realize that for two half-hours a week they cannot be given the opportunity to pace their own learning. However, if the language laboratory sessions have become somewhat more meaningful, and if opportunity for students to direct learning activities is provided in the classroom, then lab periods will nevertheless begin to make a positive contribution to foreign language learning.

3.4 MUSIC AND GAMES

Music and games offer a pleasant change of pace in the lesson. They should be selected primarily for their educational value, however, not as mere distractions or moments of relaxation.

3.4.1 *Selecting Songs*

Songs should be selected so that their lyrics reinforce a point of grammar or pronunciation. For example, the song *"Mein Hut, der hat drei Ecken"* might be used to illustrate the normal verb-second word order of German. *"Alouette"* helps the students to remember to use the definite article with parts of the body. Hit tunes may be used as well as folk songs, as long as the lyrics are appropriate to the linguistic level of the class. Certain songs such as Christmas carols and national anthems may be introduced primarily for their cultural content.

3.4.2 *Music in the Classroom*

If the teacher is musically inclined and likes to sing, he will have no qualms about leading his students in song. If in addition he plays the guitar, his problem will be rather one of refusing to let his students sing every period.

If the teacher cannot carry a tune, then there are two alternate ways of letting his class sing. Perhaps a student plays the guitar or the ukelele and would be willing to learn new songs to present them to the class. Records offer another possibility. The students can sing along with the recorded song. Moreover, there are programmed albums, often used in the elementary schools, and perhaps available from the school music department, which contain a variety of foreign as well as English songs.[1] First the students hear the entire song sung in the foreign language. Then they hear the first line, followed by the musical accompaniment of the same line, so that they can repeat the line. Then they hear the second line followed by the melody of that line, and so on. At the end of the recording they have the opportunity to sing the song in its entirety.[2]

3.4.3 *Playing Games*

Games should also be selected so that the activity contributes to furthering the linguistic aims of the lesson. Many games are suggested throughout the handbook.[3]

[1] *Exploring Music* (New York: Holt, Rinehart and Winston, Inc., 1967).
[2] See also Olivia Munoz, *Songs in the Foreign Language Classroom*, ERIC Focus Report No. 12 (1969). Available from MLA/ACTFL Materials Center, 62 Fifth Avenue, New York, N.Y. 10011, for twenty-five cents.
[3] See also William Francis Mackey, *Language Teaching Analysis* (Bloomington: Indiana University Press, 1967). Appendix B, "Language Games," contains a listing of thirty-four games.

It is important to select a game that retains the interest of all the students who are playing. If only two students are talking while the rest of the students are standing in two lines awaiting their turn, then the pace of the game must be very brisk to avoid boring the silent ones. If possible, the teacher should try to select a game in which many persons are active simultaneously.

Games which involve a limited number of people might best be selected group activities rather than whole-class activities. Some games can even be played in groups of two or four.

3.5   HOMEWORK

The primary purpose for assigning homework is to give the student additional practice in developing his language competence. It obviously takes more time to learn a foreign language than the forty to fifty minutes available in the daily school schedule.

However, before giving homework, the teacher should assure himself that the particular assignment will help the student attain the objectives of the lesson. If it is not clear that doing the assignment will be of benefit, it would be wiser not to give it.

The difficulty of the assignment must be carefully considered. If the diligent student cannot complete the work with an accuracy level of at least 80%, then the assignment should be modified. What will it profit the student to spend an hour of homework time making mistakes in the foreign language? On the other hand, "busy work," such as copying sentences several times each, will be more likely to develop negative attitudes in the student than it will contribute to his progress in the foreign language.

3.5.1   *Relating Homework to Classwork*

If possible, the homework assignment should bear directly on the next day's class. For example: "Complete the worksheet on the imperative to get ready for tomorrow's test. The solution to number 4 (horizontal) on the crossword puzzle is the answer to the first question on the test."

Sometimes the actual product of the homework may be used in the activities of the next day's class. Each student in a beginning audio-visual class might be told to find magazine pictures or to make drawings to illustrate each line of the basic dialogue. This means that he will have to read each line at least once and copy it. The following day, instead of a boring class exercise where everyone reads the dialogue from the book several times, the students are encouraged to compare notebooks. Each student will be reading the dialogue through ten or fifteen times as he discovers what kind of illustrations his friends have brought in. Perhaps the class comedian cuts out a picture of a hurricane to illustrate *Il fait beau aujourd'hui.* For the next such assignment, students will try to outdo each other in finding crazy illustrations, and motivation to read will even be greater.

Students in a more advanced class might be asked to read a selection (a magazine article, a newspaper clipping, or a textbook page), to note five unfamiliar words or idioms in their notebooks, to use each word in an original sentence, and then to prepare two or three questions on the material which they will ask their classmates to discuss the following day. This type of assignment insures that the students will have prepared the reading which is to form the basis of the classroom conversation. At the same time, since each student prepares questions for the class, he will have some say in directing the conversation into areas he finds particularly interesting.

3.5.2 *Assigning Homework*

It is necessary to make the homework assignment clear. You might announce the homework in the foreign language, then write the pertinent information in English or in the foreign language on a corner of the chalkboard so that all the students are sure to understand. The assignment should never be shouted out to the departing students after the bell has rung. For an advanced class, homework assignments for a week or two could be distributed in Ditto form.

You might allow some time at the end of the period for students to begin the homework if it entails a written assignment. In this way you are on hand to answer any questions which might arise.

3.5.2a "PIGGY-BACK" HOMEWORK

Any student who so desires may copy another student's homework. Both sets of homework are turned in together. The student who copies receives seventy-five percent of the grade given the original paper. This technique eliminates "cheating," since copying is considered acceptable. It also encourages poorer students to copy only from the better ones, thus giving them experience in writing correct sentences. In practice, few students will turn in "piggy-back" homework, since they can get a higher mark by doing it themselves or as a group. (See below.)

3.5.2b GROUP HOMEWORK

Two or more students collaborate in preparing the homework. Each student writes out the whole assignment and the group submits their homework together. If one person has done more work than the others, this fact is noted.

3.5.2c THE TWO-NOTEBOOK SYSTEM

Each student has two notebooks. The assignments are always written on the right-hand page and the corrections are entered on the left-hand page. If daily homework is assigned and corrected or reviewed by the teacher, this means that every day the student turns in one notebook and gets the other, corrected one back. The two-notebook system is most effective with college classes. It allows the student and teacher to communicate on a regular basis. Moreover, it allows the teacher to make individualized assignments for remedial work or to write out brief explanations of grammar and vocabulary.

3.5.2d OUTSIDE PROJECTS

Individual students or groups of students are given one or two weeks to prepare a special project. For example, in an elementary language class the students may be asked to research certain cultural aspects of the foreign country in English and either give brief oral reports to the class or prepare a bulletin board display. In more advanced classes students may prepare a panel discussion, a debate, or an oral presentation.

If possible, it is a good idea to have these projects coincide with topics the student is studying in another class. The home economics teacher might let a group of Spanish students prepare a Mexican dish. If the American history class is studying the French and Indian War, some of the French students might prepare a report or display describing the French point of view of the conflict. If the English class is reading a novel by Hesse, the German students might wish to work on a related project. If the biology class is studying the respiratory system, perhaps some interested French students could prepare a brief report on Laënnec and his invention of the stethoscope. If some members of the class are on the school baseball team, they might prepare a poster comparing Spanish and English sports terminology based on items in the sports pages of a Spanish-language newspaper.

This building of bridges between the foreign language class and other areas of the curriculum will help students realize that learning a language is not an isolated endeavor, but that it opens the doors to a wide variety of experiences. Cooperation between the foreign language teacher and his colleagues in other disciplines will also serve to open channels of communication which may have previously been closed. The initial effort to dovetail assignments with activities in other classes may well lead to informal exchanges between teachers. Perhaps the music teacher would be willing to give a brief presentation of Beethoven's music to the German class; in exchange the German teacher might spend fifteen minutes helping the choir improve their pronunciation of German lyrics in a song they are practicing. The economics teacher might be willing to answer questions on the French economy, while the French teacher might be able to provide this colleague with French advertisements for American products. The opportunities for such exchanges are endless and are waiting to be explored.

3.5.3 *Correcting Homework in Class*

The major drawback to assigning written exercises as homework is that the correction of such exercises can constitute an enormous waste of precious class time.

Half a class period can be lost when students write homework sentences on the board and sit back as the teacher corrects them. An entire class can fall asleep as students, one by one, read aloud their error-laden sentences for the teacher to comment on. In its most detrimental form homework dominates the language class from beginning to end: today the class laboriously goes over exercises A, B, and C, which had been assigned as homework, and for tomorrow they are to write out exercises D, E, and F, which will be similarly dissected.

3.5.3a CORRECTING VIA THE CHALKBOARD

The teacher writes the correct sentences on the board, perhaps covering them with a map. The students quickly correct their homework as the teacher reads the sentences aloud. For more objectivity, it is recommended that students exchange papers. This activity should take no more than five minutes.

3.5.3b CORRECTING VIA THE OVERHEAD

This technique is similar to the one described above. The sentences are written in advance on an overhead transparency. Using a mask, the teacher uncovers the sentences one at a time, reading them aloud. Again, this procedure should take no more than five minutes.

3.5.3c CORRECTING VIA DITTOS

The teacher distributes Dittos with the correct responses. He reads the sentences aloud as the students make the corrections.

3.5.3d READING EXERCISES ALOUD

The teacher may take a few minutes of class time to read the correct sentences aloud. The difficulty with this technique is that many students may not be able to understand by ear alone where their mistakes are. Moreover, although the better students will be able to correct their work, the poorer students—those in the greatest need of guidance—will fail to discover their errors.

3.5.4 *Collecting and Grading Homework*

The collecting and grading of daily homework for four or more classes places a considerable burden on the teacher's time.

3.5.4a EXERCISES

For beginning and intermediate classes, especially on exercises for which responses are either right or wrong, the teacher may simply use a quick correction technique in the classroom and then enter in his gradebook whether the student completed the assignment or not. From time to time the teacher may want to take a closer look at homework assignments. If time is not available to check all papers, the teacher may choose to read the papers of one class carefully and simply note whether students in other classes have done the assignment. This way the papers of each class get read carefully once a week. It is also possible to spot check at random four or five papers per class.

3.5.4b COMPOSITIONS

For compositions and other assignments where there is more than one correct form possible and, therefore, where one set of correct answers cannot be made available to all students, the teacher must plan to read each paper. As a general practice, the teacher should insist that each student rewrite his paper incorporating the suggested corrections. Unless the teacher does so, most students look at the red marks, sigh, and throw the paper away.

Some teachers write out the corrections in full and have the students copy the corrected sentences. Other teachers use a set of symbols to cover the most frequent types of errors and have the students make the corrections. Some commonly used symbols are the following: voc—vocabulary, choice of word; g—gender; ag—agreement; wo—word order.

If the classroom has cassette players, the teacher can correct a composition by recording his comments on tape (in the foreign language, if possible). The grade is given at the end. The student plays back the cassette and incorporates the suggested corrections.

In any case, the teacher should quickly reread the corrected form of the assignment to be sure that the corrections have been understood and incorporated.

3.5.4c GIVING GRADES

Some teachers give actual grades to homework assignments and others just mark whether the work has been done or not. This is a matter of personal philosophy and preference.

3.6 TESTING

For the teacher, testing is an important diagnostic instrument. Not only does it allow him to keep track of the progress of his students, but it enables him to measure his own successes and failures in the classroom and lets him know when lesson plans must be modified to meet the students' unforeseen problems.

3.6.1 Norm-Referenced Tests and Criterion-Referenced Tests

The norm-referenced test is used to rank students. Scores may be given in terms of letter grades, standard scores, percentile rankings, and the like. In other words, the test is often graded on the curve. In giving such a test, the teacher prepares some easy items and some harder items in the hope that the scores will spread out over a wide range. The broader the range, the more certain the teacher is that the letter grades assigned represent real difference in ability. Most teachers are obliged by their school systems to rank their students in some way at the end of each marking period.

The criterion-referenced test is used to determine how many students have attained a given level of mastery. In preparing such a test, the teacher includes only items that measure the skill defined by the criterion. Let us suppose that the teacher wants to know whether the students can change affirmative sentences (using familiar vocabulary) into negative sentences in writing. He would prepare a list of sentences and have the students rewrite them. His objective might be that all students should get at least nine out of ten sentences right. If one third of the class misses two or more sentences, then the teacher works with that group and gives them another test to determine whether they can now handle the transformation. This might go on for a third or even a fourth time. Another teacher might decide that his objective in this area had been attained if eighty percent of his students got nine out of ten right. It is up to the teacher to set the level of mastery, but his intention should always be that as many students as possible attain a high score.

These two types of tests may be contrasted as follows. On a norm-referenced test the teacher is upset if everyone gets 100, because he has made the test too easy. On a criterion-referenced test the teacher is upset if the grades range from 50 to 100, because that means he has failed to teach what he set out to teach; for him, if the whole class scored 100, that would be a sign of success. The norm-referenced test includes some hard questions that only the best students are expected to get right. The criterion-referenced test includes only those questions that everyone is expected to get right—and the teacher will keep teaching for that test until the students *do* get them right.

If foreign language teachers begin defining levels of learning in terms of performance objectives and teaching for mastery through the use of criterion-referenced tests, it will become imperative to establish national standards for Level I, Level II, and so on. The student's record of progress then will not only be in terms of years of study plus grades, but in terms of level proficiency as well.

3.6.2 *Formal and Informal Testing*

Much classroom testing is informal in nature. The teacher learns to tell from his students' reactions whether they have understood the meaning of a phrase. He can tell by the fluency and accuracy of their oral responses whether they have mastered a specific drill.

One question the teacher should *not* ask is, Do you understand? The question serves little purpose, since those who do not understand are usually too shy to show their ignorance and remain quiet. Others have misunderstood but are unaware of their error. The only way to check comprehension is to ask questions or plan activities which allow the student to *demonstrate* whether he has understood or not. For example, if the grammar generalization was about *ser* and *estar*, the most appropriate grammar check is to have students do an exercise where the two verbs are used. When one or more students have difficulty with a specific sentence, the teacher can diagnose the problem area.

Formal classroom tests allow the teacher to form a more precise idea of how much the students have mastered and where their areas of weakness lie. Often a quiet student performs better on a formal test than the teacher would have anticipated, while an alert, out-going student does less well.[1]

3.7   CLASSROOM MANAGEMENT

The matters of classroom management fall into two categories: maximizing available class time and maintaining discipline.

3.7.1   *Maximizing Available Class Time*

Wasted time may be kept to a minimum through the establishment of routines. Although the setting up of a routine may take a little time at the beginning of the school year, much time will be saved in the long run.

Each teacher will, of course, set up his routines as a function of the age of the students, the physical classroom environment, and the aims of instruction. Routines might be established for the following activities:

(1) The beginning of the hour: Students might be correcting homework at their places while the teacher quickly takes attendance. Certain students are assigned to distribute corrected homework and pick up new homework. If a particular arrangement of chairs is necessary, the first students to get to the classroom should be assigned this task so that the class may begin on time. If certain sentences or visuals are to be put on the chalkboard, the teacher should do this before the bell rings.

(2) Assignment to groups: If part of the class hour is to be devoted to group work, the rosters of the groups and their assignments (if appropriate) could be posted on a class bulletin board which students would consult as they entered the room.

(3) Language laboratory or electronic classroom: Procedures and seating arrangements could be made routine.

(4) Handling students' questions: Only a short part of the class hour should be devoted to answering questions, which otherwise might drag out

---

[1] For guidelines on the preparation, administration, and scoring of classroom tests, see Rebecca M. Valette, *Modern Language Testing* (New York: Harcourt Brace Jovanovich, Inc., 1967).

for fifteen or twenty minutes. Students should be encouraged to ask questions privately of the teacher during time scheduled for individual work or small group instruction. Another possible routine to establish is the following: The teacher has a question basket on his desk where students may deposit questions and requests as they come into the classroom. While one student takes roll, the teacher can read over the questions quickly, and if necessary, modify his class plan to cover the points raised. If the homework is done in a two-notebook system, students may be encouraged to write questions to the teacher in their notebooks.

(5) The end of the hour: Routines should be established for replacing furniture, shelving supplementary materials, collecting visuals, and so on. If the class has been using individual cue cards, with names of Paris monuments, for example, the teacher can stand at the door and pick up the cards as the students leave the room. Each student will say a sentence about his card: *Je voudrais visiter les Invalides.*

3.7.2 *Maintaining Discipline*

Two situations tend to give rise to discipline problems. The first is the teacher's mental set: if he anticipates having difficulties with his students, discipline problems are bound to occur. The second is class activities: if the students are actively involved in a class which is set at their linguistic level and which takes into account their interests and backgrounds, they will be so busy learning the language that discipline will, in large measure, take care of itself.

None but the most docile students will want to look only at the teacher and participate only in teacher-led activities during the entire class period, day after day. Independent work, small group conversations, interest group conversations, student-led drills, all contribute to the smoother functioning of a class. Once the teacher realizes that even his beginning students can learn a foreign language *without* his constantly playing the role of orchestra conductor, he will experience the challenge of experimenting with different types of instruction and the pleasure of seeing his students take an increased interest in class activities.

PART TWO
PRESENTING
THE LANGUAGE

CHAPTER FOUR
TEACHING
THE SOUND
SYSTEM

All foreign languages have sound systems which differ distinctly from that of English. American English is a very relaxed language. Vowels are glided and diphthongs are frequent. Vowels in unstressed syllables are reduced to an /uh/ sound. Consonants at the beginning of a word are forcefully enunciated, such as the consonants /p//t//k/, for example, which are accompanied by a puff of air (aspirated). Consonants at the end of the word are frequently unreleased.

As the American student learns to speak German, French, or Spanish, he must acquire new speech habits. He must increase the tension in his speech organs so that vowels are kept pure, even in unstressed syllables. He must eliminate the puff of air before /p//t//k/ and learn to say final consonants distinctly.

Furthermore, the American student must practice new sounds, such as the Spanish /rr/, the French /y/, and the German /x/. He must acquire new patterns of rhythm, stress, and intonation in speaking the foreign language. He must realize that even though words in the foreign language may look like English on paper, they do not sound like English when spoken aloud.

The mastery of a new sound system is one

aspect of the process of learning a second language. This chapter will suggest techniques for helping students acquire an acceptable pronunciation in the language they are studying.

4.1   GENERAL CONSIDERATIONS

Most teachers agree that early insistence on correct pronunciation can save many hours of remedial work later on. Bad habits are easily formed and very difficult to change.

The first task is to convince students of the importance of pronunciation. It should be emphasized that failure to pronounce correctly can result in not being understood. The native Spanish speaker who cannot make a distinction in English between *berry* and *very* may have trouble communicating.

The teacher may also wish to point out that poor pronunciation can be unpleasant or comical to the native speaker listening to it. Imitating a thick foreign accent while speaking English can be an effective technique.

In order to achieve the goal of good pronunciation, the teacher needs to insist on it from the outset. The first step is listening practice; it is important to remember that students must be able to hear the target sounds or they will probably never be able to make them. Next, the students may attempt to produce these sounds, most of which will seem very strange indeed. At this point the teacher needs to be fairly indulgent. With encouragement, the students gradually learn to shape the correct sounds.

Constant practice in listening discrimination, pronunciation, and intonation using a variety of drills and exercises can go far in forming good habits of correct speech. However, listening discrimination exercises must be integrated with the various devices for presenting and drilling pronunciation and intonation.

In the succeeding pages an attempt has been made to identify a few of the major problems and to propose techniques for solving them. This chapter is not a treatise on the entire sound system of any foreign language. Such studies are available in other books.[1] However, many of the techniques suggested may be applied to those pronunciation problems which have gone unmentioned here.

4.2   INITIAL PRESENTATION

The first speech samples that the student hears upon beginning his study of a foreign language almost always take the form of sentences: *Buenos días. Comment t'appelles-tu? Ich heiße Fräulein Hof.* Thus, from the very outset,

---

[1] Such as the *Contrastive Structure Series* of the University of Chicago Press.

the student realizes that a foreign language is made up of words and phrases, not of isolated sounds.

As the class continues, the student may memorize dialogues, learn sequences of sentences, answer simple questions, or repeat the script of a filmstrip or movie, depending on the type of program used. In all instances, however, he will be learning to control a new sound system within the context of phrases and sentences.

4.2.1 *Simple Mimicry*

The student's first steps in learning to speak a second language require mimicry. He listens to a model and imitates what he hears.

4.2.1a THE TEACHER AS A MODEL

The best model is the teacher who has a fluent command of the foreign language. The teacher can model a phrase as often as necessary. He can move around the room from student to student. He can vary the tempo of the sentence to be repeated, saying it more slowly at first and then progressively faster. He can break the sentence into component parts and then reassemble it. He can skip back and forth from new sentences to previously learned sentences.

4.2.1b THE RECORDING AS A MODEL

The teacher whose pronunciation is faulty can use recordings to model a phrase. The teacher can play the basic sentences on the tape recorder and then walk about the room listening to the students and encouraging their efforts. The teacher can also stay with the tape recorder, playing a sentence once and then stopping the tape so that students may repeat it several times in succession. The tape lets the student hear several voices, but it lacks the flexibility of a live teacher.

The basic tape can be put to excellent use as an aid to the teacher himself. The unsure teacher should invest in a tape recorder or a cassette player so that sentences in a particular lesson can be played over and over again in the teacher's home until they become second nature. The teacher may not feel fluent in impromptu conversation, but he should be able to model the basic sentences with confidence.

4.2.2 *Focusing on Key Sounds*

The teacher can use the basic sentences of the lesson to focus on critical sounds. As the students repeat the sentences, their attention is drawn to certain features which may present difficulties for American students.

4.2.2a THE "SEEDED" DIALOGUE

In some textbooks the initial dialogues or sentences have been built around or "seeded" with certain key sounds. Typically there is a progression from familiar sounds (with new intonation patterns and greater tension) to totally unfamiliar sounds.

The following French example is built on the vowels /a/ /i/ /u/ and consonants which are rather similar to English. The attention of the student is drawn to basic patterns of rhythm, intonation, and stress: *Voici David. Où habite David? David habite Nice.*

The following short German exchange was designed to stress the sound /x/: *Was macht Joachim? Er spielt Schach.*

4.2.2b SELECTING SOUNDS TO BE STRESSED

In other textbooks the initial sentences contain most of the sounds of the foreign language. (What "seeding" exists has been determined by grammar and vocabulary, rather than phonetic considerations.)

First the teacher prepares the dialogue or sentences by underlining those sounds that may cause difficulties. As he models each line to the class, he is especially alert to the correct pronunciation of the underlined letters:

Ramón, ¿adonde vas ahora?	trilled /rr/: *Ramón* vs. single tap /r/: *ahora*
A la Casa de Música.	pure /a/
¿Vas con Rosita?	/s/ not /z/; see also *casa* and *música*
No, voy con Paco.	nondiphthongized /o/

4.2.3 *Treating Specific Problems*

While some students can pick up the sound system of a foreign language by simple imitation, others need guidance in trying to form unfamiliar sounds.

4.2.3a DESCRIBING HOW SOUNDS ARE MADE

The teacher may tell students how to produce certain sounds:

(1) French /i/: Smile broadly, spread your lips, tighten your facial muscles, press the tip of your tongue against your lower teeth and say *qui, ici, fit.*

(2) German /y/: Round your lips, draw them tightly together, pretend you are drinking from a straw, say /i/ and you will really be saying /y/: *fünf, für, Füller*

(3) Spanish /o/: Round your lips, push them forward, tighten your facial muscles and say *mo, no, mono, fo, to, foto.* Hold your lips in this position and keep them from sliding to another sound. As you say /o/, you should feel a vibration in your throat.

4.2.3b USING A MIRROR

The students are asked to bring pocket mirrors to class. The teacher pronounces a difficult sound or contrasts an English sound with a foreign language sound. As the students imitate the teacher, they look into the mirror and compare their lips with the teacher's. This technique is especially helpful in eliminating the tendency to diphthongize vowels at the end of a word. Students are told to freeze their mouth position and not to change it until they have stopped speaking.

The teacher might contrast English *no* with Spanish *no*; English *key* with French *qui*; English *coo* with German *Kuh*.

4.2.3c GIVING ENGLISH NEAR-EQUIVALENTS *last + least*

Beginning with familiar words or sounds, the teacher models them so that he brings his students to pronouncing a key sound in the foreign language:

(1) Spanish /r/: The teacher starts with *pot of tea* and then rapidly pronounces it *pot' a tea*. Gradually he shapes the phrase to come to *para ti* and finally the word *para*. Using nonsense syllables, the teacher can also build on *kot' a tea*, *sot' a tea*, and so on.

(2) French /r/: The teacher starts with the name *Bach* and then adds a vowel, such as /i/. The sequence becomes *Bach Bach-i* and finally *Barry*. Similarly, *Pach-i* leads to *Paris*, *Lach-ou* leads to *la roue*, *Kach-é* leads to *carré*.

(3) German /ts/: The teacher begins with *cat soup*. Gradually he encourages students to go from *cat soup* to *ca-a-a-at soup* to *ca-a-a-at su* to *ca-a tsu* ending with the word *zu* once the *ca* has been dropped.

4.2.3d BREAKING UP DIFFICULT SOUND COMBINATIONS

Sometimes students have difficulty pronouncing in combination sounds which they have mastered individually. These tricky clusters can be broken up and then rebuilt.

(1) Spanish /r/ plus consonant: In words like *árbol*, the teacher adds a schwa between the /r/ and the following consonant: a /rə/ bol. As the students repeat the word many times, they are asked to accelerate. Finally they say *árbol*.

a /rə/ ma ⟶ arma
a /rə/ te ⟶ arte
a /rə/ co ⟶ arco[1]

(2) German /x/ plus consonants—the choo-choo train technique: In pronouncing the word *sechzig*, the teacher separates the two long syllables

[1] Robert L. Politzer and Charles N. Staubach, *Teaching Spanish* (Waltham: Blaisdell Publishing Co., 1965), p. 79.

with a long pause. Students repeat. Then, as the teacher says the two syllables several times, he increases the speed and shortens the pauses. (The accent marker indicates stress.)

nách————ts	séch————zig
nách————ts	séch————zig
nách——ts	séch——zig
nách—ts	séch—zig
nách-ts	séch-zig
náchts	séchzig[1]

(3) French nasals—eliminating /n/ or /m/ before a consonant: American students have a strong tendency to insert a nasal consonant between a nasal vowel and the following consonant sound, for example, to pronounce the /m/ of *tomber* or the /n/ of *demander*. The teacher separates the nasal vowel and the following consonant by reversing the order of the syllables and having students repeat them rapidly:

bé—tom—bé—tom—bé—tom—bé—tomber
dé—deman—dé—deman—dé—deman—dé—demander
pression—im—pression—im—pression—impression

(4) Eliminating the /ʃ/ sound: A persistent problem is the American student's tendency to introduce a /ʃ/ into cognates of English words in *-tion*.

Spanish:	nación	ci	ci	ci	ción	ción	nación
German:	Nation	zi	zi	zi	zion	zion	Nation
French:	nation	si	si	si	sion	sion	nation

4.2.3e ELIMINATING ASPIRATION

Americans tend to pronounce /p//t//k/ with a slight puff of air when these consonants occur at the beginning of a word. Since these same consonants are not aspirated in the combinations /sp/ /st/ and /sk/ in English, these clusters can serve as a point of departure for helping students produce /p//t//k/ without the air. For example, to get the Spanish student to pronounce *pan*, tell him to put an *s* before the word and say *span*. Then have him think the *s*, but not say it.

The student may use one of the following techniques to keep track of his progress:

(1) Hold the back of your hand near your mouth. You should hardly feel any air on it if you are saying /p/ /t/ /k/ correctly.

(2) Put a piece of paper in front of your mouth. As you say the consonants /p//t//k/, the paper should scarely move. If you pronounce the consonants the American way, the paper will flutter.

---

[1] Eberhard Reichmann, "Tackling Cluster and Juncture Problems in Pronunciation Drill," in *Die Unterrichtspraxis*, I (1968), p. 45.

(3) Place a lighted candle or match in front of your lips. The flame will not go out if you pronounce the consonant correctly.

4.2.3f TAPPING OUT THE RHYTHM

The teacher demonstrates how to tap out the rhythm of a French word and its English equivalent. He takes a pencil and taps evenly: *pá-rá-gráphe* (French), then taps out one long and two short syllables for *pár-a-graph* (English). Then he calls on individuals to tap out other words in French and in English: *Mississippi, impossible, composition, nationalité, correspondance.*

4.2.3g ADOPTING A "FOREIGN" ACCENT

Some students feel silly and uncomfortable speaking a foreign language and compensate by maintaining an American accent, especially when using cognates. Often it is possible to help students over this psychological hurdle by training them to speak English with a heavy French or German or Spanish accent. After the student learns to purify his vowels, substitute one sound for another, and maintain a foreign intonation pattern while speaking broken English, he can then apply this new "accent" to the foreign language:

German: Vee vant to vait here.
French: Eet eez eemposseebla to speak Eengleesh.

4.2.3h USING HAND SIGNALS

The teacher can use hand and arm motions to make students aware of intonation patterns, raising his hand when the intonation rises and bringing his hand down when the intonation falls. This is particularly useful in teaching the continuing intonation pattern of French: *Je vais en ville* (arm moves up) *avec Pierre* (arm moves down).

In teaching Spanish and German words where students have trouble accentuating the appropriate syllable, the teacher can develop a hand signal, such as a forward motion of the wrist, with which to emphasize stressed syllables. For example: *au - to - mó* (hand signal) - *bil; Kon - zért* (hand signal).

4.2.3i DRAWING SYMBOLS ON THE CHALKBOARD

Sometimes a visual representation helps clarify a pronunciation problem.

(1) Sketching mouth positions: A simple side view of the mouth can illustrate the relative position of the tongue and teeth. Here are two French examples:

A To pronounce /i/ and /e/: keep your tongue rounded and hold the tip of your tongue against the lower front teeth. Now say /i/ and round

your lips. Do not change the tongue position (result: /y/). Say /e/
and round your lips. Do not change the tongue position (result: /ø/.

B When you pronounce /t/ or /d/, be sure your tongue touches the upper
front teeth.

(2) Arrows: A rising arrow is used to indicate a rising intonation. A
falling arrow is used to indicate a falling intonation:

Je ne travaille pas. ↓

Je ne travaille pas ↑   à la maison. ↓

(3) Musical notes: Musical notes may be used to indicate intonation and
diphthongs:

Finissez vite: *b*eau versus *beau*

El hombre viene.   ca fé versus ca fé
INTONATION   DIPHTHONGS

(4) Contour lines: A continuous line may be superposed on a sentence to
show intonation:

¿Dónde está mi lápiz?

Se fué para el centro.

(5) Marking liaison and linking: Symbols may be used to remind students
of sounds that are added or dropped within a group of words.

French: Où est votre ami?

/z/
D'où est-ce que ces‿amis viennent?

Spanish: para‿escribir

4.3 DEVELOPING LISTENING DISCRIMINATION

Students must learn to discriminate between correct and incorrect pronunciations in learning to speak the foreign language with an acceptable accent. This aural sensitivity is usually developed by means of "minimal pairs." These are words or phrases that differ from each other by one sound or by a general feature such as intonation or stress.

4.3.1 *Contrasting English and the Foreign Language*

Through discrimination exercises the student is brought to realize that the sound system of the foreign language differs from that of English.

4.3.1a GROUP PRACTICE

The teacher reads a list of words. Some are German and some are English. The students mark G or E on a piece of paper. The list is read a second time and correct responses are given: *Du, die, Lee, day, See.*

Similarly the students mark F or E for French or English as they hear the following list of words: *motor, motor, moteur, moteur, motor, moteur, letter, lettre, lettre, letter, lettre, letter, television, télévision, television, télévision, télévision, television.*

4.3.1b INDIVIDUAL RESPONSES

The teacher reads a random series of English and French words. After each word he pauses to point at an individual student who replies either *"anglais"* or *"français,"* as appropriate: *feel, ville, mille, meal, sel.*

4.3.1c USING MINIMAL PAIRS

The teacher reads aloud a pair of contrasting Spanish and English words. The students raise their right hand if the first word was Spanish. They raise their left hand if the second word was Spanish: *day—de, lo—low, mi—me.*

4.3.1d DETECTING AN AMERICAN ACCENT

The teacher reads a series of words. Students shake their heads if the teacher mimics an American accent. In this example, the teacher randomly switches between an American /r/ and a French /r/. Except for the /r/, the words are pronounced to sound like French: *arrive, garage, parc, Richard, Albert.*

4.3.2 *Contrasting Words in the Foreign Language*

In learning a second language, students must be made aware of phonemic distinctions, that is, those differences in sound which change the meaning of a word or phrase. Through exercises of the following types, the students soon realize that in some cases making distinctions between single sounds is necessary for comprehension.

4.3.2a RAISING HANDS

The teacher reads a series of words containing the vowel /u/ or the vowel /y/. Students raise their hands when they hear the sound /y/: *loup, lu, du, trou, fou, tu, bu, boue.*

4.3.2b RHYMES

The teacher pronounces groups of three words. As the students listen, they circle on their answer sheets the letter of the word that does not rhyme. At the end of the exercise, the teacher rereads the list and gives the correct answers: *son—main—ton, lu—tu—fou.*

4.3.2c SAME OR DIFFERENT

The students listen to pairs of words. Some are the same, others are different. They are asked to mark S (same) or D (different) on their papers: *mira—mire, mucha—mucha.*

4.3.2d INTONATION PATTERNS

The teacher prepares a set of sentences including commands, questions, and statements. As the teacher reads each sentence, the student writes a period if he hears a statement, an exclamation point if he hears a command, and a question mark if he hears a question: *Carlos, ¡trabaja María trabaja. ¿Ana trabaja?*

4.3.2e FLASH CARDS

The teacher prepares flash cards, each containing one of the words to be contrasted, for example, *pero* and *perro*. In the classroom the teacher calls two students forward and gives each a card to hold. He then reads sentences which contain one of the two words. If the students hear *pero*, they point to the student on the left who is holding that word. If they hear *perro*, they point to the student on the right. The teacher's sentences might utilize unfamiliar vocabulary, for example, *Pero no bebe leche.*

For more advanced students, this exercise can be made more difficult if both words in the minimal pair are the same part of speech: *le dessert* vs. *le désert.* Sample sentence: *Je n'aime pas le désert.*

4.3.3 *Contrasting Sentences in the Foreign Language*

The most important minimal contrasts in a language are those which carry grammatical meaning. While a French student should hear the difference between a nasal vowel and a non-nasal vowel plus /n/, this distinction becomes critical if he is to distinguish between *Il vient demain* and *Ils viennent demain*. Similarly the German student should hear the difference between *Er kommt zu spät* and *Ihr kommt zu spät*, and the Spanish student should be sensitive to distinctions between *Hablo español* and *Habló español*. In drilling these contrasting sounds, the teacher could ask the students to signal whether they heard *singular* or *plural* (French), *he* or *you* (German), *present* or *past* (Spanish).

4.3.3a SPOKEN RESPONSES

The teacher directs the students to listen for a specific distinction and say what they hear. For example, in presenting new vocabulary, the teacher may hold up pictures of nouns and say what each picture represents. Students say whether the noun is masculine or feminine: *Es un gato. C'est une fleur.*

4.3.3b PHYSICAL RESPONSES

In this technique the student makes a physical response to show whether he has heard the sentence correctly.

(1) Fingers: The students raise one finger if the sentence is singular, two fingers if the sentence is plural, and a closed fist if they cannot tell: *Ils finissent demain. Elle aime son frère. Ils(s) parle(nt) anglais.*

(2) Body movement: (For young junior high school students.) The teacher writes across the top of the chalkboard *faire avoir être aller*. A student goes to the front of the room. The teacher reads a sentence containing *font, ont, sont,* or *vont,* for example, *Ils ont deux frères*, and the student moves to stand under the correct verb, *ont.*

The headings on the board can be varied to suit the type of listening discrimination being practiced. They might be present and imperfect: *nous dansons* vs. *nous dansions*; masculine and feminine: *Mes amis sont américains* vs. *Mes amies sont américaines*; and so on.

(3) Cards: (For young junior high school students.) Students color a blue circle on one index card and a red circle on the other. The teacher reads a set of sentences and students indicate whether they heard *le* (blue card) or *la* (red card) : *J'aime la danse. J'aime le théâtre.*

In Spanish, students could color circles white and black. If the sentence they hear contains a verb in the present tense, they raise the white card. If the verb is in the past, they raise the black card. This exercise measures the student's sensitivity to a shift in stress as indicative of a shift in verb tense and subject: *Estudió español. Hablo bien.*

4.4 PRONUNCIATION PRACTICE

When the student can discriminate among the sound features of the language he is learning, and when he has received specific suggestions about how to produce certain sounds and sound combinations, he must be given the opportunity to practice his pronunciation. The memorization of basic sentences or a dialogue already furnishes one of these opportunities, but frequently additional pronunciation practice is needed. Some oral exercises do not lend themselves well to pronunciation practice because their main stress is on structure. In communication exercises the emphasis is on fluency of expression and a teacher's highly critical attitude toward pronunciation may stifle the student's willingness to speak. In the following sections, some further ways of introducing pronunciation practice are suggested.

4.4.1 *Tongue Twisters*

Most students enjoy tongue twisters and do not mind repeating them frequently for practice.

Spanish /rr/: Erre con erre cigarro,
Erre con erre barril.
Rápido corren los carros
Por la línea del ferrocarril.
French /ʃ/ and /s/: Un chasseur sachant chasser chasse sans chiens.
German /ʃ/ and /s/, /fr/ and /f/: Fischer frißt frische Fische.
French vowels: Didon dîna, dit-on, du dos d'un dodu dindon.

4.4.2 *Songs*

There are many foreign language songs which contain frequent repetitions of difficult sounds.

French /r/: "Il était un' bergère"
Il était un' bergère
Et ri et ron, petit patapon
Il était un' bergère
Qui gardait ses moutons -ton -ton.

French /ɔ̃/ vs. /ã/: "Sur le pont d'Avignon"
Sur le pont d'Avignon
L'on y danse, l'on y danse
Sur le pont d'Avignon
L'on y danse tout en rond.

Spanish /rr/: "Corrocloclo"
Una gallina con pollos
Cinco duros me costó
Corrocloclo, corrocloclo, corrocloclo, corrocloclo
La compré por la mañana
Y a la tarde se perdió
Corrocloclo, corrocloclo, corrocloclo, corrocloclo.

German /r/ and /l/ :   "O wie wohl ist mir am Abend"
O wie wohl ist mir am Abend,
Mir am Abend,
Wenn zur Ruh
Die Glocken läuten,
Glocken läuten,
Bim, bam, bim, bam, bim, bam!

4.4.3   *Poems*

Many teachers have used poetry to practice pronunciation. As students memorize poems, they acquire a feeling for the music of the language. It is not necessary to have students memorize a poem in its entirety; often just a stanza may be introduced.

French /œ/ :   "Il pleure dans mon cœur"
Comme il pleut sur la ville.
Quelle est cette langueur
Qui pénètre mon cœur?
Verlaine

Spanish /rr/ /r/ and /v/ /b/ :   "Ñapas"
El cielo está emborregado
quién lo desemborregará
el emborregador que lo ha emborregado
buen desemborregador será.

Tres, tristes tigres
comián trigo
en la triga
de un trigal.

De la viña de Valencia
vino el vino
a dar vida
al bien viejo
don Benito.

4.4.4   *Cheers*

When there is a forthcoming football or basketball game, some students might enjoy writing and practicing foreign language cheers. For example, an equivalent of *Hit 'em again, harder!* is *Encore—Plus fort!*

4.5   SOUND-SYMBOL CORRESPONDENCES

At some point in a student's language program he learns to associate the spoken word with its written form. This initiation to the sound-symbol correspondences of a second language may begin on the first day of class, or it may be postponed several weeks or months. The teacher may either present sound-symbol correspondences directly, in sequential order, and let students read unfamiliar words aloud (the symbol-to-sound approach) or he may select known words containing a given sound and bring the student's attention to the different spelling patterns (the sound-to-symbol approach). First, however, many teachers have their students learn the alphabet in the foreign language.

4.5.1 *Teaching the Alphabet*   *Controversal matter*

alphabet is words

If students can use the foreign alphabet, the talk about sound-symbol correspondences and about spelling may, at least in part, be carried on in the foreign language. Furthermore, if the teacher uses a deductive approach in teaching sound-symbol correspondences, the sounds of the alphabet may be used frequently as models.

4.5.1a MEMORIZATION

The alphabet may be memorized chorally in recitation or by song. A common problem is that students who know the letters in sequence often have difficulty thinking of the name of the letter when it is presented in isolation.

4.5.1b GROUPING LETTERS

(This exercise is mainly for young junior high school students.) The teacher may prefer to teach groups of letters which sound alike, and then later put together the alphabet in sequence. Each group can also be coded with its own color. Once a group of letters has been taught, the teacher can point to letters and have students name them. The letters can be put on index cards, shuffled, and distributed to students for a variety of oral activities: Who has A? Susie, show me who has D. Joe, trade letters with Dick: What letter do you now have?

French:	B C D G P T V W	F L M N R S Z	I J X Y	A H K
	Q U O E			

German:	B C D E G P T W	F L M N R S Z	I X	A H K
	Q U O V Y			

4.5.1c INITIALS

To practice the letters of the alphabet, the teacher can dictate initials of famous people, for example J.F.K., and have the students identify these people by name. Initials can be dictated to students placed at the board. Students themselves can dictate initials to their classmates. This type of practice can be turned into a game, and gradually students grow to feel at ease with the foreign alphabet.

4.5.2   *The Symbol-to-Sound Approach*

The teacher presents sound-symbol correspondences in a step-by-step manner. For example, in teaching French the teacher might explain that the letter *a* usually represents the sound /a/ (the name of that letter in the alphabet). The letter *i* usually represents the sound /i/ (the name of the letter in the alphabet, too). Final *e* is usually silent. Then the teacher lets the students read aloud new words: *salade, Alice, maladie, Annie.* A sentence using these sounds might read: *Annick va à la piscine.* A subsequent lesson might introduce the symbols *ou*, silent *h* and *ch* in sentences such as *Où habite Milou? Il habite la Chine.*

The advantage of this presentation is that the student masters the sound-symbol correspondences in a sequential, cumulative manner. The presentation may be made more inductive if the teacher holds up cards and reads certain key words aloud and then asks students what letter or letters are used to represent the sounds they hear.

4.5.3   *The Sound-to-Symbol Approach*

The students first practice and control sentences orally. Once they can say them readily, they are allowed to see how these sentences are written. Building on this global approach to reading, the teacher uses known words to present sound-symbol correspondences.

The global approach has the advantage that the student controls certain words and sentences orally before learning to read them. However, since basic dialogues and core sentences are rarely developed around considerations of sound-symbol presentation, the student may encounter dozens of sound-symbol patterns, plus some exceptions, in learning to read one line of dialogue.

The following techniques help the teacher build on the student's familiarity with certain sentences and words by focusing on sound-symbol correspondences one by one.

4.5.3a   SOLICITING WORDS CONTAINING A GIVEN SOUND

The teacher asks the class for known words containing a given sound. He puts these words on the chalkboard or on the overhead and guides the students in discovering which symbols are used to represent that sound. Sometimes there is a one-to-one correspondance, as in the German example below. Sometimes there is a one-to-two correspondance, as in the Spanish example, where both *ú* and *u* represent the same sound. Sometimes the relationship is more complex, as in the French example, where one sound has a variety of written representations.

Teacher: Nennen Sie mir sieben Worter mit /ʃt/.
Class: Strasse, Stein, stoßen, Bleistift, aufstehen, bestellt

Teacher: Dénme Vds. una lista de palabras que tienen el sonido /u/.
Class: tu, mucho, música, gusto, azul, busca, lunes

Teacher: Donnez-moi une liste de mots qui contiennent le son /e/.
Class: mes, bébé, thé, café, des, parlez

4.5.3b   FELT BOARD TECHNIQUE

On the left-hand side place cards with words that contain one particular letter combination, such as *ch*: *mich, ich, nicht, dich, noch, braucht, euch, nach, acht, Mädchen*. On the right-hand side place cards with words that contain a contrasting letter combination, such as *sch*: *Schiff, schon, schenkt, Schnee, Schier, Schere, schuldet*. The letter combinations under consideration could be underlined, or in capital letters, or in some way made prominent. The teacher asks: What sounds do the letters *ch* represent in the words on the left-hand side of the board? Do the letters *ch* on the right-hand side of the board represent either of these sounds? What letter appears before the *ch* in the words on the right-hand side? What sound do the letters *sch* represent?

4.5.3c   MAGNETIC BOARD TECHNIQUE

On the left side of the board, place a magnet over each of the following cards: *paPEL, capiTAL, aZUL, nacioNAL, hoTEL*. Generalization questions: How do all the above words end? What do you do with your voice when the word ends in an *l*?

Now, on the right side of the board, place a magnet on each of the following cards: *FÁcil, HÁbil, autoMÓbil, Ágil*. Generalization questions: These words are not stressed on the last syllable, even though they end in *l*. What difference do you see in how they are written? What must you do with your voice when an accent mark appears over a vowel?

4.5.3d   TRANSPARENCY: COLOR CODING

On a transparency write the following words. The underlined letters should appear in orange: *qui, café, cinq, d'accord, kilo*. The teacher asks the student to name the different spellings of the sound /k/.

4.5.3e   CHALKBOARD

The teacher prints two columns of words on the chalkboard, writing the underlined letters in colored chalk. The teacher reads each word as he prints it, and the students repeat.

Then the teacher asks: What sound is represented by both *ç* and *c*? What vowels occur after *ç*? Do you see those same vowels after *c*? What vowels occur after *c*? Do you se these vowels after *ç*?

4.5.3f POSTERS AND WALL CHARTS

(1) One poster shows a penguin and a stork and reads: *El pingüino no puede volar como la cigüeña.* Another poster depicts a guitar and a gourd and reads: *Sé tocar la guitarra y el güiro.*

The teacher points to the pictures and asks: When you hear /gwi/ as in *pingüino* and *güiro*, how do you write it? When you hear /gi/ as in *guitarra*, how do you write it?

Similarly, a poster showing money and ointment and reading: *Pagué por el ungüento* could be used to illustrate /ge/ and /gwe/.

(2) The following poster can remind students of the names of accents in French. Upon putting it up the teacher tells the class: This poor man had an acute attack of appendicitis and fell back into his grave.

(3) A small poster with the words *hi̲s* and *hi̲s̲s̲* can serve as a reminder that in French one *s* between vowels represents the sound /z/, whereas a double *s* between vowels represents the sound /s/.

4.5.4 *Phonetic Transcription*

Some teachers introduce the phonetic alphabet to help their students use foreign language dictionaries to look up the pronunciation of new words. This is particularly useful in the case of French, where the general rules of sound-symbol correspondence are often insufficient for predicting the pronunciation of a word. Other teachers feel that a formal introduction to the IPA alphabet is too time-consuming.

If the teacher does not want to spend time on a formal presentation of IPA symbols, he might prepare Ditto sheets for independent work by those students who are interested.

4.5.4a SAME OR DIFFERENT

The teacher can have the students look up the following pairs of words and indicate whether the underlined letters represent the same sound or different sounds: *vers—fils, femme—dame, examen—lentement*. This could also be a lab drill with printed materials and taped exercises.

4.5.4b SILENT OR NOT

The teacher can have the students look up the following words and circle those final consonants which are *not* pronounced: *sac, estomac, flirt, vert*.

4.6 REMEDIAL WORK *stressing / sound a week*

Once students have acquired bad habits of pronunciation, the process of correction is difficult and very time-consuming. However, with patience and effective teaching techniques, it is possible to attain positive results.

4.6.1 *General Procedures*

The teacher of any language class of second-year level or higher is faced with the general problem of how best to improve his students' ability to discriminate among the sounds of the language and to produce these sounds in an acceptable manner. His problem is compounded by the fact that some students control the sound system better than others, and that each has individual pronunciation difficulties. The following sections suggest some general techniques for doing the necessary remedial work.

4.6.1a LISTENING FOR OTHERS' MISTAKES

The first step in improving one's pronunciation is becoming aware of mistakes. Since another's mistakes are often more noticeable than one's own, the teacher can encourage students to become more critical of one another's speech. If students are giving short presentations, or if pairs of students are reciting a dialogue, the rest of the class might note down errors on slips of paper, not indicating students' names. Another possibility is to assign two or three students per day to be "umpires" and listen for mistakes. After all the presentations have been given, the teacher collects the slips and points out the errors without mentioning the individuals who committed them. Throughout these activities the teacher must maintain a friendly and cooperative atmosphere in the classroom.

In a less personal way, the teacher can play a tape recording prepared by another group of students, identified only by number, and have the class pick out pronunciation errors. It is also possible to exchange tapes: Section A criticizes a tape made by Section B, and vice versa.

4.6.1b LISTENING FOR ONE'S OWN MISTAKES

On any recorded listening test or exercise, the students are required to listen to their own recording. Any mistake they catch and note down is scored −1. Any mistake they do not catch, but that the teacher catches, is scored −5. Such a system encourages critical listening.

4.6.1c INDIVIDUALIZED PRONUNCIATION OBJECTIVES

At the beginning of a quarter, the teacher has the students record fifteen sentences containing most of the sound and pronunciation features of the language being taught. The teacher listens to the tape and assigns each student two mistakes to be corrected by the end of the quarter: success in correcting the two mistakes (even if other mistakes persist) is rewarded by an A for that part of the course. This system gives the poorer student a reachable goal and requires the better student to work just as diligently in overcoming less obvious phonological problems. Moreover, the students help each other out, since they are not competing against each other, but rather aiming for a fixed objective.

4.6.1d THE SOUND-A-WEEK SYSTEM

The teacher stresses one sound or phonological feature (such as rhythm or stress) per week. Only mistakes in that area are corrected each time they occur, and only they are counted if spoken activities are graded.

4.6.1e RECORDED SENTENCES: PASS-FAIL

The teacher prepares five sentences containing one or more phonetic features. The students one by one record these sentences (at a tape recorder in the language lab, at the back of the classroom, or at the teacher's desk while others are doing written exercises). The teacher then grades the tape, noting each student's mistakes on a check list. Students making more than one or two mistakes must practice the sentences and then record them again. Only pass marks are recorded.

4.6.1f RECORDED SENTENCES: CLASSROOM EXERCISE

Students record a single sentence one after the other. The sentence contains two or more examples of a critical sound. For instance, *As-tu bu du jus?* The tape is then played back to the students who judge whether the sounds are right or wrong. The teacher is the final arbiter.

Alternate judging technique: Students each have a red and a green card. If they accept the sound, they raise the green card. If they do not accept the sound, they raise the red card. The teacher can tell at a glance if there is unanimity or if the sentence should be played over.

4.6.1g LISTENING DISCRIMINATION DRILLS PREPARED BY STUDENTS

In more advanced classes, the students can take turns preparing a set of listening discrimination sentences (such as those suggested in sections 4.3.2 and 4.3.3). One student reads his sentences while his classmates mark down, for example, whether they heard the article *ce* or *ces* before the direct object.

4.6.2 *Specific Techniques*

Sometimes a student needs special help in specific areas. Many of the techniques suggested for initial presentation (see section 4.2) and for listening discrimination (see section 4.3) may also be adapted for remedial work. In addition, some teachers might want to experiment with the following techniques.

4.6.2a PARTIAL CORRECTION

Many students have difficulty with the German *ü* and the French *u*, for which they substitute the English *oo*. Such students may be encouraged to substitute an /i/ for the /y/. In German, *vier mich* is much more acceptable than *fuhr mich* as a mispronounced *für mich*. Similarly, in French *ti viens* is better than *tout viens* as a substitute for *tu viens*. Since the American has a tendency to round his lips for the *u* he sees on paper, the chances are good that the /i/ sound will gradually come to resemble the /y/.

4.6.2b WORKING WITH COGNATES

Often the worst pronunciation mistakes occur when students are using cognates. The teacher might prepare a tape on the following pattern:

1. (pause) téléphone (pause)
2. (pause) télégraphe (pause)

The student receives a Ditto sheet containing the words. The first time he practices with the tape he repeats the French cognate after he has heard it. When he is more sure of himself, he reads the word in the pause between the number and the voice on the tape. He may repeat it a second time after the voice if he so desires.

In speaking Spanish, the student tends to transfer the English to the pronunciation of cognates. Thus the American is likely, for example, to say *tele-FOno* rather than the correct *teLEfono*. A contrastive drill may help the student realize his errors.

English	Spanish
TElephone	teLEfono
uniVERsity	universiDAD

English	Spanish
PASSport	pasaPORte
aMERican	ameriCAno
MEXican	mexiCAno
CAnada	CanaDA

4.6.2c UNSTRESSED VOWELS

The introduction of the unstressed vowel, or schwa, into French or Spanish is a very prevalent error. Strong insistence by the teacher on clearly articulated vowels will help students become aware of their mistakes. Whenever the teacher has noted several such mispronunciations in the course of a speaking activity or a small pronunciation test, he might have a brief full-class session, proceeding as follows: he reads some pairs of words; the students repeat the one that is French: *uh-méricain—américain, difficile—diff-uh-cile*. The students know immediately which is the right form and usually cooperate good-naturedly as they recognize the very words they were mispronouncing only a few minutes before.

Very often a student can be helped to make the proper sound if the teacher repeats both the sound he is making and the proper one. He often has to hear the contrast modeled by someone else before he can produce the sound accurately. This can be a one-second individual correction device as well as a brief full-class session.

CHAPTER FIVE
TEACHING GRAMMAR: GENERAL PROCEDURES

Foreign language teachers, especially teachers of beginning and intermediate classes, spend a considerable portion of their time teaching grammar. The terms may vary: grammar, generalizations, sentence patterns, structure, transformations, verb forms, conjugations, declensions, but the basic consideration is the same. Knowledge of vocabulary alone is insufficient for communication.

This chapter presents several approaches to the teaching of grammar. Should the student be presented with a pattern, rule, or generalization and then be given the opportunity to practice it (a deductive approach)? Or should he practice a set of patterns and then be led to derive his own generalization (an inductive approach)? Should the student be guided through a series of pattern drills of increasing difficulty in an effort to form correct language habits (a habit-formation or stimulus-response approach)? Or should he be allowed to apply generalizations and form original sentences in the foreign language (a cognitive or generative approach)? Although these approaches represent different philosophical positions about the nature of learning, the teacher will probably adapt techniques from each of them. Sometimes an approach that works with two-thirds of the class is not as effective with the remaining third, who would learn more readily from a different type of presentation.

The teacher should be encouraged to try out a variety of approaches and discover which work best for him and for his students.

5.1   GENERAL CONSIDERATIONS

The word "grammar" brings to the minds of many high school students a formal and often uninteresting analysis of language. Some students think only of conjugations, paradigms, declensions, and diagraming, all of which appear to be an end in themselves. If, on the other hand, students are eager to communicate their thoughts, and if to do so they must select the proper forms and put them in the correct order, grammar study takes on a new meaning.

Preparing students for a grammar lesson is just as important as choosing the exercises and drills to be used. The teacher who begins the lesson by saying, "Today we are going to study interrogatives," may lose many of his students. If, however, the students are conversing and need to ask questions of their teacher or classmates, they will want to learn the interrogative forms. Let us assume they can use affirmative forms and are able to say *Paul is going to the movies tonight.* If they want to ask Mary if she is going to the movies tonight, they need to learn this new structure. Similarly, in role playing, the student who is at a dinner party and does not have a fork must be able to use the negative when reporting this information to his hostess.

These kinds of situations and many more can serve as a point of departure for the study of grammar.

5.2   SUPPLEMENTING THE TEXTBOOK

The textbook, or basic program, including wall charts, films, or film strips, determines the order of presentation of grammar. Moreover, most textbooks are accompanied by a teacher's manual which gives many suggestions for teaching the grammatical patterns included in each lesson.

However, even the most thorough teacher's manual cannot provide complete guidelines for the teaching of grammar, guidelines which take into consideration differences among students, differences in school populations, differences in teachers, differences in scheduling, and physical environment. The teacher himself must assume the creative role of bridging the gap between the materials and the students, of teaching those things which the materials fail to teach adequately, and of providing supplementary activities where and when needed. The teacher may even discover that the type of presentation suggested in the teacher's manual is not appropriate for his particular students and may consequently modify those suggestions.

5.2.1 *Determining and Checking Requisite Knowledge*

Language learning, particularly at the early levels, is a cumulative process. The student must know the gender of a noun before he can make the article and adjectives agree with that noun. He must know the different forms of auxiliary verbs before he can be expected to produce compound tenses. This kind of basic knowledge is called *requisite learning*.

Although textbooks do present grammar in a sequential manner, they frequently do not have the space to review requisite knowledge before presenting a new point of structure. Recent research has indicated that the student's mastery of requisite knowledge is a greater factor in successful language learning than length and type of practice or the teacher's method of presentation. In other words, if the foreign language teacher wants his students to learn a specific point of grammar, such as the use of the subjunctive after *Pensez-vous que* and *Croyez-vous que*, he must first make sure that the students remember the forms of *penser* and *croire* in the present tense, and then that the students can handle the subjunctive forms of the verbs that will be used in the dependent clauses. This time spent for review of requisite knowledge is never wasted. If all students remember the forms, then the review has built up their confidence and prepared them for the new material. If some students have forgotten certain things, then the teacher is in the position immediately to review the difficult points in the old material before going on to the new lesson.

The following chart gives some examples of requisite knowledge which should be reviewed before introducing the new material:

New Material	Requisite knowledge
agreement of adjectives	genders of nouns to be used
irregular adjectives	forms of regular adjectives; genders of nouns to be used
direct-object pronouns (accusative)	forms of the direct object (accusative), genders of nouns to be used
position of object pronouns	forms of object pronouns; forms of verbs to be used
French: conditional tense	formation of future stems; imperfect endings or review of imperfect tense
German: prepositions of place	accusative and dative forms of nouns to be used
Spanish: subjunctive forms	imperative
French and Spanish: imperfect vs. preterite, *passé composé*	forms of the imperfect and the past tense

New Material	Requisite Knowledge
French: *passé composé* with *être*	present tense of *être*; forms of regular adjectives; past participles of *-er* verbs
inverted word order	regular word order; forms of verbs to be used

For each lesson in the textbook, the teacher should establish for himself which previous material the student must master if he is to understand the new material.

The form of the review will vary from lesson to lesson. For example, let us assume the new German lesson will introduce the conversational past with *haben*. The teacher might ask each student to pick up an object and hold it in his hand.

Teacher: Was hast du in der Hand?
Student: Ich habe ein Buch.

Various question-and-answer patterns will allow a review of *ihr habt, wir haben, er hat, sie hat, sie haben.* The review of familiar material has provided a warm-up session in spoken German. The students have been able to demonstrate how fluently they command the verb *haben*, and the teacher has been able to refresh the memories of those students who needed the review. From this positive beginning, the teacher can move on to a presentation of the past tense.

5.2.2   *Anticipating Areas of Interference*

The manuals on applied linguistics usually point out areas of interference which may present problems to the second-language learner.

One area of interference is the student's native language. The student of French, for example, will want to pronounce the final *s* on noun plurals, because this is the English pattern. The student of German will want to impose English word order on the German sentence. The student of Spanish will forget to use the *a* with a personal direct object. Some teachers explicitly present the English pattern and contrast it with the foreign language pattern to make students aware of the difficulty. Others prefer concentrating on drill and practice in the foreign language to strengthen the proper foreign language pattern. In the latter case drills containing the areas of interference will need much more practice than those containing patterns which parallel English.

The second type of interference arises within the foreign language itself. Here the textbooks often fail to contrast similar patterns explicitly, and the teacher must introduce supplementary exercises. For example, when beginning French students have learned the present tense of *faire*, they should be given ample opportunity to distinguish between the present tense of *faire* and that of *être*, *avoir*, and *aller*. When they learn the adjectival forms *ce, cet, cette, ces*, they should also review the pronoun *ce*, which becomes *c'* before a vowel sound. In German, <u>der gute Mann</u> should be contrasted with <u>der</u> guten *Frau* and <u>der Mann, der</u> *hier war*.

5.2.3   *Finding Alternate Presentations*

When the teacher has taught a unit and given the unit test, he may discover that not all students have attained the desired level of mastery; some remedial work from alternate sources may therefore be necessary.

5.2.3a   OTHER BOOKS

The department may have other textbooks on hand. Students may be asked to review the presentation of the same grammar points in another book. Often a second, slightly different, presentation seems clearer than the first.

5.2.3b   OTHER TECHNIQUES

The teacher may work with the students who need help while the rest of the class is engaged in another activity. At this time he might experiment with another technique, since the first one failed to produce the desired result.

5.2.3c   OTHER STUDENTS

Other students, either from the same class or from a higher class, may work as tutors with those who need assistance. Sometimes another student's explanation is more effective than the teacher's in clarifying a difficult structure (see section 5.7.2).

5.3   PRESENTING RULES: A DEDUCTIVE APPROACH

In a deductive approach, the rules, patterns, or generalizations are presented to the student, and then he is given ample opportunity to practice the new feature of grammar. This approach is most effective for the presentation of irregular patterns or exceptions to general patterns, for these by their very nature cannot be discovered through analogy. In the hands of a good teacher, the approach can save class time. There are also some students who prefer having the rule presented and then being allowed to demonstrate their comprehension by applying it to new sentences.

The drawback of the deductive presentation is that it may become dry and technical. The student may feel that he is being lectured and stop paying attention. If the examples are too tricky, the student is frustrated in his attempts to apply the rule. Learning a second language becomes a purely intellectual exercise instead of being a means to communication.

5.3.1 *Procedure*

The deductive presentation of grammar follows this general pattern: 1. Statement of the rule or pattern, 2. Sample sentences which students repeat, 3. Ample opportunity for students to practice the new pattern.

The first presentation is usually made orally. When the students can handle the spoken pattern, they are introduced to the written form. For more complex patterns at the intermediate levels, the teacher may present the written patterns first and then allow for oral practice afterwards.

Teacher: A simple way of turning a statement into a question in French
is by beginning the sentence with *est-ce que* and letting your
voice go up at the end. /
Listen: *Paul travaille. Est-ce que Paul travaille?* /
Repeat: *Paul travaille. Est-ce que Paul travaille?* /
Here is another example: *Marie travaille aussi.* /
The question: *Est-ce que Marie travaille aussi?* /
Now I will make a statement, and you turn it into a question:
  Robert travaille.
You ask the question.

Class: *Est-ce que Robert travaille?* /

5.3.2 *Techniques*

The teacher may use a variety of techniques to emphasize the essential aspects of the rule or pattern he is presenting. The teacher may speak in English (as in the following examples) or in the foreign language.

5.3.2a FLASH CARDS

The teacher is presenting inverted questions in German. He prepares sets of flash cards:

As he shows the regular statement he holds up a subject card and a verb

card: er arbeitet . He explains that to turn the statement into a question

you just invert, or reverse, the subject and the verb. In saying this he crosses his hands so the flash cards read ⟨ arbeitet ⟩ ⟨ er ⟩. With the other cards he presents additional examples.

5.3.2b   TRANSPARENCY AND OVERHEAD PROJECTOR

The teacher prepares the following transparency:

```
hablar
hablo
hablas
habla
hablamos
habláis
hablan
```

In class he first rapidly reviews forms of *hablar*, using a question-answer technique. Then he puts the transparency on the projector. He asks the students to read each form aloud, indicating which syllable is stressed. He circles the stressed syllable with a grease pencil (so that the circles may be erased and the transparency reused with another class).

Then he writes (in grease pencil) the infinitive *cerrar* on the right-hand side of the transparency. He gives the meaning of the new word. He elicits the forms *cerramos* and *cerráis*, which are regular. Then he explains that in these two forms the accent falls on the next-to-last syllable and asks the students to look at the root vowels of *hablar* and *cerrar*. The *a* of *hablar* appears in all the present tense forms. The root vowel *e* becomes *ie* when that vowel carries the accent of the word. He writes *e ie*. Therefore we say *Yo cierro*. He writes in the form *cierro*. Then he lets students generate the remaining forms of the new verb.

All the forms of *cerrar* are then practiced orally. Other radically changing verbs that follow the same pattern may be introduced so that the students may apply the pattern to an unfamiliar verb.

5.3.2c   PROPS AND CHALKBOARD

The teacher has a boy and a girl come forward, bringing their books with them. The forms of the possessive adjective are reviewed orally:

Teacher: Est-ce que c'est ton livre?
Student: Oui, c'est mon livre.

He asks the question of both the boy and the girl. Then he explains that the possessive adjective *son*, which can mean either *his* or *her*, follows the pattern of *mon*. He picks up the boy's book, points to the boy, and says: *C'est son* livre—*It's his book.* Then he takes the girl's book and says: *C'est son livre—It's her book.* Class repeats.

Then he gives the boy and girl each a piece of chalk.

Teacher: Est-ce que c'est ta craie?
Student: Oui, c'est ma craie.
Teacher: (Takes back the chalk.)
          How would you say: It's her (his) chalk?
Class: C'est sa craie.

He asks a boy to come forward, placing him between the other two students.

Teacher: (To girl.)
          Est-ce que Larry (student's name) est ton ami?
Girl: Oui, Larry est mon ami.
Teacher: (To class.)
          How do you say Larry is her friend?
Class: Larry est son ami.

The teacher continues, with another girl (*son amic*), Larry and the second girl (*ses amis*), two notebooks (*ses cahiers*).

On the chalkboard, he presents the written forms; students may dictate some of the sentences.

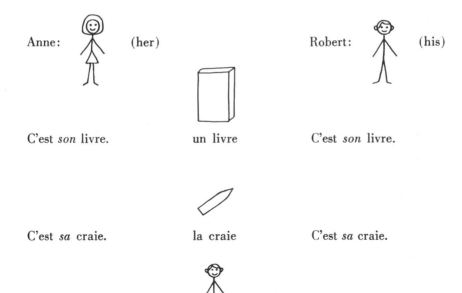

Anne: (her)   Robert: (his)

C'est *son* livre.   un livre   C'est *son* livre.

C'est *sa* craie.   la craie   C'est *sa* craie.

C'est *son* ami.   un ami   C'est *son* ami.

C'est *son* amie.   une amie   C'est *son* amie.

Ce sont *ses* amis.   des amis   Ce sont *ses* amis.

Ce sont ses cahiers.   des cahiers   Ce sont ses cahiers.

5.3.2d PUTTING PARADIGMS TO MELODY

Paradigms, or other forms to be learned by rote memory, may be more enjoyable if set to music.

The affirmative, interrogative, and negative forms of the verb *aller*, for example, may be sung to the music of the "Mexican Hat Dance." (For young students.)

Je vais, tu vas, il   va,   nous allons, vous allez, ils   vont.

Est-ce que je   vais? vas-tu? va - t - il?   allons-nous? allez-vous? vont-t-ils?

Je ne vais   pas, tu ne vas pas, il ne va   pas,   nous n'allons pas,

vous n'allez pas, ils ne vont   pas.

It is of course necessary to go beyond paradigms, so that students can use the new forms in full sentences. The paradigm is only a preliminary step in presenting a new irregular form.

Variation: Finger-snapping and other rhythmical techniques, such as hand-clapping, may also be used to liven up paradigms.

5.4 PRESENTING RULES: AN INDUCTIVE APPROACH

In an inductive approach, the teacher first gives the students examples of the grammatical structure to be learned. After the examples have been practiced, the student is guided in forming a generalization about the grammatical principle he has been working with. This approach works best with regular grammatical patterns.

The advantage of the inductive approach is that the student participates in the formulation of the grammatical principle. He has been saying or writing sentences using a specific pattern, so that the generalization is meaningful to him in terms of his previous activity. The disadvantage is that it often takes more time than a deductive presentation. Furthermore, some students prefer knowing the generalization before practicing the examples.

5.4.1 *Procedure*

The inductive presentation of grammar follows this general pattern: (1) Presentation of examples. (2) Pattern drills, question-answer practice, oral or written drilling. (3) Generalization or rule that grows out of the previous activity. Either the teacher states the rule or the students formulate it with his help. The rule may be in English or in the foreign language. 4 more practice

5.4.1a SELECTING THE MODEL SENTENCES

The careful choice of examples is the key to success in this approach. Often the use of paired sentences helps to make the grammatical point clear. For example, to teach the past tense in English, the teacher might give a series of examples like the following: *Today I want to play football. Yesterday I wanted to play baseball.*

In selecting sentences for a generalization, it is important to use only those which illustrate the grammatical point of the lesson.

(1) If the lesson had been on the partitive, it would be unwise to include nouns of different gender and number:

Good Choice

Je voudrais du pain.
Je voudrais du beurre.
Je voudrais du sucre.
Je voudrais du sel.

Here the teacher can ask what the nouns have in common. (They are all masculine.) Then the teacher can ask what word is used to express the idea of "some" before these masculine nouns (*du*).

Poor Choice

Je voudrais du pain.
Je voudrais de la viande.
Je voudrais des carottes.
Je voudrais de l'eau.

Here we have partitives of different gender and number. The way they are grouped makes it difficult to ask simple questions.

(2) For a lesson on the imperative, only regular verbs of the same conjugation should be used:

Good Choice

Juan <u>mira</u> la televisión.	Juan, ¡no <u>mires</u> la televisión!
Carlos <u>habla</u> inglés.	Carlos, ¡no <u>hables</u> inglés!
María <u>toma</u> el libro.	María, ¡no <u>tomes</u> el libro!
Carmen <u>compra</u> dulces.	Carmen, ¡no <u>compres</u> dulces!

Here the teacher could ask what the underlined words in the first column had in common. (They all end in *a*.) What kind of sentences are they? (Declarative.) What happens to these underlined words (or verbs) when they are used to make negative commands? (They drop the *a* and add *es*.)

Poor Choice

Juan <u>mira</u> la televisión.	Juan, ¡no <u>mires</u> la televisión!
Carlos <u>escribe</u>.	Carlos, ¡no <u>escribas</u>!
María <u>sale</u>.	María, ¡no <u>salgas</u>!
Carmen <u>va</u> a la ventana.	Carmen, ¡no <u>vayas</u> a la ventana!

These sentences contain both regular and irregular verbs of different conjugations. The only thing they have in common is that they are used in the negative imperative. It would be very difficult to ask any other questions on these groups of sentences.

5.4.1b PROCEEDING FROM KNOWN TO UNKNOWN GRAMMAR

Hier ist der Mantel.	Ich brauche den Mantel.
Hier ist der Bleistift.	Ich sehe den Bleistift.
Hier ist der Mann.	Ich kenne den Mann.
Hier ist der Brief.	Ich schreibe den Brief.

In the first column all the nouns are singular, masculine, and occur in the nominative case. The students must know this information before using the nouns in the accusative case (in the second column). In every case the noun marker changes from *der* to *den*.

Je parle français.	J'ai parlé français.
Il regarde la télévision.	Il a regardé la télévision.
Nous cherchons le cinéma.	Nous avons cherché le cinéma.
Tu dînes à sept heures.	Tu as dîné à sept heures.
Ils étudient l'espagnol.	Ils ont étudié l'espagnol.

Before teaching the material in the second column, the teacher should have given a lesson on the verb forms of *avoir*, and he should review the forms of regular verbs in the first conjugation (in the first column).

5.4.1c PREPARING THE QUESTIONS LEADING TO THE GENERALIZATION

(1) Oral presentation: In French there is a grammar of the spoken language which is very different from that of the written. The types of questions that a teacher would ask about the oral forms of the language would reflect this difference. (An IPA transcription as used here would not be used with students.)

[pɔl e mark]	[liz]	Paul et Marc lisent.
[pɔl e mark]	[part]	Paul et Marc partent.
[pɔl e mark]	[ekriv]	Paul et Marc écrivent.
[pɔl e mark]	[sɛrv]	Paul et Marc servent.
[pɔl e mark]	[finis]	Paul et Marc finissent.
[pɔl e mark]	[bwav]	Paul et Marc boivent.
[pɔl]	[li]	Paul lit.
[pɔl]	[par]	Paul part.
[pɔl]	[ekri]	Paul écrit.
[pɔl]	[sɛr]	Paul sert.
[pɔl]	[fini]	Paul finit.
[pɔl]	[bwa]	Paul boit.

The questions for the generalization refer only to the forms that appear in brackets. It is assumed that the class has never seen the language in its written form (this is the prereading stage).

The teacher might ask the following questions:

Teacher:	How many boys' names did you hear me pronounce in the first set of sentences?
Students:	Two.
Teacher:	How many in the second set?
Students:	One.
Teacher:	What happened to the verb when I used it with only one person?
Students:	You dropped off the last sound.

In an oral generalization it is essential that the teacher ask questions about sounds, and not letters.

(2) Written presentation: *good to demonstrate*

holen	Ich	habe	das	Buch	geholt.
suchen	Ich	habe	das	Kind	gesucht.
kaufen	Ich	habe	die	Uhr	gekauft.
machen	Ich	habe	den	Tisch	gemacht.
fragen	Ich	habe	den	Mann	gefragt.
bauen	Ich	habe	das	Haus	gebaut.
decken	Ich	habe	den	Tisch	gedeckt.

In these examples the teacher will need to ask questions: 1. about the presence of the auxiliary and its position in the sentence, 2. about the position of the direct object, 3. about the position and formation of the past participle. Notice that all the verbs selected are weak. In another lesson there could be a list of strong verbs.

Teacher: How many words make up the verb in each sentence?
Students: Two.
Teacher: Which one is the same in every sentence?
Students: *Habe.*
Teacher: Where does *habe* appear in the sentence?
Students: After the subject.
Teacher: Look at the infinitives in the list. What do we do to them when we use them in sentences?
Students: We drop off the *en* and replace it with a *t*. We also add *ge* to the beginning of the word.
Teacher: Where is its position in the sentence?
Students: At the end.
Teacher: Where do we place the direct object?
Students: Before the second verb (or past participle).

5.4.2   *Techniques for Presenting Model Sentences*

It is possible to use a variety of media in making the generalizations.

5.4.2a   CHALKBOARD

(1)   Using only the chalkboard, the teacher presents the Spanish subjunctive. He writes the following sentences on the board and covers them with a map until they are needed. As he uncovers them, he uses the same question-and-answer technique described above:

Vd. *habla* español.	Yo quiero que Vd. *hable* español.
Vd. *termina* el libro.	Yo quiero que Vd. *termine* el libro.

Vd. *toma* el dinero.   Yo quiero que Vd. *tome* el dinero.
Vd. *entra* por aquí.   Yo quiero que Vd. *entre* por aquí.

(2) Writing sentences while students watch or dictate: The teacher writes the first column and lets the students dictate the second:

Il est arrivé.   Elle est arrivée.
Il est tombé.   Elle est tombée.
Ils sont rentrés.   Elles sont rentrées.
Ils sont revenus.   Elles sont revenues.

(3) The board plus a prop: To teach the direct object in German, the teacher could use the following technique: He writes on the board,

Ich   habe   getrunken.

Holding a glass, he places it in several positions against the board: before the auxiliary, after the past participle, between the auxiliary and the past participle. Then he asks, Where must *ein Glas Wasser* be placed? (Between *habe* and *getrunken*.)

(4) The board plus index cards with masking tape or double-adhesive tape: Each card contains either a picture of a drink or the German word: *eine Tasse Kaffee, eine Tasse Tee, ein Glas Milch, ein Glas Wasser, ein Glas Schokoladenmilch, Limonade*. One by one the teacher sticks the index cards between *habe* and *getrunken*, for example, *Ich habe Limonade getrunken*.

5.4.2b WALL CHART

A wall chart with drawings may be used to present adjective agreement in Spanish.

5.4.2c FLANNEL BOARD

The object of the lesson is to teach the dative case with location (German). Cut out pieces of flocking paper and draw or paste the following pictures on them: a cat, a car, and a garage.

As the cat is placed in various positions on the flannel board, the teacher says:

mouse + cheese

snoopy + dog house is good idea

Die Katze ist
$\left\{ \begin{array}{l} \text{auf} \\ \text{vor} \\ \text{hinter} \\ \text{in} \end{array} \right\}$
dem Wagen.

Die Katze ist
$\left\{ \begin{array}{l} \text{auf} \\ \text{vor} \\ \text{hinter} \\ \text{in} \end{array} \right\}$
der Garage.

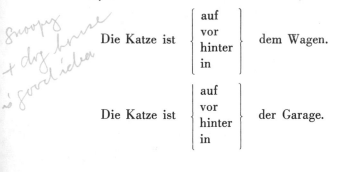

5.4.2d OVERHEAD TRANSPARENCIES

(1) A single transparency prepared in advance: This transparency is used to teach Spanish verb endings, present and preterite. The present endings are in blue, the preterite in red.

Hoy	Ayer
El come	El comió
El escribe	El secribió
El bebe	El bebió
El sale	El salió

(2) A prepared transparency with prepared overlays: This set of transparencies teaches the position of object pronouns in Spanish.

Basic Transparency: El   LEE.
Overlay #1:   lo
Overlay #2:   se

(3) Strips of acetate above a paper grid: This technique can be used in teaching German word order. Take a piece of paper the size of a transparency. Cut four slits in it and place it on the overhead projector.

The slits serve as windows through which various words are made to appear. Then take four narrow acetate strips and print on them the list of words that could be used in each part of the sentence. The loose strips are placed on top of the windows and moved up and down to form a variety of possible sentences. From time to time the teacher may move the strips to different positions making certain that the verb always appears second.

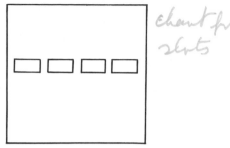

Jetzt	trinkt	Inge	Milch
Später	bestellt	er	Kaffee
Morgen	bekommt	sie	Wasser
	kauft	Hans	

(4) Writing on the overhead in front of the students: The teacher writes the sentence on the left, and the students dictate the sentence on the right.

J'ai acheté les fleurs.	Je les ai achetées.
J'ai vu les dames.	Je les ai vues.
J'ai trouvé les stylos.	Je les ai trouvés.
J'ai perdu les cahiers.	Je les ai perdus.

5.4.2e A PREPARED DITTO SHEET

Each student receives the following sheet:

De el dinero a los niños!	Déselo!
De el retrato a la señora!	Déselo!
De el lápiz al estudiante!	Déselo!
De el chocolate a los chicos!	Déselo!

De la muñeca a la nina!	Désela!
De la carta al cartero!	Désela!
De la propina a los criados!	Désela!
De la cartera al chico!	Désela!

The student is asked to draw one line under the direct objects and two lines under the indirect objects, or he may underline the direct objects in purple and the indirect objects in orange.

5.5   PATTERN DRILLS

Pattern drills offer a way of practicing new grammatical features. These drills, also referred to as structural drills or patterned-response exercises, are found in most current textbooks.

The pattern drill consists of two parts: the stimulus (or cue) and the response. The model, or initial set of utterances, establishes the pattern for the remainder of the exercise. Pattern drills are designed so that the student will almost always give the correct response. Through intensive practice, these responses become natural and the student acquires correct language speaking habits.

5.5.1   *Drills with Spoken Cues*

Traditionally pattern drills use only spoken cues. The teacher reads the stimulus or the tape gives it. The student then responds and the correct response is confirmed.

5.5.1a   TYPES OF PATTERN DRILLS

There are many types of pattern drills. Briefly, the principal kinds of drills are:

(1) Simple repetition
   Stimulus: Paul sees Mary.
   Response: Paul sees Mary.
(2) Simple substitution
   Stimulus: Paul sees Mary.   Alice.
   Response: Paul sees Alice.
(3) Multiple substitution
   Stimulus: Paul sees Mary.   David. Alice.
   Response: David sees Alice.
(4) Simple correlation
   Stimulus: Paul sees Mary.   Paul and David.
   Response: Paul and David see Mary.
(5) Multiple correlation
   Stimulus: He hurts himself.   They.
   Response: They hurt themselves.
(6) Transformation
   Stimulus: Paul sees Mary. (negative)
   Response: Paul doesn't see Mary.
(7) Joining sentences
   Stimulus: Paul sees Mary. Mary is waiting for a bus.
   Response: Paul sees Mary who is waiting for a bus.

(8) Rejoinder
Model: Paul sees Mary. That's nice, but I don't see her.
Stimulus: Paul sees David.
Response: That's nice, but I don't see him.
(9) Expansion drill
Stimulus: Paul is buying a house.   New.
Response: Paul is buying a new house.
(10) Translation drill
Stimulus: Paul needs Mary.
Response: Paul a besoin de Mary.

For the teacher who is looking for new ideas for language drills, there are books which contain only pattern drills.[1]

5.5.1b USING DRILLS IN THE CLASSROOM

The success of classroom language drills depends on their implementation. Nothing is deadlier than a difficult drill that bogs down because students are unable to respond quickly. The drill should either be simplified or dropped on the spot.

(1) Tape-cued drills: The teacher plays the tape recorder and points to individuals to respond.

(2) Teacher-cued drills: The teacher reads the cues and points to individuals to respond.

(3) Student-cued drills: A student is asked to prepare and lead a specific drill. This encourages student participation. Moreover, a student can lead a drill with one half the class while the teacher is working with the other half.

(4) Working in pairs: One student reads the cue while the other student answers. At the end of the drill the roles are reversed. This method has the advantage of involving the entire class actively in the drill.

5.5.1c USING DRILLS IN THE LANGUAGE LABORATORY

For suggestions on livening up drills in the language laboratory, see section 3.3.3d.

5.5.2 *Drills with Visuals*

Often drills can be made more meaningful to the students by the introduction of visuals.

5.5.2a OVERHEAD PROJECTOR

The teacher prepares a transparency showing figures that represent all the pronoun subjects.

[1] See for example, Mavis Beal, *French Language Drills* (New York: St. Martin's Press, 1967), and James Etmekjian, *Pattern Drills in Language Teaching* (New York: New York University Press, 1966).

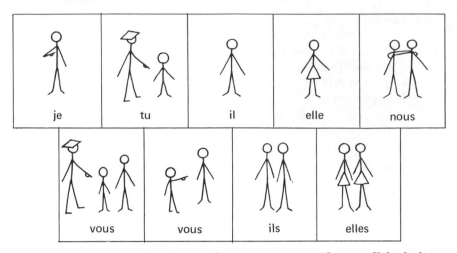

The teacher points to the boy in the transparency and says: *Il lit le livre.*
Then while the teacher points to each of the other figures in turn, the class
gives the sentence with the various forms of the verb *lire*: *Je lis le livre.*
Nous lisons le livre. Vous lisez le livre, and so on.

5.5.2b INDEX CARDS WITH PICTURES

Each index card contains a line drawing of a beverage: milk, water, beer,
and so on. This drill is to practice the verb *to drink.*

Teacher: (Holds up a card.)
          Qu'est-ce que tu bois?
Student: Je bois du lait.

5.5.2c INDEX CARDS WITH SYMBOLS

Each index card contains a symbol.

The teacher gives a model sentence in the plural: *Ils font du ski.* Then he
flashes a card with the drawing of one finger. The students say: *Il fait du ski.*
The teacher next flashes the card with the question mark. The students say:
Fait-il du ski? Then he shows them the card with the drawing of plural
fingers. The students say: *Font-ils du ski?* And then the card with the period.
The students say: *Ils font du ski.* Finally, the teacher flashes the card with X,
meaning negative. The students say: *Ils ne font pas de ski.*

5.5.2d THE USE OF INDEX CARDS WITH WORDS

The teacher prepares index cards containing German nouns in the nominative. The model sentence is *Ich sehe das Buch*. The purpose of this pattern drill is to practice the definite article in the accusative case.

As the first card appears, the students say: *Ich sehe den Bleistift*. Next, *Ich sehe die Karte*, and so on.

5.5.2e WALL CHARTS WITH PICTURES

The teacher displays a wall chart with the drawing of a body. The purpose is to practice *le duele*. . . . The teacher points rapidly to each part of the body and the class says: *Le duele la nariz. Le duele la mano. Le duelen los dedos*, and so on.

5.5.2f WALL CHARTS WITH WORDS

The teacher displays a wall chart with columns containing the elements of the sentence. The teacher points to the words in the last column, and the students give the correct form of the sentence using that word.

$$
\text{Jean va}
\begin{cases}
\text{au} \\[2pt]
\text{à l'} \\[2pt]
\text{à la}
\end{cases}
\begin{cases}
\text{épicerie} \\
\text{école} \\
\text{bibliothèque} \\
\text{lac} \\
\text{boulangerie} \\
\text{église} \\
\text{cinéma} \\
\text{restaurant} \\
\text{maison} \\
\text{café}
\end{cases}
$$

For example, the teacher points to *école*. The students say: *Jean va à l'école*.

5.5.2g PROPS

(1) The teacher displays a dish containing plastic fruit. He picks up one fruit at a time and the class says: *Pásame la manzana. Pásame el plátano, las uvas*, and so on. The purpose of the drill is to practice the gender of the nouns.

(2) The teacher displays doll clothes. He holds up each article of clothing and the class says: *Je voudrais une robe verte. Je voudrais un pantalon noir,* and so on. The purpose of this drill is to give the students practice in placing the adjective after the noun.

5.6 QUESTION-ANSWER TECHNIQUES

The question-answer techniques enable the students to practice points of grammar and structure by asking questions. The actual questions are often as closely structured as the stimulus lines in a pattern drill. The drill is artificial, in that the students are placed in a situation where they must give a specific response.

Yet, while the question-answer technique has all the qualities of a good pattern drill (intense oral practice, sequential presentation of new elements, and specific desired responses), it has one additional feature in its favor: student involvement.

When the student goes through a series of drills, *He bought a hat, He bought a coat, He bought a jacket,* all the sentences seem irrelevant. After all, *he* didn't really buy all those things. The question-answer technique introduces an element of role-play, of student participation. For example, the teacher may wish to drill the above sentences. He prepares index cards with pictures of items of clothing and distributes them to the students. He then asks the class: *What did Bob buy?* Bob holds up his card, and another student (or the entire class) replies: *He bought a jacket.*

5.6.1 *Index Cards*

The use of index cards, as described in the example above, is the simplest way to implement a question-answer drill. The teacher can walk around the room, holding up cards for all to see and having students exchange cards, thereby introducing an element of movement into the class.

The cards may contain symbols, line drawings, words, or initials. Students may be asked to bring blank index cards to class and prepare their own upon the instructions of the teacher.

5.6.1a ELICITING THE NEGATIVE

The teacher asks a student who holds a card labeled *math*: *Do you like English?* The pattern, given by the teacher in a model, requires the student to reply: *No, I don't like English. I like math.*

Students hold cards depicting pastimes. Two boys have cards showing a swimming pool.

Teacher: Are they going to the movies?
Student: No, they're not going to the movies. They're going swimming.

5.6.1b CHANGE OF TENSE

Students have cards depicting places.

Teacher: Are you going downtown today?
Student: No, I went downtown yesterday.

5.6.1c OBJECT PRONOUNS

Students have cards depicting objects.

Teacher: Sue, give Jane the record.
           (Student carries out the action.)
Teacher: What did you do with the record, Sue?
Student: I gave it to Jane.

5.6.2 *Grouping*

Roles, or "tags," may be assigned to entire groups. For example, whatever the boys plan to do, the girls will do tomorrow. The boys are given cards depicting sports.

Teacher: What are you doing this afternoon, Jim?
Jim: I'm going to play baseball.
Teacher: And you girls?
Girls: We're going to play baseball tomorrow.

5.6.3 *Directed Dialogue*

The use of groups or cards may also furnish cues for directed dialogue.

Teacher: Jonathan, ask Sally what she's drinking.
Jonathan: Sally, what are you drinking?
Sally: (According to her card.)
           I'm drinking lemonade.

5.6.4 *Chain Drill*

The chain drill may also be adapted to the question-answer technique. In the above example, Sally would then turn to her neighbor and ask him what he is drinking.

5.6.5 *Free Responses*

When the teacher feels that the students can handle a grammatical structure and the vocabulary well in controlled drills, he may wish to ask questions which elicit a free response from the students. This technique develops the students' conversational skills. (Further variations are presented in Chapter 9.)

5.7 WRITTEN EXERCISES

Students must be given the opportunity to practice new structures in written form as well as orally. Writing, however, is primarily an individual activity, whereas speaking requires two or more people. Written exercises lend themselves well to homework, while spoken exercises are more effectively carried out in the classroom. The following section gives some suggestions for activities designed to develop written control of structures.

5.7.1 *Types of Written Exercises*

5.7.1a COPYING

Students copy material from a model. A variation of this activity is unscrambling sentences and rewriting them in logical order. Matching exercises may be developed where the student writes the appropriate caption, selected from among several given possibilities, under each of a group of pictures. Students may also play "Who said what" by selecting a statement and placing it next to the picture of the person who most likely made it.

5.7.1b PATTERN DRILLS

Students write the responses to pattern drills. The model may be written on the board, and the teacher may dictate the stimulus sentences.

5.7.1c QUESTION-ANSWER TECHNIQUE

The students write the answers to the teacher's questions instead of giving them orally.

5.7.1d DICTATION

The teacher dictates familiar or unfamiliar material to the class. (For examples, see section 11.3.)

5.7.1e COMPLETION EXERCISES

The student completes a written phrase by filling in blanks or adding a new word to the sentence.

5.7.1f GRAMMAR COMPOSITIONS

The students, individually or in small groups, write brief compositions incorporating several examples of a specific grammar point: verb tenses, descriptive adjectives, relative clauses, and so on. For example, students may write about weekend plans (using the future), or they may use the conditional to complete a paragraph beginning with *Si j'étais président.*

5.7.2 *Techniques for Utilizing Written Exercises in the Classroom*

5.7.2a INDEPENDENT WORK

Any written exercise which is self-contained, that is, which is based on only written instructions, may be assigned as independent work. The teacher may wish to let students talk quietly together and help each other with the work.

Written exercises which are correlated with a tape program may be used in the language laboratory. If the recorded material is on cassettes, and if the classroom is equipped with cassette recorders, the students may work individually in the classroom. A group of students may work on this type of exercise together if the classroom has a tape recorder with several headsets.

5.7.2b TEACHER-LED WORK

The teacher can work with a group of students or with the entire class in directing written exercises.

(1) Using the chalkboard: Some students may be asked to put the written work on the chalkboard. The teacher corrects these sentences with the help of the other students while those at their seats correct their own work.

(2) Using the overhead: One student may be given an acetate sheet and a grease pencil. He does his written work, a dictation for example, on the transparency. The rest of the class writes the sentences on paper. At the end of the exercise, the transparency is projected on the overhead. The teacher corrects the work and answers questions.

Variation 1: A student may write at the overhead with the light turned on, so that others may immediately see what he is doing.

Variation 2: The teacher may prepare a transparency with blanks to be filled in. As the students give the correct answers, the teacher fills in the blanks on the transparency with a grease pencil. A similar Ditto is then handed out for homework.

Variation 3: The teacher gives the oral cue to a pattern drill or a question-answer exercise. The students give the oral response and the teacher writes it on the lighted overhead. Students copy the correct written response.

5.7.3 *Techniques for Correcting Written Exercises in the Classroom*

The techniques suggested for correcting homework may be used for correcting written exercises. (See section 3.5.3.)

5.8   REMEDIAL WORK

With intermediate and advanced classes the teacher is faced with the problem of remedial work. There are always some students who continually make mistakes with noun-adjective agreements. Others have trouble with irregular verbs, or even regular verbs.

5.8.1   *Whole-Class Technique*

Announce the "Error of the Week," for example, subject-verb agreement. When correcting written work that week, the teacher deducts one point for each error, *except* errors in subject-verb agreement, which cost the student five points.

5.8.2   *Individualized Techniques*

Each student is given a personal error to correct over a two- or three-week period. Small groups of students may be allowed to work on the same error.

5.8.2a   POSTER

The student makes a poster to illustrate the structure he is having difficulty with. These posters may be put up in the classroom. The teacher may also wish to use them with other classes.

5.8.2b   DITTOS

The student prepares a Ditto master on his error, perhaps illustrating the correct form with a drawing or cartoon. He may wish to write five or six exercises based on that point of grammar. The teacher will check the Ditto master for accuracy and then let the student run off copies for his classmates. The student gives out the Dittos to the whole class (or part of the class) and then corrects their answers.

5.8.2c   TUTORING

The student is asked to tutor a beginning student on his particular difficulty. He prepares a short test (approved by the teacher) which he gives to his tutee when he feels the latter has mastered the structure.

5.8.2d   CORRECTING PAPERS

The student corrects exercises on the grammar point with which he has difficulty for the teacher. These may be exercises done in a beginning class.

5.8.2e TEACHING

The student prepares a mini-lesson on the grammar point and teaches it to another class or to a group of students. This mini-lesson might also be the joint project of two or three students.

CHAPTER SIX
TEACHING GRAMMAR: TECHNIQUES ARRANGED BY GRAMMATICAL CATEGORIES

This chapter offers a range of techniques for teaching specific elements of grammar. Each technique makes use of media: flash cards, felt board, magnet board, pocket chart, overhead projector, or opaque projector. Games, songs, and crossword puzzles are also included.

The catalogue of suggested techniques is far from exhaustive; it is merely illustrative. It is hoped that the teacher will be inspired to apply some of these suggestions to other grammatical problems—that he will begin experimenting with a variety of activities and eventually invent new approaches or new variations to old approaches. In other words, the teaching of grammar will cease to be a "grind" and will rather become a challenge to the teacher to express his creativity.

6.1 NOUN PHRASES

Noun phrases include nouns as well as determiners (definite, indefinite, and partitive articles, possessive and demonstrative adjectives, expressions of quantity), adjectives, and adverbs used as intensifiers.

6.1.1 *Noun-Adjective Agreement*

6.1.1a COLOR CARDS PLUS WALL CHART

For a French class, for example, prepare a wall chart with line drawings of articles of clothing. The articles of clothing of masculine gender are outlined in blue, while those of feminine gender are outlined in red. Next prepare a stack of 4 × 6 index cards with a colored square in the center of each. For the colors given below add a red superscript on the card: green (*vert*) :/t/; white (*blanc*) :/ʃ/; gray (*gris*) :/z/. The cards for red, blue, yellow, orange, black, brown (marron) have no superscripts.

The teacher reviews the articles of clothing with questions like: *Qu'est-ce que c'est? C'est une jupe.* Then he reviews the names of the colors with the flash cards. Next he holds the red card next to the pants and asks: *De quelle couleur est le pantalon?* He models the response: *Il est rouge.* With the card next to a shirt he asks: *De quelle couleur est la chemise?* He models the response: *Elle est rouge.* Then he varies the questions, using all the cards without superscripts.

When the students can alternate freely between responses with *Il est . . .* and *Elle est. . .* , the teacher selects a card with a superscript, for example, the green card, holds it next to a masculine article of clothing, and asks: *De quelle couleur est le manteau?* He gives the answer: *Il est vert.* Then he asks the class to listen carefully as he says: *De quelle couleur est la robe? Elle est verte.*

He goes from one drawing to the next saying: *La jupe est verte. Le pantalon est vert.* The students notice, or he points out, that the red *t* on the green card means that the t sound must be pronounced when the adjective modifies a feminine noun (outlined in red on the chart).

Holding up the gray card, he asks: *De quelle couleur est la cravate?* Generally the students can give the correct reply: *Elle est grise,* for they notice the /z/ on the gray card.

In a subsequent lesson the students learn how to spell the adjective forms and see the correspondence between the sound /z/, for example, and the spelling "se."

6.1.1b PIECES OF PAPER

Have the girls in the Spanish class write an A on a piece of paper. Have the boys write an O. Divide the class into two groups, Mexico and Norteamérica. When asked their nationality, the girls answer: *Soy mexicana* or *Soy norteamericana.* Boys give the masculine form. By bringing two boys from the same country together, the teacher can drill *Son mexicanos.* A variety of questions may be asked of the students; for example, *Are you North American? Is María Mexican? Ask Joe if he is North American. Are Pablo and Teresa Mexican? Ask Inez and Carlita if they are North Ameri-*

can? At the end of this oral practice, the students can easily develop the generalization that masculine adjectives end in *-o* and form a plural in *-os* and that the equivalent feminine forms end in *-a* and *-as.*

6.1.2 *Definite Articles*

6.1.2a POSTER

Speakers of French, Spanish, and German use the definite article for parts of the body; speakers of English use the possessive adjective. Draw a picture of a body on the chalkboard.

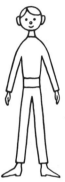

As the teacher points to each part of the body he says:

Jacques s'est cassé la jambe, le pied, la tête, and so on.
Juan se rompió la pierna, el pie, la cabeza, and so on.

The class repeats in chorus, then individually.

6.1.2b A GAME FROM COSTA RICA: "¿VAS CON LA LUNA O CON EL SOL?"

The class is divided into two teams: *Los Rojos* and *Los Blancos.* A student at the board keeps the score—one point for each correct answer. The teacher utters a noun without its gender. He then turns to a student on one team and asks: *¿Vas con la luna o con el sol?* If the word is feminine, the student must say *Voy con la luna;* if maculine, *Voy con el sol.*

6.1.3 *Possessive Adjectives*

6.1.3a ARTICLES OF CLOTHING

Teach some of the articles of clothing and all of the colors. Say while pointing to your own skirt: *Ma jupe est bleue. Mi falda es azul.* The class repeats several times. Then ask individuals: *De quelle couleur est votre jupe? ¿De qué color es su falda?*

The French examples might be all feminine at first. After a time introduce the masculine form *mon. Ma chemise, ma ceinture, ma jupe, ma cravate; mon pantalon, mon sac, mon pull,* and so on.

Plural forms are presented the same way: *Mes chaussures sont noires. De quelle couleur sont vos chaussures? Mis zapatos son negros. ¿De qué color son sus zapatos?*

After these forms are mastered, the students could be directed to ask one another the same question. This will require using the familiar forms: *De quelle couleur est ton pull? Mon pull est vert. ¿De qué color son tus zapatos? Mis zapatos son negros.*

6.1.3b CLASSROOM OBJECTS

English-speaking students confuse the different forms of possessive adjectives in French and German because English uses fewer forms. For practice in the comprehension of the forms corresponding to *my, his,* and *your,* the teacher asks individuals to hand objects to one another: *Jean, donnez votre crayon à Pierre. Marc, donnez à Hélène son crayon. Marie, donnez mon crayon à Paulette. Hans, gib Fritz deinen Bleistift! Inge, gib Georg seinen Blesitift! Heinz, gib Karl meinen Bleistift!*

6.1.4 Demonstrative Adjectives

Place objects on the desk in front of you: a green book, a black notebook, a white pencil. Draw on the chalkboard a stick figure of a short boy and a tall boy.

In the back of the room there are objects on a window sill or table: a red book, a blue notebook, a green pencil, a tall boy and a short boy (stick-figure pictures).

While pointing to objects near and far from you, say:

Ce livre-ci est vert.	Ce livre-là est rouge.
Ce cahier-ci est noir.	Ce cahier-là est bleu.
Ce crayon-ci est blanc.	Ce crayon-là est vert.
Ce garçon-ci est petit.	Ce garçon-là est grand.
Ce garçon-ci est grand.	Ce garçon-là est petit.

After these forms are mastered, do the same thing with feminine objects.

Draw on the front board a white rose, a yellow apple, a tall girl and a thin girl. Draw on the back board a yellow rose, a red apple, a little girl, and a stout girl.

Cette rose-ci est blanche.	Cette rose-là est jaune.
Cette pomme-ci est jaune.	Cette pomme-là est rouge.
Cette fille-ci est grande.	Cette fille-là est petite.
Cette fille-ci est mince.	Cette fille-là est grosse.

6.1.5 Partitive Articles

6.1.5a PROPS

Use one candy bar and index cards with the following pictures:

bave
thun
play thum

The teacher first shows the students the cards on the left while giving the question and the answer: *Qu'est-ce que vous aimez? J'aime le lait, le sucre, le pain, le beurre, la salade, la viande, la glace, l'eau.* The students then answer the questions individually.

After the genders have been mastered, the teacher shows the cards on the right while giving the question and answer: *Qu'est-ce que vous voulez? Je voudrais du lait, du sucre, du pain, du beurre, de la salade,* and so on.

The teacher holds up the candy bar and says: *Aimez-vous le chocolat? Oui, j'aime le chocolat.* Then she breaks off a piece and asks individuals: *Voulez-vous du chocolat?* Individual students respond: *Oui, je voudrais du chocolat.*

6.1.6 *Possessive Pronouns*

6.1.6a WALL CHART

The teacher displays a wall chart or a transparency depicting many objects of different genders. He points to a house and says: *Es para mí.* Then he says: *Es mía. Es para Juan. Es suya. Es para nosotros. Es nuestra. Es para tí. Es tuya.* He does likewise for the masculine forms.

6.1.6b GAME: BASEBALL

The teacher divides the class into two teams: *Los Rojos* and *Los Blancos.* He puts two baseball diamonds on the board—one for each team.

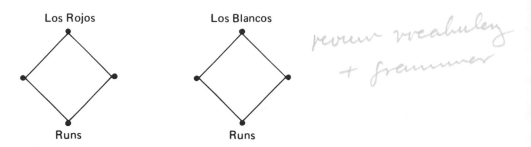

The teacher points to a picture of a hat on the chart (or transparency) and says: *Es para mí.* Then he points to a student on *Los Rojos* team. If the student says *Es mío*, he advances to first base, and the teacher indicates this on the diamond by making a mark with red chalk along the side of the first base. Then the other team has a chance. No one advances if there is a wrong answer.

Runs are scored after a team gets four correct answers, thus arriving at home base. The team having the largest number of runs wins.

6.1.7 *Demonstrative Pronouns*

Index cards, spread along the chalkboard, contain line drawings of people in different colored clothing.

Teacher:	Regardez ces jeunes filles. Qui est la plus grande? (Points to one.)
	Celle en rouge.
Class:	Celle en rouge (several times).
Teacher:	Qui est la plus petite?
Student:	Celle en bleue.
Teacher:	Qui est la plus jolie?
Student:	Celle en vert.

Another next set of pictures is of boys or men.

Teacher:	(Gives both question and answer. Class repeats.)
	Qui est le plus grand?
	Celui en bleu.
	Qui est le plus beau?

Student: Celui en vert.
Teacher: Qui est le plus fort?
Student: Celui en noir.

6.2 VERB FORMS

This section suggests techniques for teaching verb forms and the use of various tenses.

6.2.1 *Subject-Verb Agreement*

6.2.1a OVERHEAD TRANSPARENCY

Draw the following stick figures on a transparency. Write the pronouns themselves on an overlay, so that they will fall below the figures.

First it may be necessary to clarify the use of the symbols. Put the basic transparency (stick figures minus the words) on the overhead and explain the pronouns. With seventh graders, the concept of personal pronouns might have to be explained in English: *The first figure is talking about himself. What pronoun do you use when you talk about yourself? (I). In German you say* ich. After having presented the pronouns, the teacher can practice them rapidly, pointing to one and having the students give the German equivalent. Finally the overlay may be placed on the overhead so that the students see how the pronouns are spelled.

The transparency may also be used from time to time in order to provide cues for verb drills:

Teacher: Ich gehe in die Stadt.
            (Points to *er*.)
Student: Er geht in die Stadt.

6.2.1b LARGE SYMBOLS

The teacher prepares symbols, on 8½″ × 11″ pieces of cardboard, to represent the known verbs:

aimer   détester   compter   travailler   habiter

Five students, each holding up a symbol, come to the front of the class. The teacher has a deck of index cards containing each of the pronoun symbols that have been presented up to that time. He holds a pronoun symbol over the head of the student holding the verb card. The class responds appropriately: *Tu travailles. Il compte.* Short complements should be included for the transitive verbs: *Nous aimons Paris. Nous détestons Paul. J'habite ici.*

6.2.1c FLASH CARDS

The teacher prepares flash cards with infinitives: *entrar, estudiar, hablar, esperar.* He holds up a card and announces a pronoun. The students give the appropriate verb form.

6.2.1d CUE CARDS

The teacher prepares enough cue cards for the entire class. These cards have pictures: a football, a basketball, a baseball, a ping-pong paddle, a volleyball. The cards are distributed and the nouns are reviewed.

Teacher: A quoi joues-tu?
Student: Je joue au football.
Teacher: Marie et Pierre, à quoi jouez-vous?
Student: Nous jouons au volleyball.
Teacher: Et Robert, à quoi joue-t-il?
Student: Il joue au ping-pong.

This type of conversation drill of verbs is often very effective. The same pictures may also be used to elicit sentences of the type: *J'aime le football. Je déteste le basketball. Je fais souvent du baseball. Hier j'ai joué au football. J'aime faire du volleyball. Je n'aime pas le baseball. Je n'aime pas faire du basketball. Je ferai du volleyball demain.*

6.2.1e GAME: A RELAY RACE

Eight students go to the chalkboard. Each stands under a pronoun: *elles, tu, vous, je, il, nous, ils, elle.* At a given signal each writes a sentence with *être* in the *passé composé*, starting with the pronoun above. As each individual finishes his sentence, he moves to the next pronoun and writes a sentence using it. All students keep rotating. The student at the far right of the board takes the place of the student at the far left. After three or four minutes, the teacher says *Halte!* and all sit down. Then the teacher, with the help of the class, counts the correct sentences. To add to the excitement, two teams could play, perhaps the boys against the girls.

Variation: All eight students are assigned the same verb and the same tense, for example, *se lever* in the *passé composé*. The teacher signals *Commencez!* and the students each write a sentence. As soon as they are finished, they move to the left and write another sentence. When the teacher calls *Halte!* all sit down, and the number of correct sentences are counted.

6.2.2 *Present to Past*

6.2.2a CALENDAR

The teacher points to a calendar and says: *Aujourd'hui Paul dîne à sept heures. Hier il a dîné à six heures. Hier, moi, j'ai dîné à six heures et demie.*

Then the teacher asks each person: *A quelle heure avez-vous dîné hier?* Individual students respond: *Hier, j'ai dîné à six heures,* and so on.

6.2.2b CROSSWORD PUZZLE

Change all verbs to the preterite.

bad example

Horizontal

1. llegan
4. lava
5. entro
6. ven
7. anda
8. rompe
9. hablo
10. niegan

Vertical

1. llevan
2. oye
3. nadas

¹L	L	E	G	A	R	²O	³N
⁴L	A	V	O	▨	▨	Y	A
⁵E	N	T	R	E	▨	O	D
⁶V	I	E	R	O	N	▨	A
⁷A	N	D	U	V	O	▨	S
⁸R	O	M	P	I	O	▨	T
O	▨	▨	⁹H	A	B	L	E
¹⁰N	E	G	A	R	O	N	▨

6.2.3   Passé composé *with* être

6.2.3a   WALL CHART OR TRANSPARENCY OF TWO HOUSES

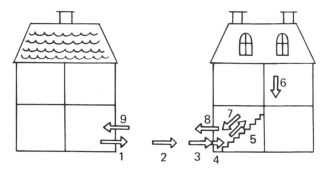

Teacher says while class repeats:

1. Je suis sorti de chez moi.
2. Je suis allé chez ma grand-mère.
3. Je suis arrivé chez elle.
4. Je suis entré dans la maison.
5. Je suis monté au premier étage.
6. Je suis resté une heure dans la chambre de ma grand-mère.
7. Je suis descendu.
8. Je suis parti.
9. Je suis rentré chez moi.

When the class is familiar with the sentences, the teacher randomly points to a number and individual students respond.

When the class can control the *passé composé* with the subject *je*, other pronoun subjects can be introduced.

Variation: An overlay can be prepared which places the written infinitive next to each number on the basic transparency.

6.2.3b   LA PETITE HISTOIRE TRAGIQUE DE JACQUES

Verbs that do not connote motion to or from can be presented by having students memorize: *Jacques est né. Jacques est tombé. Jacques est mort.*

6.2.4   *Imperfect versus Preterite (or* Passé Composé*)*

6.2.4a   OVERHEAD PROJECTOR

Each transparency has a second one hinged to it so it can be used as an overlay.

The first transparency is of María talking on the phone. The overlay is of her mother entering the room.

Teacher: (showing first transparency) María hablaba por teléfono (adding second transparency) cuando su mamá entró.

Other sentences that lend themselves to similar presentation are: La mamá preparaba la cena cuando el teléfono sonó. Merendaban cuando empezó a llover.

6.2.4b CHALKBOARD

Ask a student to stand at the chalkboard holding a piece of chalk high above the ledge. The eraser becomes a train and is moved by the teacher along the chalkboard ledge.

Teacher: Le train allait à Paris (continues to move eraser) quand une bombe est tombée dessus!
Student: (Drops chalk.)

6.2.4c FLASH CARDS

Make flash cards of different actions: boy eating, drinking, reading, writing, and so on. As each card is flashed, the students say: *El comía cuando su mamá llegó. El escribía cuando su mamá llegó. Il mangeait quand sa mère est entrée. Il buvait quand sa mère est entrée.*

6.2.4d SONG

Cantaba la rana.
La rana *cantaba,*
Sentada debajo del agua
cuando la rana *se puso* a cantar
Vino la mosca y la *hizo* callar.

6.2.5 *Subjunctive*

6.2.5a WALL CHARTS OR TRANSPARENCIES

A series of visuals could be used to depict two actions: the first a child behaving in a certain way, and the second, his mother wanting him to behave in another way. These could be on wall charts or transparencies with overlays. Teacher points to each visual and says: *Marie ne fait pas la vaisselle. La maman veut que Marie fasse la vaisselle. Le bébé ne dort pas. La maman veut que le bébé dorme. Marc ne va pas chez le dentiste. La maman veut que Marc aille chez le dentiste.*

6.2.5b DIRECTED DIALOGUE GAME

Teacher: María ¿qué quieres que Juan haga?
María: Quiero que Juan vaya a la puerta.
(Juan must execute this order.)

Teacher: Carlos, ¿qué quieres que Pablo haga?

Carlos: Quiero que Pablo escriba su nombre en la pizarra.

(Pablo executes the order.)

Teacher: Ricardo, ¿qué quieres que Carmen haga?

Ricardo: Quiero que Carmen se levante.

(Carmen executes this order.)

6.2.5c FLASH-CARD DRILL

Teacher holds up a set of cards on which nouns and pronouns appear:

| él | | tú | | ellos | | Juan y María |

The model sentence is *Quiero que ella venga conmigo*. The class responds chorally and then individually: *Quiero que él venga conmigo. Quiero que tú vengas conmigo. Quiero que ellos vengan conmigo. Quiero que Juan y María vengan conmigo.*

Variation: Use index cards with stick figures instead of words.

6.2.6 *Conditional with If-Clauses*

6.2.6a GAME

The teacher distributes several slips of paper to each student. He then divides the class into two groups. On the separate slips of paper, one group writes only *si*-clauses in the imperfect tense with the subject pronoun *vous*. The other writes only independent clauses in the conditional with the subject pronoun *je*. The teacher writes an example on the board: *Si vous prépariez un repas, je ne le mangerais pas.* Then the teacher collects all the pieces of paper and puts them in two separate hats.

Several students are sent to the board and asked to take one of the pieces of paper from each hat. Then they proceed to copy the two clauses and make a sentence. The results can be hilarious. Such combinations as the following are not uncommon: *Si vous étiez le professeur, je vous donnerais une bonne fessée. Si vous étiez riche, je vous épouserais.*

The same game can be played in Spanish using the imperfect subjunctive: *Si Vd. fuera el profesor, yo le daría una bofetada. Si Vd. fuera rico, yo lo casaría.*

A similar game can be played in German: *Wenn Sie Geld hätten, würde ich ein Buch schreiben.*

6.3 COMPLEMENTS

This section deals with direct and indirect objects, prepositional phrases, infinitive clauses, relative clauses, and predicate adjectives.

6.3.1 *Direct and Indirect Objects*

6.3.1a MAGAZINE PICTURES

The teacher cuts the following pictures out of magazines and pastes them on index cards: a book, a car, a glass of milk, a house, a loaf of bread, and so on. (Line drawings could also be used, if the teacher can draw.)

As the teacher flashes each card, he asks a question and answers it. The students first repeat the answer chorally and then individually.

Teacher: (Shows picture of book.)
               Was hat Karl gelesen?
               Karl hat das Buch gelesen.
Students: Karl hat das Buch gelesen.
Teacher: (Shows picture of bread.)
               Was hat Inge gegessen?
               Inge hat das Brot gegessen.
Students: Inge hat das Brot gegessen.
Teacher: (Shows picture of glass of milk.)
               Was hat Helga getrunken?
               Helga hat ein Glas Milch getrunken.
Students: Helga hat ein Glas Milch getrunken.

6.3.1b OVERHEAD TRANSPARENCY

On a transparency make a series of line drawings with a number alongside each.

The teacher says one of the numbers (from 1 to 10), and individual students respond with either *Je le vois, Je la vois,* or *Je les vois.* If he says *deux,* for example, the answer is *Je le vois.*

Variation: The first few times, the masculine nouns may be colored blue and the feminine nouns red. If washable ink is used, this color coding may be erased as the students become surer of the genders.

6.3.1c INDEX CARDS

Draw figures of different people on index cards.

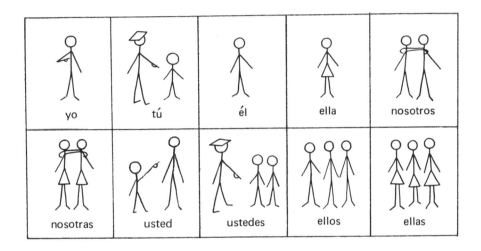

As the teacher shows each card to the class, he uses the English model sentence *He gives it to_____.* If the card depicts the first person singular, the teacher says: *Me lo da.* The class repeats chorally and then individually. The answers will be: *Te lo da. Se lo da. Nos lo da. Me lo da.*

6.3.1d SONG

The Spanish song, "*Me gustan todos,*" may be introduced to emphasize the position of indirect object pronouns:

Me gustan todas   (Repeat.)
Me gustan todas en general;
Pero esa rubia   (Repeat.)
Pero esa rubia me gusta más.

6.3.2. *Prepositional Phrases*

6.3.2a USE OF MAGNETIC BOARD

Most chalkboards are magnetized, especially in the newer school buildings. If not, a regular magnetic board is easily obtainable.

The teacher can cut out pictures from magazines (preferably foreign ones) of a railroad station, pastry shop, bakery, bookstore, restaurant, café, school, church, theater, and so on. He places each one on the chalkboard with a magnet. The object is to practice the forms of the preposition plus article.

The teacher points to each object and says: *Je vais au café, au restaurant, au cinéma, au musée, à la bibliothèque, à la boulangerie, à la gare, à l'école,* and so on. Then he asks individuals: *Où allez-vous?* Using the same pictures, the teacher can practice: *Je viens de. . . .*

6.3.2b USE OF FLANNEL BOARD

The teacher places on a flannel board photographs of famous landmarks, such as the Eiffel Tower, Big Ben, the statute of Don Quijote and Sancho Panza, the Statue of Liberty, Fujiyama, the Kremlin. (Good sources are *National Geographic* and *Holiday* magazines.)

These visuals can be used to teach *Je vais à Paris, à Londres, à New York, à Madrid; Je vais en France, en Angleterre, aux Etats-Unis, au Mexique, au Japon; Je viens de Paris, de Londres, de New York;* and *Je viens de France, d'Angleterre, des États-Unis.*

The teacher asks questions: *Dans quelle ville allez-vous? Dans quel pays allez-vous? De quel pays venez-vous? De quelle ville venez-vous?*

6.3.2c CLASSROOM OBJECTS

The teacher can use his desk and a book to teach the use of the dative and the accusative with German prepositions such as *auf, unter* and *zwischen.*

The teacher picks up a book. *Ich habe ein rotes Buch.* He puts it on the table, saying: *Ich lege das Buch auf den Tisch.* He steps back from the table and says: *Jetzt liegt das Buch auf dem Tisch.*

Other objects may also be used. For example, the teacher shows the class some coins: *Ich habe viel Geld.* The teacher puts the money in his pocket, saying: *Ich stecke das Geld, in meine Tasche.* The teacher holds up his empty hands: *Wo ist das Geld? Es ist in meiner Tasche.*

6.3.3 *Infinitive Clauses*

6.3.3a INDEX CARDS AND MAGNETIC BOARD

The teacher prepares index cards with the following pictures. The cards are then placed with magnets on a magnetic board or the chalkboard.

1

2

3

4

5

ford to fit
sentences out
of students

As the teacher points to each figure, he indicates the present, then the immediate future:

1. Jean mange maintenant.
   Il va manger ce soir aussi.
2. Jean écoute la radio maintenant.
   Il va écouter la radio ce soir aussi.
3. Jean étudie maintenant.
   Il va étudier ce soir aussi.
4. Jean parle au téléphone maintenant.
   Il va parler au téléphone ce soir aussi.
5. Jean joue au tennis maintenant.
   Il va jouer au tennis ce soir aussi.

Then pointing to each of the cards in turn, the teacher asks individuals: *Qu'est-ce que Jean va faire ce soir?*

Note: All the infinitives in these sentences were from the first conjugation.

Later lessons could use verbs from other conjugations as well as irregular verbs.

6.3.3b POSTER

The visuals suggested in section 6.3.3a may all be placed on a poster. As the teacher points to each drawing, he describes the action first in the present and then in the future:

1. Hans ißt jetzt.
   Er wird auch heute abend essen.
2. Hans hört jetzt Radio.
   Hans wird auch heute abend Radio hören.
3. Hans studiert jetzt.
   Er wird auch heute abend studieren.
4. Hans telefoniert jetzt.
   Er wird auch heute abend telefonieren.
5. Hans spielt jetzt Tennis.
   Er wird auch heute abend Tennis spielen.

Models may also be presented with the same poster: *Er kann später essen. Er will immer Radio hören. Er soll bald studieren.*

6.3.4 *Relative Clauses*

6.3.4a CHALKBOARD AND COLOR CODING

(1) The teacher asks the class for a list of noun subjects. As the class dictates them, he writes them in yellow on the left-hand side of the board: *la dame, le garçon, les maisons, un homme, une jeune fille, les étudiants.* Then the teacher takes the first example and writes it in a sentence on the right-hand side. The words *la dame* and *qui* are written in yellow, the rest of the sentence in white: *Voilà* la dame qui *parle français.*

The class is then asked to create the remaining sentences using the noun subjects on the left. Possible answers are: *Voilà* le garçon qui *joue au football. Voilà* les maisons qui *sont laides. Voilà* un homme qui *est intelligent. Voilà* une jeune fille qui *sait le français.*

(2) On another section of the chalkboard the teacher writes the same nouns in purple chalk. He then writes a model sentence using the first noun and writes it and *que* in purple: *Voilà* la dame que *je connais.*

The class is asked to create sentences of the type above using the nouns in purple. Possible answers are: *Voilà* le garçon que *vous aimez. Voilà* les étudiants que *nous avons vus. Voilà* les maisons que *Paul a vendues. Voilà* une jeune fille que *tu devrais inviter.*

6.3.4b USING LINE DRAWINGS PLUS SENTENCES

The teacher places the following drawing and the two sentences on the blackboard or on an overhead transparency. In each sentence the subject and relative pronoun are circled in yellow or purple chalk, as appropriate.

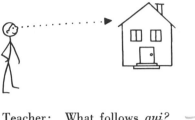

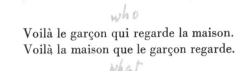

Voilà le garçon qui regarde la maison.
Voilà la maison que le garçon regarde.

Teacher:	What follows *qui?*
Student:	A verb (or action word).
Teacher:	What follows *que?*
Student:	A subject (or noun).

6.3.5 *Predicate Adjectives*

6.3.5a FLANNEL BOARD: DOLL AND CLOTHES

The teacher puts a cut-out doll on a flannel board and dresses it. As different articles of clothing are placed on it, he asks: *¿De qué color es la falda, la blusa, la camisa, el pantalón? ¿De qué color son los calcetines, los zapatos, los guantes?*

6.3.5b FLANNEL BOARD: "EL CABALLERO DE LA CALABAZA"

The teacher puts a large, cut-out figure of a head on a flannel board. The hair and the eyes are missing. He has in hand several cut-out flannel eyes and hair pieces of different colors which he places on the head.

Teacher:	¿De qué color es el pelo?
Student:	El pelo es rubio (moreno, gris, blanco) or Es pelirojo.
Teacher:	¿De qué color son los ojos?
Student:	Los ojos son azules, verdes, negros, cafés. . . .

6.4 BASIC SENTENCE PATTERNS

This section deals with problems of word order as well as imperative, negative, and interrogative sentences.

6.4.1 *Word Order*

6.4.1a FLANNEL BOARD PLUS CARDS

On the flannel board the teacher places index cards with German words on them. They should be arranged in statement word order.

Adverb	Verb	Subject	Complement
immer	trinkt	er	Milch
morgen	kauft	Inge	Fußball
jetzt	besucht	Hans	ein Buch
später	spielt	sie	Wasser
manchmal			ein Auto
			Kaffee
			den Lehrer
			einen Pullover
			die Tante
			Tennis
			ein Kleid
			seinen Freund

The teacher takes one card from each group and forms a sentence: *Morgen spielt Hans Tennis.* After he has formed others, he puts the cards back and asks for volunteers. He is careful to see that all sentences are correct and make sense.

6.4.1b LARGE CARDS

The teacher prepares large cards on the following model:

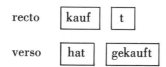

recto | kauf | t |

verso | hat | gekauft |

Four students are called to the front of the class. The middle two students are each given one of the verb cards which they hold so that the present tense is visible. The fourth student holds an object, such as a book.

The teacher explains the sentence: *Hans* (or the name of the first student) *kauft das Buch.*

To form the past tense, the two middle students turn their cards over, and the second of the two walks around to the end of the line. The new sentence reads: *Hans hat das Buch gekauft.*

6.4.1c OVERHEAD

See the example of the puzzle technique to teach word order in section 2.4.2e.

6.4.2 *Interrogative Sentences*

6.4.2a CHALKBOARD

The teacher writes a sentence on the board. First he reads it as a declarative sentence and writes at the end an arrow pointing down. Then he reads it as a question and makes the arrow point upward. Finally individual students are asked to go to the board and write in the arrows.

La maison est jolie. ↓
La maison est jolie? ↑
Il est à la maison. ↓
Il est à la maison? ↑

Juan viene con nosotros. ↓
¿Juan viene con nosotros? ↑
Tiene que comprar algo. ↓
¿Tiene que comprar algo? ↑

6.4.2b CHALK LEDGE AND CARDS

On separate index cards, the teacher prints verbs, subjects, and complements and arranges them in affirmative sentences on the chalk ledge. (Cards with question marks and periods should be included.) Then he switches the subject and verb cards to make the sentences interrogative. Finally, the students are asked to come forward and rearrange the cards to form questions.

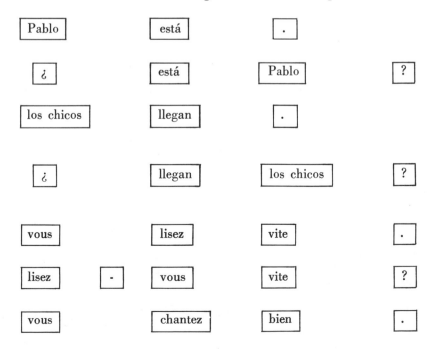

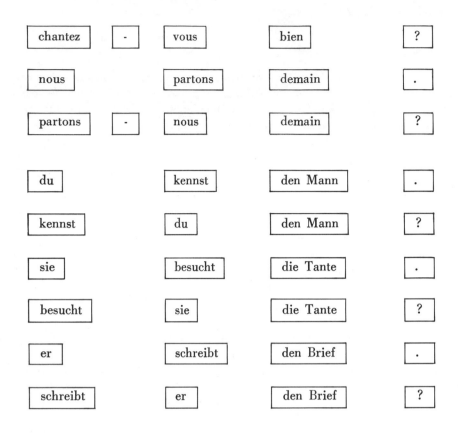

6.4.3 *Negative Sentences*

6.4.3a POCKET CHART

The teacher makes cards containing the following words:

The cards can be inserted in the pocket chart to form the following sentences:

Jean		parle		français
Jean	ne	parle	pas	français
Jean	ne	parle	jamais	français
Jean	ne	parle	plus	français
Jean	ne	voit	personne	

The teacher substitutes other cards containing different verbs and subjects.

Then the students are asked to come forward and make negative sentences. Other important changes are:

Jamais	Jean	ne	parle	français
Personne	ne	voit	Jean	

6.4.3b SONGS

The teacher can use songs to teach negative word order patterns. For example, in "*Au clair de la lune*" is the pattern *Je n'ai plus de feu,* and in "*Dansons la Capucine,*" *Mais ce n'est pas pour nous.*

6.4.3c TRANSPARENCY PLUS OVERLAY

The teacher prepares a basic transparency with a picture plus an affirmative sentence. The overlay introduces the negative in a contrasting color.

Basic Transparency   Overlay   Composite Picture

Similar transparencies may be prepared in French and German.

6.4.4 *Imperative Sentences*

6.4.4a CHALKBOARD

The teacher writes a sentence on the board, using *vous* as a subject. He erases the pronoun to form the imperative sentence.

Vous parlez français.
    Parlez français!
Vous allez dans votre chambre.
    Allez dans votre chambre!

6.4.4b   MOVEMENTS

The teacher addresses the German class as *Sie*. When he makes a statement, the students do not move. When he gives a command, they all obey: *Sie stehen auf.* No one moves. *Stehen Sie auf!* The class stands. *Setzen Sie sich!* The class sits down.

CHAPTER SEVEN
TEACHING
VOCABULARY

Words are essential to communication. Little children learn to speak in isolated words and then in chains of nouns and verbs. The child who says "Daddy go bye-bye car" is easily understood by English-speaking adults.

We expect students of a second language, however, to control the grammatical features of that language as well as its vocabulary. The foreign language teacher does not generally accept childish speech in his classroom.

Teaching the structure and the sound system of a language is the primary focus of the first years of language instruction. Intensive vocabulary building is usually postponed until after a solid grammar foundation has been established, that is, until the third and fourth years of instruction. Standardized examinations, such as the College Board Achievement Tests in foreign languages, tend to measure primarily breadth of vocabulary.

While not its main focus in the early stages of instruction, vocabulary is nonetheless an important factor in all language teaching. Students must continually be learning words as they learn structures and as they practice the sound system. This chapter offers suggestions for teaching vocabulary at both the beginning and the more advanced levels.

113

7.1   GENERAL CONSIDERATIONS

Concrete words are the easiest to learn. Neither younger nor older students have trouble in learning numbers, days of the week, colors, names of objects, and the like. The difficulty arises with using these words in sentences. For this reason, words are generally taught in the context of sentences.

Adverbs and adverbial expressions are difficult to learn. Even intermediate students confuse *souvent* and *surtout, tout de suite* and *tout d'un coup*. Much practice with adverbs is necessary in all languages.

Students also tend to forget the basic forms of nouns, adjectives, and verbs. Unless they learn the gender and plural form of a noun or the correct forms of an adjective, for example, they will be unable to use that noun or adjective accurately in a sentence. Unless they know the forms of a verb, they cannot use the verb properly in speaking or writing. The section on improving students' retention suggests ways to help students remember basic forms.

As students progress in their language learning, they discover that words in the foreign language do not have identical meanings in English. Even numbers do not always mean the same thing in different languages. In French, for example, the equivalent of *dozens* of something is *des dizaines* or *tens* of something. The number 36 in French has the additional meaning of *a great many*, an indefinite, large number of things. The question of equivalency or nonequivalency is an even greater problem with cognates.

The final part of this chapter focuses on techniques for vocabulary building.

7.2   TECHNIQUES OF PRESENTATION

In presenting new vocabulary, the teacher must first convey the meanings of the words he is teaching. Then he must bring the students to use the words properly in full sentences.

7.2.1   *Conveying the Meanings of New Words*

Some teachers give the English equivalents of new words. This is often the most direct way to teach adverbial expressions and abstract terms. Other teachers use a variety of techniques to convey the meanings of new words without recourse to English.

The careful use or complete avoidance of English is a matter to be decided by each individual teacher. Some beginning students feel more comfortable when they can mentally assign an English equivalent to a word. They seek the reassurance of a vocabulary in their textbook and will ask friends to tell them what a word means if the teacher refuses to do so. Other students learn more rapidly if the entire class period is conducted in the foreign language. They don't mind feeling a bit unsure about the meaning of a new word, for they know that gradually they can figure out what it means. Some students like to discover the meaning of a new word that has been presented without recourse to English and then are so proud of their discovery that they announce the English equivalent aloud to show that they have understood.

In any case, the use of English must be minimized in the classroom. Once students know the meaning of a new word, they must use it often and correctly in the foreign language in order to master the word and make it part of their personal vocabulary.

7.2.1a USING VISUALS

(1) Labels: For a beginning class the teacher can prepare labels for objects in the classroom. For example, in a German classroom the door might have a label reading *die Tür*; above the chalkboard might be a sign saying *die Tafel*.

(2) Magazine pictures: The teacher cuts out magazine pictures that illustrate words in a dialogue or basic sentences. These are placed on the chalkboard or on a magnetic board with magnets. The teacher points to the objects and gives their foreign language equivalents: *Das ist eine Küche* or *Voici la cuisine.*

(3) Props: If the lesson is about foods, the teacher could bring to class a basket of plastic fruit.

Teacher: ¿Qué es esto?
Class: Es una papa; es un tomate; es una pera; es una naranja.

In teaching about the house, a doll house with furniture can be used to teach the names of rooms, floors, parts of the house, and articles of furniture.

(4) Classroom objects: The calendar may be used to teach *today, yesterday, tomorrow,* as well as *last week, next week, next month, in two weeks,* and so on.

(5) Slides: Slides furnish an excellent medium for conveying the connotative cultural meanings of ordinary words in the foreign language.

The word *house,* for example, to an American student, denotes an American type of house. Even if he lives in an apartment, he has seen American houses in the movies and on television and has developed a concept of what a *house* is. The word *casa* to a Spanish-speaking person does not evoke an American-style house, but a Spanish-style house. A slide, or several slides, showing what Spanish houses look like can be shown in the classroom to help teach the word *casa.*

Slides of daily contemporary scenes, taken by the teacher on a trip abroad or by students or friends who have traveled in the foreign country, can frequently be used in teaching vocabulary. Items of clothing might be taught first, with the help of drawings or pictures. A slide of several people going shopping provides an opportunity for the students to talk about what the people are wearing. In this way, foreign words slowly absorb the connotations which they have in their culture.

7.2.1b USING GESTURES

Gestures may be used to convey the meanings of some words. Certain descriptive adjectives, such as *tall, thin, fat, happy, dumb,* lend themselves to pantomime and gesture. Prepositions of place can also be effectively taught by movements: *Le livre est sur la table. Le crayon est sur le livre. Le livre est sous le crayon. Maintenant le crayon est derrière le livre.*

Action verbs can be acted out: *El profesor come. El profesor bebe. El profesor lee.*

Teacher: ¿Qué hace el profesor? (Teacher pretends to be chewing.)
Class: El profesor come.

7.2.1c USING KNOWN VOCABULARY

The teacher can use known vocabulary to teach the meanings of new words.

(1) Synonyms and antonyms out of context:

Un sinónimo de *aprisa* es *rápidamente.* ¿Cuál es un sinónimo de rápidamente?

Das Gegenteil von *groß* ist *klein.* Was ist das Gegenteil von klein?

Le contraire de *chaud* est *froid.* Quel est le contraire de *froid?*

(2) Synonyms and antonyms in sentence context: Use the new word in sentences that contain an antonym or contrary expression:

Cette viande est *dure.* Je ne peux manger que de la viande *tendre.*

Pablo era *perezoso* mientras su hermano, Carlos, era *industrioso.* Carlos trabajba todo el tiempo.

Use the new word in sentences that contain a synonym or equivalent expression:

Madeleine était *épuisée.* Solange, elle aussi, était *extrêmement fatiguée.*

¡Hombre! ¿Por qué dices eso tan *aprisa?* Los americanos no te comprenden cuando hablas *rápidamente.*

(3) Categories: Names of categories can be taught verbally if the students know some names of items that belong within a particular category.

Teacher: Le café est une boisson.
Le Coca-Cola est une boisson.
Le thé est une boisson.
Donnez-moi d'autres exemples de boissons.
Student: Le lait est une boisson.

Teacher: El tenis es un deporte.
El soccer es un deporte.
¿Cuál es otro deporte?
Student: El fútbol es un deporte.

(4) Definitions and paraphrases: Definitions and paraphrases may be given in the foreign language. Foreign language dictionaries are useful to the teacher, especially those dictionaries prepared to help foreigners learn the second language.[1]

Un chanteur est une personne qui chante.
Une fille qui est *moche* n'est pas très belle. Elle est laide.

7.2.1d USING ENGLISH

The use of English to convey meaning may be direct or indirect, that is, the English may simply give the meaning of a word or phrase, or it may explain a gesture or symbol which will later be used to evoke the word or phrase.

(1) Direct use of English: The question *Quelle heure est-il?* means *What time is it? Wir sprechen Deutsch* means *We're speaking German.*

(2) Indirect use of English—gesture: A beckoning of hands means *repeat: répétez, répétez.* A hand cupped behind the ear means *listen: écoutez, écoutez.* Subsequently, when the teacher wants to tell students to listen, he will simply say *écoutez* and, if necessary, accompany the word with the gesture to reinforce the meaning of the command.

(3) Indirect use of English—symbols: The teacher can give the meaning of written symbols quickly in English and subsequently use the symbols to teach the new words in the second language. Students readily remember the meanings assigned to simple drawings.

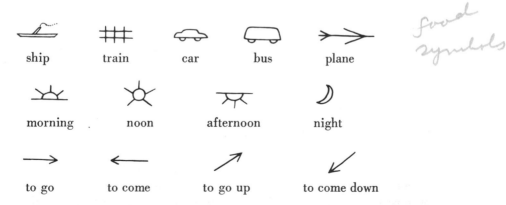

food symbols

| ship | train | car | bus | plane |

| morning | noon | afternoon | night |

| to go | to come | to go up | to come down |

[1] See, for example, Georges Gougenheim, *Dictionnaire fondamental de la langue française* (Paris: Didier, 1958). See also Pierre Fourré, *Premier Dictionnarie en images* (Paris: Didier, 1962). Distributed by Chilton Books, Philadelphia.

7.2.2   *Teaching Series and Word Sequences*

Some of the words taught in elementary language courses occur naturally in sequences, such as numbers, names of months, days of the week. Students readily memorize the series, but they then have difficulty using the words out of sequence. The following techniques help students practice elements in a series.

7.2.2a   FLASH CARDS

The items, or abbreviations of the items (days of the week and months of the year), can be put on flash cards. For example, all the letters of the alphabet are put on cards. The teacher shuffles the cards to present the letters out of sequence for drill.

7.2.2b   CLOCK FACE

Using a toy clock, or a face of a clock drawn on the board, the teacher randomly points to the numbers 1 through 12 while the students say them aloud. The numbers 13 to 24 may also be added.

7.2.2c   CHALKBOARD

The teacher writes the first letter or foreign abbreviation of the days of the week across the chalkboard. After teaching the new words, the teacher points to the letters on the board in random order, eliciting the days of the week from the students.

7.2.2d   TRANSPARENCY

The teacher prepares a transparency with the abbreviations of the months of the year. Once the names of the months have been taught, the teacher randomly points to an abbreviation, and the students name the corresponding month.

7.3   IMPROVING STUDENTS' RETENTION

The presentation of new words is only the first step in the process of language learning. The student must subsequently remember these words and make them part of his own vocabulary. Retention is a product of frequent practice. The following techniques suggest ways in which students' retention can be improved.

7.3.1 *Color Coding*

Learning the gender of nouns is a problem for all language students. Eye-minded students remember gender more easily if they mentally associate gender with color, for example, blue—masculine, red—feminine, green—neuter. This association may be reinforced in a variety of ways.

7.3.1a CONSTRUCTION PAPER

Pictures of masculine objects are mounted on blue construction paper. Pictures of feminine objects are mounted on red construction paper. Pictures of neuter objects are mounted on green construction paper.

7.3.1b COLORED DISCS

A blue disc is pasted in the corner of a magazine cut-out of a masculine object. Similarly, a red disc codes feminine, and a green disc codes neuter.

7.3.1c COLORED SYMBOLS AND LINE DRAWINGS

Homemade drawings or symbols are used on flash cards, cue cards, posters, and overhead transparencies. Use blue felt pens for masculine objects, red for feminine, and green for neuter.

7.3.1d COLORED CHALK

In writing sentences on the board in which noun and adjective agreement is being stressed, use blue chalk for the masculine forms, red (or pink) chalk for the feminine forms, and green chalk for the neuter forms.

7.3.1e DITTOS AND STUDENTS' NOTEBOOKS

Students who have difficulty with gender should be encouraged to color code nouns (and related forms such as articles, adjectives, and past participle endings) on homework and handouts. This may be done with crayons, colored pencils, felt pens, or water-soluble felt markers. Colored Ditto masters may also be used.

7.3.2 *Grouping*

Many textbooks present vocabulary items in random order. Some books have alphabetical lists of new words. In either case, new words may be further grouped to point out similarities and differences among them. The bright student does this automatically, but often the slower student experiences difficulty precisely because he does not notice the obvious groupings.

The teacher can prepare Ditto handouts which group words to help students remember them more easily.

(1) Nouns: Nouns can be grouped by gender. In German, the groups could be further subdivided by how the plurals are formed. For more advanced classes, nouns may be grouped by endings to bring out gender patterns (for example, *-tion* words are feminine, *-age* words are usually masculine in French).

(2) Verbs: Verbs can be grouped by conjugation patterns. The general groupings may be further refined to group similar irregular forms together (stem-changing verbs, compound tenses formed by *to be* or *to have*, forms of the past participle, and so on).

(3) Adjectives: Adjectives can be grouped according to the way the feminine and plural forms are generated.

(4) Pairs of words: Synonyms and antonyms can be grouped. Root words may be paired with forms using prefixes or suffixes.

7.3.3 *Asterisks*

Asterisks are sometimes used in dictionaries to show specific types of irregularities (the aspirate *h* in French). Visuals and lists likewise might carry the asterisk. For example, a picture of ice hockey would be coded blue and carry an asterisk: *le hockey*.

7.3.4 *Type Face*

In Spanish and German, American students often stress the wrong syllable of a word. In Dittoed lists, the stressed syllable could be lettered in heavier writing, or in capitals, or underlined. Students who tend to mispronounce words by shifting stress could be required to underline the stressed syllable on all written assignments.

7.3.5 *Drawings*

Drawings illustrating vocabulary may be hung around the classroom. These are especially effective if they illustrate points where learning problems tend to occur.

ils sont en classe

ils vont en classe

7.3.6 *Prepared Visuals by Students*

Students should be encouraged to prepare visuals for words or expressions which they find difficult. These visuals can then be displayed in the classroom or integrated into language learning activities. If a second- or third-year student still mixes up some basic vocabulary words, he might prepare a visual plus a "mini-lesson" and be asked to teach those vocabulary words to some students in a lower class.

These visuals may take the form of posters, flash cards, Ditto handouts, and so on. An art student might like to make a mobile with vocabulary forms.

Students should also be encouraged to put their problem words into sentences. A drawing of a fat person eating several ice cream sundaes could carry the caption *Er hat Eis* besonders *gern* or *Il aime* surtout *la glace.* Such drawings help students remember adverbs which often present difficulty.

7.4 COGNATES

The presence of many cognates in the foreign language facilitates the learning of vocabulary.

7.4.1 *Cognate "Fit"*

The "fit" between cognates refers to the similarity that exists between the English word and the foreign language word.

7.4.1a FIT IN MEANING

For those cognates whose fit is near-perfect, usually scientific or technical terms such as *les mathématiques,* the student has no trouble learning the meaning of the new word. The more common words, however, often have slightly different ranges of meaning in the two languages: *voyage* means any kind of trip in French, but in English it refers to a trip by boat. Here the new word should be presented in a variety of different sentences to show its range of meaning.

In false cognates the meanings of the two words are completely different. These words are especially hard for students to learn. Making visuals often helps them learn the differences between words that look alike but have different meanings.

7.4.1b FIT IN SPELLING

Cognates are sometimes spelled differently. Spelling changes can be made more obvious to the students by underlining the letters which differ in English and the foreign language.

7.4.1c FIT IN PRONUNCIATION

Even cognates that look exactly alike *never* have exactly the same pronunciation in the two languages. Students must be given ample opportunity to practice spoken cognates.

7.4.2 *Recognizing Written Cognates*

Students readily recognize obvious written cognates. The average student, however, needs help in learning to recognize cognates which have undergone some spelling modification. The teacher prepares lists of cognates which follow a similar pattern and presents these to the students.

7.4.2a PREFIXES

Before class begins, write the following list of French words on the board and cover them with a map:

décharger	désagréable
décourager	désenchanter
dédain	déshonorer
défaveur	désorganiser

Ask the class what English prefix *dés-* and *dé-* correspond to. Ask which French prefix is used before a consonant sound (left column) and which is used before a vowel sound (right column). You might also point out that sometimes the French prefix *dé-* corresponds to the English prefix *de*, as in *détacher, déplorer, décider, délivrer, déléguer.*

7.4.2b SUFFIXES

Show the following list of words on the overhead projector:

curiosidad	brutalidad
humildad	dignidad
oscuridad	familiaridad
responsabilidad	prosperidad

Ask what letters all the words end in. What suffix does this correspond to in English? Say the words in English.

7.4.2c PREDICTABLE SPELLING CHANGES

(1) Prepare a cue card like the following: $\boxed{(\hat{S})}$

Explain that the circumflex accent frequently means that an *s* was dropped over three hundred years ago and that English still has the *s*. Let students give the meanings of words, such as *la bête, la fête, le mât, de la pâte, honnête.*

(2) Prepare a transparency indicating a sound shift: | t → d |

Then show flash cards with words that exemplify the sound shift and have students provide the English equivalents of *Gott, das Bett, der Ritter.*

7.4.3 *Recognizing Spoken Cognates*

Students who recognize written cognates often fail to recognize the same cognates when they hear them spoken. Since most commercial programs offer little practice in the recognition of spoken cognates, the teacher must develop his own exercises.

7.4.3a INDIRECT EXERCISES

Cognates may be used in listening exercises designed to develop students' awareness of structural signals. As the students listen for gender markers, number markers, tense markers, and the like, they will indirectly become aware of what the cognates sound like.

(1) Indicate on your worksheet whether the noun is masculine, feminine, or neuter:

(tape)   1. Da ist der Bus.
           2. Da ist der Fisch.
           3. Da ist die Garage.
(worksheet)

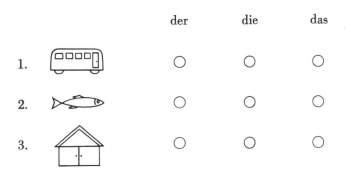

good for elementary

(2) Indicate on your answer sheet whether the verb expresses past time or near future:

1. Paul va inviter sa soeur.
2. Nous avons autorisé cette action.
3. Vous allez observer cette classe.

As the sentences are read a second time, and the correct answers announced, the printed sentences are projected on the overhead screen. This allows the students to see the written cognates and helps them understand the words they did not get the first time they heard them. (All the verbs are cognates unfamiliar to the students.)

7.4.3b DIRECT EXERCISES

The student is given a Ditto sheet with ten English words (or the written foreign language cognates) in alphabetical order. He then hears ten sentences, each containing one of these words, and writes the number of the sentence in which the word appeared next to the word. At the end of the exercise, each sentence is read again, followed by the word in isolation. Then the sequence of the ten numbers is read. Example: *Sa grand-mère s'occupait de son éducation.*

7.4.4 *Generating Written Cognates*

Producing cognates is more difficult than understanding them. Even when the student knows the basic patterns cognates follow, there is the chance that he will generate a nonexistent word. This does not mean, however, that the student should be prevented from trying to form cognates. To help him, the teacher should teach the basic transformations and then the exceptions, that is, those English words which do not have predictable cognates in the foreign language.

7.4.4a DEVELOPING AN AWARENESS OF WRITTEN PATTERNS

Whenever the students are given a reading assignment to prepare, they can be given one cognate assignment:

1. Make a list of all words in the passage beginning with *mé-* and give the English cognates where appropriate.
2. Make a list of all words in the passage ending in *-ción* and give the English cognates where appropriate.

These lists can be used in class the next day for cognate study.

7.4.4b PREDICTING GENDER

It is not enough simply to predict the form of a noun cognate. The proper gender must also be predicted. Students should be taught those cases where gender patterns are regular and should be put on their guard for those words where gender varies unpredictably:

English words in *-em* often have cognates in *-ème*. These cognates are masculine: *system—le système.*

1. It's a good system.   C'est un bon système.
2. It's a big problem.   C'est un grand problème.
3. It's a difficult theorem.   C'est un théorème difficile.

Students write the French sentences, some at their seats and some at the chalkboard. The teacher then corrects the sentences on the board, and students correct their own work at their seats.

7.4.4c WRITING COGNATES: BASIC FORMS

The teacher prepares a list of English cognates which are related in a predictable way to French cognates. As he dictates the English word, the student writes the French equivalent:

English verbs in *-ate* frequently have French cognates in *-er: operate— opérer.* English verbs in *-cate* have cognates in *-quer: syndicate—syndiquer.* Remember: the letter *e* in English when followed by one consonant or by another vowel is usually *é* or *er* in French: *cooperate, indicate, penetrate, celebrate, ventilate, initiate, marinate, generate, liberate, educate.*

When the students have written the cognates, the teacher places the correct forms on the overhead projector.
Variation: Students do the homework on Ditto sheets and then correct their own papers, using an answer key provided by the teacher.

7.4.4d WRITING COGNATES: IN CONTEXT

The teacher prepares a set of sentences in which cognates have been left out. The student supplies the appropriate form of the cognate. It is better to give the entire English sentence, rather than just the single cognate, so that students notice that there is not a word-to-word correspondence between the other elements of the sentence:

Many English verbs in *-ish* have French cognates in *-ir*. Remember: a single *e* in English is usually written *é* in French.

1. The Indians perished.
   Les Indiens _____.
2. They are demolishing that wooden house.
   Ils _____ cette maison en bois.

7.4.5 *Generating Spoken Cognates*

Before the student can generate spoken cognates, he must first learn how to pronounce known cognates accurately. (See also section 4.6.2b.) Once he commands the sound system of the foreign language, he may be introduced to spoken cognate exercises.

7.4.5a LEARNING EXERCISES

At first the teacher guides the student in the pronunciation of cognates:

Teacher: Répétez après moi: *nation, action, émotion, condition, éduca-*
tion, destruction.
A quel son /sjɔ̃/ correspond-il en anglais?

Student: /ʃən/

Teacher: Bien. Maintenant, je vais vous donner un mot en anglais et
vous allez le prononcer en français: *nation, station, decoration,*
munitions.

Teacher: Pronuncien: *perfect—perfecto, active—activo, future—futuro,*
service—servicio. Where do we put the stress on the English
words we just pronounced?

Student: On the first syllable.

Teacher: Correct. And on the Spanish words?

Student: On the next to the last syllable.

Teacher: Correct. Now I shall give you a list of English words. You are
to put them into Spanish. Remember, the Spanish words end in
-o: absolute, modest, human, ordinary.

7.4.5b PRACTICE DRILLS

Once the students are aware of the patterns, they need much practice:

Teacher: Comment dit-on *receive* en français?

Student: On dit *recevoir.*

Teacher: Comment dit-on *conceive* en Français?

Student: On dit *concevoir.*

Teacher: ¿Cómo se dice *explosion* en español?

Student: Se dice *explosión.*

Teacher: ¿Cómo se dice *expression* en español?

Student: Se dice *expressión.*

7.4.5c FREE CONVERSATION

In free conversation practice (see section 9.6) students tend to use cognates
to express themselves. As the teacher listens to the students speaking with
each other, he makes note of mispronounced and incorrect cognates. This
list of errors forms the basis of cognate study at the end of the conversation
hour.

7.5   VOCABULARY BUILDING

As students advance in their study of the foreign language, they must continue to build their vocabularies. Some helpful techniques for vocabulary expansion are given in this section.

7.5.1 *Word Families*

If the student learns to recognize the key parts of words, he will increase his comprehension of unknown vocabulary items and spend much less time thumbing in the glossary or dictionary.

7.5.1a COMPOUND WORDS

Students of German must learn to form compound nouns.

(1) Put the following chart on the board:

der Mittag   der *Vor*mittag
der Mittag   der *Nach*mittag

Ask students how Germans create the words for forenoon and afternoon:

Teacher: If you know *der Tag*, how would you say *the day before?*
Student: Der *Vor*tag.
Teacher: If you know *der Weg*, how would you say *the way (to) home?*
Student: Der Nachhauseweg.[1]

(2) Nominalized verbs often form compounds with other verbs or nouns:

Auto fahren—to drive a car   das Autofahren—(the) driving of a car
einkaufen gehen—to go shopping   das Einkaufengehen—(the) shopping
Kuchen backen—to bake a cake   das Kuchenbacken—(the) baking of a cake
Wasserschi laufen—to waterski   das Wasserschilaufen—(the) waterskiing
zu Mittag essen—to eat lunch   das Mittagessen—(the) lunch, dinner

(3) An adjective and a noun are often combined to form a compound noun:

deutsch + das Land: Deutschland—Germany
gross + der Unternehmer; der Grossunternehmer—big-businessman
fett + das Gedruckte: das Fettgedruckte—boldface type

7.5.1b NOUNS FROM ADJECTIVES

The teacher makes a transparency with the following words:

schön	schwierig
krank	wirklich
gesund	billig
echt	freundlich
beliebt	ähnlich
schwach	gemütlich
dunkel	selig

[1] *A-LM German: Level III* (New York: Harcourt Brace Jovanovich, Inc., 1964), p. 191.

With a grease pencil he writes *die Schönheit* after *schön*, explaining that *die Schönheit* is the noun based on the adjective *schön*. He does the second example also, unless students already want to generate *Krankheit* from *krank*. As the students dictate, the teacher writes on the board the nouns made by adding -*heit* to the adjectives in the first column.

Then he uncovers the second column and asks the students to listen as he reads the series of adjectives aloud. He asks what sound all the adjectives end in. He explains that the suffix added to adjectives ending in -*ig* and -*ich* is not -*heit*, but -*keit*, which is easier to pronounce; for example, *Schwierigkeit* is much easier to pronounce than *Schwierigheit* would be. He writes *Schwierigkeit* on the transparency. Students dictate the other nouns according to the model.

7.5.1c WORDS BUILT ON A COMMON STEM

Students work in pairs on the following Ditto. Then they check their answers against the answer key on the teacher's desk.

L'ensemble de toutes les feuilles d'un arbre s'appelle le *feuillage*. Un arbre qui a beaucoup de feuilles est *feuillu*. Arracher les feuilles d'un arbre c'est l'*effeuiller*.

1. *Feuillu* veut dire *qui a des feuilles*. Que veulent dire les mots suivants:

   a. barbu   b. chevelu   c. poilu

2. *Feuillage* veut dire *une collection de feuilles*. Que veulent dire ces mots:

   a. branchage   b. plumage   c. herbage

3. Effeuiller veut dire *enlever les feuilles*. Que veulent dire les mots suivants:

   a. ébrancher   b. effruiter   c. écrémer[1]

7.5.2 *Paraphrasing*

In paraphrasing, students realize that there are frequently several ways of expressing roughly the same idea in the foreign language.

The students complete sentences by furnishing a synonym or equivalent of an underlined term:

(1) This exercise provides practice in using *por* and *para*. After the students have completed the exercise, pass out a sheet with the answers, or put them on the overhead projector.

[1] Adapted from L. Seibert and L. Crocker, *Skills and Techniques for Reading French* (New York: Harper and Row, 1958), pp. 13–14.

En los ejercicios que siguen reemplace las palabras (Subrayadas) (under-lined) con *por* o *para*.[1]

Modelos: El avión salió en direción a Mexico.
El avión salió para Mexico.

Los mexicanos cruzaron en balsa a través del río.
Los mexicanos cruzaron en balsa por el río.

1. A cambio de dinero, Judas vendió a Cristo.
_____ dinero, Judas vendió a Cristo.
(Por)

2. Salió de la clase a fin de pegarle a Tom.
Salió de la clase _____ pegarle a Tom.
(para)

(2) Review orally the synonyms in this exercise before asking the students to fill in the blanks. Each blank in the second part must contain a paraphrase of the words in the first part.

Sylvie et Nicole sont chez Jacqueline. Jacqueline parle trop rapidement, mais tout le monde la trouve gentille. Sylvie ne dit pas un mot, mais elle est extrêmement jolie. Les trois camarades regardent la télévision. Nicole dit, "Je déteste les films de guerre. A quelle heure est-ce que le western commence?" Jacqueline répond, "Immédiatement."

Sylvie et Nicole sont _____ Jacqueline. Jacqueline parle trop _____, mais tout le monde la trouve _____. Sylvie ne dit _____, mais elle est _____. Les trois _____ regardent la télévision. Nicole dit, "Je _____ les films de guerre. _____ est-ce que le western commence?" Jacqueline répond, "_____."

7.5.3 *Techniques of Inference*

Students should be taught to infer the meanings of new words from the context in which they are used.

7.5.3a MULTIPLE CONTEXT

The new word is used in several different sentences.
Put the following sentences on the overhead projector. Tell the students to try to guess the English equivalent of the word *trabaja*. Ask them not to call out the meaning, but to wait until everyone has had a chance to read the sentences and figure it out.

1. El profesor *trabaja* en la escuela.

[1] Poston, Jr., Lawrence, et al., *Workbook Accompanying Continuing Spanish II* (New York: American Book Company, 1967), pp. 7–12.

2. El presidente *trabaja* en Washington.
3. El agricultor *trabaja* en su rancho.
4. El gato no *trabaja*; él duerme mucho.
5. El caballo *trabaja* mucho; él transporta a personas y mercancías.
6. El estudiante que *trabaja* mucho recibe una A. El estudiante que no *trabaja* recibe una F.
7. El inválido no *trabaja*; es físicamente imposible.

7.5.3b SINGLE CONTEXT

Prepare sentences for the overhead projector or write them in grease pencil while the students watch. Then ask questions about the sentences.

Hier soir j'ai entendu un rossignol. Sa chanson était très belle.

Teacher: Vous ne savez pas ce que c'est qu'un rossignol. Mais qui peut me dire ce qu'un rossignol peut faire?

Student: Il peut chanter.

Teacher: Oui, et il a une belle voix. Maintenant je vais vous donner encore une phrase à lire.

Teacher: (Writes, or lowers mask on prepared overhead.)
Je ne pouvais pas le voir, mais il était probablement dans l'arbre près de ma fenêtre. Maintenant, pouvez-vous deviner ce que c'est que ce rossignol?

Student: C'est un oiseau.

Teacher: Oui, très bien. En anglais nous appelons cet oiseau un *nightingale*. On le trouve en Europe mais pas aux Etats-Unis.

7.5.4 *Vocabulary Lists*

7.5.4a LISTS PREPARED BY THE TEACHER

New vocabulary may be presented in list form. This method of presentation (or review) is most effective when the words all relate to a topic that the class is studying.

For example, if the students are given an assignment to describe their bedroom, a vocabulary list would contain the words and expressions they might need to use. The list is most useful if the words are given in all their basic forms and then included in sample sentences.

Vocabulary lists might also be distributed for debate topics and prepared oral conversations.

7.5.4b LISTS PREPARED BY STUDENTS

(1) Whenever a student looks up a word in the end vocabulary, he enters a checkmark by the word. When a word has three checkmarks, he copies that word in a notebook and uses it in a sample sentence. He is encouraged to try to memorize the words he has listed in his notebook.

(2) For each reading assignment, the student selects five words or idioms he is unsure of and considers useful. He writes these in a notebook and uses each word in an original sentence.

7.5.5 *Game: Jeopardy*

The TV game "Jeopardy" may be adapted for foreign language classes.[1] It gives the students practice in using their newly acquired vocabulary in varied contexts. The teacher, or the class as a whole, selects four or five categories. Students then write questions and answers for these categories.

The questions are grouped in order of difficulty, from simple questions worth ten points each to hard questions worth fifty points each. There should be five questions for each category. The answers are written in columns on the board and covered with large pieces of manila paper which carry the numbers 10, 20, 30, 40, and 50.

Students compete in teams. The first student on a team picks a category and a value. He is then shown the answer and must supply a question.

Category: Geografía
Answer: La capital de Missouri
Question: ¿Qué es Jefferson City?

If the student gives the correct question, his team gains the designated number of points. If he misses, the points are deducted from his team's score.

7.6 PROBLEM AREAS

Vocabulary problems arise when words in English and the foreign language do not cover the same range of meaning. The most troublesome cases are those where the foreign language makes distinctions that English does not make, for the student must learn to reorganize his way of viewing reality. It is also essential that students become aware of the cultural meanings of words. (See section 12.4.2b.) For example, in teaching the names of animals, the French teacher can point out that camels, rather than skunks—which do not exist in Europe—are used to designate unpleasant people: *quel chameau!*

Although it is beyond the scope of this handbook to treat the many problem areas that exist, techniques are suggested for teaching two difficult points.

7.6.1 *Ser vs. Estar*

Using the two forms of *to be* correctly in Spanish always creates difficulties for American students. Prepare a transparency or wall chart with the following figures:

[1] Adapted from Clarice Ritthaler and Donna Gregory, "Jeopardize Your Foreign Language Classes," *Show-Me, News and Views (Missouri Foreign Language Newsletter)*, Vol. II, No. 2 (February 1971), p. 18.

The teacher points to each figure and describes him:

(A) El muchacho *es* alto, pequeño, inteligente, americano, gordo, flaco.

(B) Hoy el muchacho *está* enfermo, feliz, triste, sentado.

While it is true that in several of these situations either *ser* or *estar* could be used, one way to present the concept is by contrasting permanent with transitory characteristics.

A pattern drill of the following sort might follow the presentation:

Teacher	Students
El muchacho es alto	El muchacho es alto.
gordo	El muchacho es gordo.
triste hoy	El muchacho está triste hoy.
enfermo hoy	El muchacho está enfermo hoy.
americano	El muchacho es americano.
sentado	El muchacho está sentado.

7.6.2 *Savoir vs. Connaître*

The teacher can explain that *savoir* means *to know* in the sense of to have learned or to know by heart, whereas *connaître* means *to know* in the sense of to be acquainted with.

The distinction between the two verbs becomes clearer, however, if the students see that certain complements *require* one or the other verb. This can be shown on a wall chart.

CONNAÎTRE	SAVOIR
une personne (M. Blot) un endroit (Paris) un objet (le "Penseur") $\Big\}$ je le connais	infinitif (jouer au football) que . . . comment . . . pourquoi . . . quand . . . où . . . si . . . $\Big\}$ je le sais
CONNAÎTRE ou SAVOIR une chose qu'on apprend: une réponse, une leçon	

PART THREE
DEVELOPING
THE SKILLS

CHAPTER EIGHT
LISTENING
COMPREHENSION

The teaching of listening comprehension as a separate skill is a recent innovation in language teaching. Even at present most commercial language programs do not focus on a sequential and methodical development of the listening skill. Listening is simply considered as an adjunct of the speaking. Tape programs contain models for repetition, cues for spoken drills, and recordings of reading selections. Only a few programs contain exercises for listening discrimination, and even fewer contain listening comprehension selections, which appear only on tape (and not in the student's book).

This chapter presents techniques for the development of the listening skill, arranged in order of increasing difficulty.

8.1   GENERAL CONSIDERATIONS

Developing the ability to understand the spoken foreign language is a long, continuous process. It is a skill that must be taught and that does not happen automatically. One of the teacher's most important tasks is to provide a variety of purposeful listening activities throughout the entire language course.

The students must be given a reason for listening to one another. If the teacher requires individuals to respond to each other, the students will make an effort to listen more carefully for the information requested. In order to accomplish this, the teacher must insist that everyone speak up.

It is also important that teachers not repeat their questions and comments. Those teachers who repeat each utterance a dozen times find that their students stop listening altogether. Even more boring is the teacher who repeats each student's response or question. Obviously the teacher cannot react in silence to a student's utterance, and repeating what has just been said is an easy but unfortunate way to say something. The alternative is for the teacher to develop a large repertory of responses to students' utterances. Even the not-too-fluent teacher can practice a list of possible rejoinders in the foreign language, such as: Great. Wonderful. That's better, but not quite perfect. I see you've been practicing at home. Hey, you got it right. Now if I hear you make that mistake again you have no more excuses. Say that once more. That was perfect.

At the intermediate and advanced levels, the teacher must make the effort to find suitable taped material for listening activities. It is not enough for students merely to listen to each other and the teacher. They must also have frequent opportunities to listen to a variety of different speakers talking at a normal conversational speed.

8.2   UNDERSTANDING INDIVIDUAL WORDS

One of the first things that the language student learns to understand is individual words, either in isolation or more usually in the context of sentences.

8.2.1   *Numbers*

Numbers are taught early in the language course, yet even advanced students have difficulty understanding them. An easy way to drill numbers is with flash cards. The teacher reads off ten cards, previously shuffled. The students write down the numbers, in digits. Then the teacher rereads the cards one by one, showing the card to the students so that they can correct their list.

For advanced classes, the teacher can prepare forty or fifty index cards with three- and four-digit numbers. These are shuffled, and every day the teacher dictates ten numbers to the students at the beginning of the class hour.

Page numbers and line numbers in the textbook should also be given in the foreign language to reinforce listening comprehension.

8.2.2 *New Vocabulary*

The teacher uses magazine cut-outs, cue cards, or whatever visuals have been used to teach the new vocabulary (see Chapter 7).

The teacher says a word and holds up or points to a visual. If the word identifies the visual, the students mark *true* on their papers. If it does not, they write *false*. The teacher says each word only once.

Then he goes through the list once more, pausing after each word. The class responds *true* or *false*. If the answer was *false*, the teacher asks a student to identify the visual properly.

By calling for a quick raising of hands, the teacher can check whether the students understood the words or whether they need more oral listening practice.

8.2.3 *Minimal Pairs*

Intermediate and advanced students often mix up words that sound almost alike, even though the same students could probably identify the words in written form.

To check this kind of listening comprehension, the teacher distributes sheets on which there are line drawings of objects or events. As he pronounces one in each pair, the students identify it with A or B.

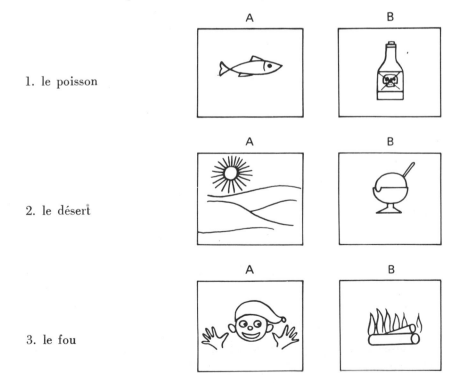

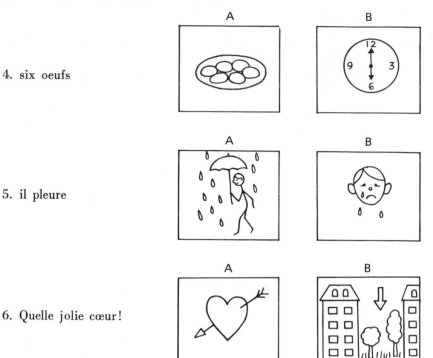

4. six oeufs

5. il pleure

6. Quelle jolie cœur!

8.3 IDENTIFYING AND UNDERSTANDING SENTENCES

Students quickly learn to recognize sentences, especially if they are required to demonstrate their comprehension. (On the other hand, it is possible for students to memorize sentences and forget what these sentences mean if comprehension is not reguarly checked and reinforced.)

8.3.1 *Giving a Physical Response*

Students carry out some kind of action to show that they understand the meaning of the sentence.

8.3.1a EXECUTING ORDERS

The teacher gives a series of rapid commands to the entire class. The students perform each act as rapidly as possible: *Levez-vous. Levez la main droite. Baissez-la. Levez le pied gauche. Baissez-le. Tournez-vous. Asseyez-vous.*

8.3.1b DRAWING PICTURES

The teacher calls on individuals to draw pictures on the board. The other students practice at their seats:

Jean, allez au tableau. Dessinez une maison avec six fenêtres.

Marie, dessinez un arbre à droite de la maison.

Marc, mettez une cheminée sur le toit de la maison.

Variation: Students can draw pictures on the overhead projector with the light on.

8.3.1c USING THE MAGNETIC BOARD

The teacher puts various cutouts of buildings on the board with magnets. The students listen to the directions and move the buildings around:

Paco, la biblioteca se queda detrás del banco.

María, la peluquería se queda enfrente del banco.

Carlos, el cine se queda a la izquierda del banco.

Juana, la iglesia se queda a la derecha de la biblioteca.

8.3.1d USING THE FLANNEL BOARD

(1) On the left-hand side of the flannel board are several objects; the right side is bare. The teacher asks individuals to come forward and put various objects from the left side to the right:

Pierre, mettez la chaise sur la table.

Monique, mettez la jeune fille sur la chaise.

Claude, mettez le balai dans les mains de la jeune fille.

Claire, mettez une souris devant la table.[1]

(2) On the left side of the flannel board are the following objects: a cup, a hat, a dog, a pair of shoes, a table, the frame of a house, a chair and a bed (scattered about haphazardly). The right side of the flannel board is bare. The teacher calls on individual students to come forward and make the following pictures:

Ich habe meine Tasse auf den Tisch gestellt.

Ich habe meinen Hund ins Haus gebracht.

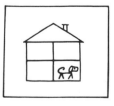

[1] *Le Tableau de Feutre dans la Classe de Langue Vivante*, Bureau Pour l'Enseignement de la Langue et de la Civilisation Françaises à l'Etranger (Paris: Librairie Istra, 1969).

Ich habe meinen Hut auf den Stuhl gelegt.

Ich habe meine Schuhe unter das Bett gestellt.

8.3.1e GAME: SIMON SAYS

Commands are given to the entire class. Students obey commands which are preceded by "Simon says" and do not move when the simple command is given. Students who make the wrong movement or who move at the wrong time are sent to the back of the room, where they continue to participate. The game continues until only one student is left in the front:

Simon dit: "Les mains sur la tête."
Mettez les mains sur les épaules.
Simon dit: "Mettez les mains sur les épaules."

At first the teacher carries out all the actions, so that the students can concentrate on the absence or presence of the phrase *Simon dit*. When the class knows the parts of the body well, the teacher can give a command to touch the knees while he himself touches his head. Students who fail to touch their knees are eliminated.

Variation: The teacher addresses individuals:

Marta, ¡levántate!
Carlos, Simón dice, "¡levántate!"
Carlos, ¡siéntate!
Carlos, Simón dice, "¡siéntate!"
Roberto, ¡abre tu libro!
Ricardo, ¡cierra tu cuaderno!

8.3.1f CHARADES

This game may be played boys against girls. The scorekeeper at the board marks a point for each person who correctly acts out the statement made by the teacher:

Teacher: J'ai froid.
           (Points to first boy on team.)
(Boy shivers.)
Teacher: J'ai mal à la tête.
           (Points to first girl on team.)
(Girl rubs her head.)
Teacher: J'ai faim.
(Boy rubs his stomach.)
Teacher: J'ai sommeil.
(Girl yawns.)

8.3.1g FOLLOWING LONGER INSTRUCTIONS

(1) The teacher gives a long, rather complicated set of directions to various individual students to develop their listening comprehension. Each attempts to execute the commands:

Hans, stehe auf, gehe an den Tisch, setze dich hin, nimm den roten Bleistift und schreibe das Wort *gut* auf das Papier! Dann falte es, und stecke es in dein Buch! [1]

(2) The teacher distributes maps of a city. He then gives a series of directions in the foreign language and asks students where they have ended up on their maps:

Teacher: Trouvez l'église. Vous y êtes? Ecoutez bien. Vous sortez de l'église et vous tournez à droite. A la rue Nationale vous prenez à gauche. Vous continuez tout droit. Puis vous prenez la deuxième rue à droite. Quel bâtiment se trouve immédiatement à votre droite?
Students: Le bureau de poste.

8.3.2 *Using Visual Cues*

Students listen to a sentence and indicate whether or not it fits a visual cue.

8.3.2a DIALOGUE POSTERS

The teacher recites a line of dialogue and points to a picture on the poster. Students indicate whether or not the line corresponds to the picture.

[1] Based on James J. Asher, "The Learning Strategy of the Total Physical Response Approach: A Review," *The Modern Language Journal*, Vol. L, No. 2 (February, 1966) pp. 79–84.

8.3.2b CUE CARDS

The teacher makes a statement about each cue card. The students reply *yes* or *no* to indicate whether the statement is appropriate or not:

Teacher: (Holds a picture of a tall boy.)
           El chico es alto.
Students: Sí
Teacher: (Holds a picture of a fat boy.)
           La chica es gorda.
Students: No.

8.3.2c WALL CHARTS

The teacher puts up a wall chart showing different kinds of weather. The teacher asks a question and points to a picture. The students answer *yes* or *no:*

Teacher: (Points to a snow picture.)
           Regnet es?
Students: Nein.

8.3.2d CLOCK WITH MOVABLE HANDS

The teacher moves the hands of the clock and then asks if it is a certain time. Students respond *yes* or *no:*

Teacher: (Moves the hands of the clock to 2:15.)
           Il est deux heures moins le quart, n'est-ce pas?
Students: Non.

8.3.2e SEQUENCING EVENTS: DRAGNET

The teacher reads an adaptation of the detective serial *Dragnet.* Eleven events occur in the story. The class must remember the sequence of events. Then the teacher distributes Dittoed sheets on which there are eleven sketches depicting each of the events. The students are asked to write the numbers of the pictures in the correct order:

1. Ich kam bei Fritz an.
2. Ich ging die Treppe hinauf.
3. Ich ging in sein Zimmer hinein.
4. Ich sah Fritz auf einem Stuhl sitzen.
5. Ich näherte mich ihm.
6. Er richtete eine Pistole auf mich.
7. Ich erfaßte die Pistole und warf sie aus dem Fenster.

8. Fritz lief auf die Tür zu.
9. Ich lief ihm nach.
10. Er fiel die Treppe hinunter.
11. Am Fuß der Treppe saß ich auf ihm bis die Polizei ankam.

8.3.3 *Giving English Equivalents*

Students can also show their comprehension by using English.

8.3.3a ORAL TRANSLATION

The teacher says a sentence aloud or plays a sentence on the tape. The students, in chorus or individually, give the English equivalent.

8.3.3b PRINTED TRANSLATION

The teacher prepares Dittos with English sentences. The foreign language sentences are read aloud or taped.

(1) The Ditto contains five English sentences. The teacher reads five French sentences, each preceded by a number. The students write the appropriate number next to each English sentence:

Voice: 1 Donnez-le-moi.

Ditto: ___ Give them to me.
       1 Give it to me.
      ___ Give it to them.
      ___ Give it to him.
      ___ Give them to him.

(2) The Ditto contains four English sentences for each taped sentence in Spanish. The last option is *I don't know:*

Voice: Vivo aquí desde abril.
Ditto: a. I have been living here since April.
      b. I will be living here until April.
      c. I was living here until last April.
      d. *I don't know.*

8.4   HEARING STRUCTURE SIGNALS

Students are often so busy listening for content words and trying to determine "who is doing what" that they fail to listen to structure signals. They might identify a scene as occurring in a restaurant because they have heard key vocabulary items, but they do not know whether the couple has just ordered, whether they are planning to order, or whether they have already finished eating.

While intermediate and advanced students often fail to listen for verb tense or for whether the conversation has shifted from the formal *you* to the familiar *you*, beginning students often need much practice even in recognizing verb subjects, singular-plural markers, and case differences.

The teacher may easily prepare exercises that help students listen for structure signals. In class, the teacher reads aloud ten sentences containing the structural feature while the class mark their responses on a piece of paper. Then the ten sentences are read again, and answers are corrected. Such exercises may also be recorded and used in the language laboratory.

Advanced students may be asked to prepare their own sets of sentences. At the beginning of the class, one student is assigned to read his ten sentences and then to correct his classmates' answers.

The following examples show some of the types of exercises which can be devised by the teacher.

8.4.1   *Listening for Number*

8.4.1a   NOUN MARKERS

The teacher reads a series of sentences. As the students hear the plural, they raise their hands or mark their papers:

1. Le garçon parle français.
2. Les filles parlent français.

3. L'homme parle français.
4. Les enfants parlent français.

8.4.1b VERB FORMS

The teacher reads sentences with *il* or *ils* as a subject. Students mark whether the sentence is definitely singular, definitely plural, or whether it could be either:

1. Ils boivent du lait.
2. Il essuie les verres.
3. Ils partent.
4. Il(s) découvre(nt) le trésor.

3.4.2 *Listening for Gender*

8.4.2a NOUN MARKERS

(1) The teacher reads a series of sentences. The students write on their sheets M for masculine and F for feminine:

1. Es un animal.
2. Es una canción.
3. Es una radio.
4. Es una amiga.

(2) For the German exercise the students write M, F, or N (for neuter):

1. Ich habe ein Auto.
2. Ich habe eine Kamera.
3. Ich habe einen Hut.
4. Ich habe ein Rad.

8.4.2b ADJECTIVE AGREEMENT

(1) The students raise their hands when the adjective describes a girl:

1. Mon ami est petit.
2. Mon amie est intelligente.
3. Mon amie est grande.
4. Mon ami est méchant.

(2) The students listen to a series of sentences. On their papers they have two columns—one marked Boy, the other Girl. As they hear the adjectives, they put a check mark in the proper column:

	Boy	Girl
1. ¡Qué simpática es!		✓
2. ¡Qué alto es!	✓	

3. ¡Qué bonita es!   ✓
4. ¡Qué linda es!   ✓

(3) The teacher reads sentences from a conversation between a boy and girl on the telephone. The students are told to listen to the adjectives in order to find out who is talking—a boy or a girl. On their papers the students write B for boy, G for girl:

1. Maman dit que je suis trop grande pour cela.
2. Mon ami me dit, "Que tu es méchante!"
3. Dis-moi où tu es; je suis très curieux.
4. Moi, parresseuse! Tu es fou!
5. Papa croit que je suis malheureux.

8.4.3 *Pronouns*

8.4.3a PERSONAL PRONOUNS

The teacher reads a series of sentences. The students have a paper with groups of three pronouns for each item. They circle the correct one:

1. Voy a casa.   (yo)   tú   él
2. No estudias mucho.   yo   (tú)   él
3. Sale temprano.   yo   tú   (él)
4. Necesito una blusa.   (yo)   tú   él

8.4.3b OBJECT PRONOUNS

The students hear a series of sentences with the object pronouns *le, la, les*. On their papers they have three columns: *le cadeau, la radio, les skis*. They are to put a check mark under the column which refers to the object mentioned:[1]

1. Je ne le vois pas.   (le cadeau)
2. Elle ne les trouve pas.   (les skis)
3. Il ne la porte pas.   (la radio)
4. Tu ne le prends pas.   (le cadeau)

8.4.4 *Verb Tenses*

The teacher asks the class to raise their hands when they hear a sentence in the immediate future:

1. Il va partir.
2. Nous venons de manger.

---

[1] Based on *A-LM French, Level One, Teacher's Edition,* 2d ed. (New York: Harcourt Brace Jovanovich, Inc., 1969), p. T73.

3. Elles vont venir.
4. Je viens de déjeuner.

8.4.5   *Identifying Subject and Object*

The student hears a sentence. On his paper he sees two nouns. He marks S beside the noun which was the subject of the sentence and O beside the noun which was the object:

Voice: Den schwarzen Hund wird der Mann nicht kaufen.
Paper: Hund   O   Mann   S
Voice: Die Mutter wird einen Kuchen backen.
Paper: Mutter   S   Kuchen   O

8.5   LISTENING TO UNFAMILIAR MATERIAL

In most language classes students get little opportunity to listen to difficult and totally unfamiliar material. Many do not know what to do when they suddenly hear an onslaught of the foreign language—on a standardized listening test, for example, or when traveling abroad.

The following activities introduce the student to foreign speech which he is not expected to understand.

8.5.1   *Identifying the Language*

Even beginning students should be taught to identify the foreign language when they hear it spoken and not to mix it up with other unknown languages.

8.5.1a   USING LESSON TAPES

The foreign language department in a school can make composite tapes containing snatches of material from the French program, the Spanish program, the Italian program, the German program, and so on. Sample publisher's tapes for languages not offered in the school also have foreign speech samples.

As students hear short snatches of a foreign language, they pick out samples of the language they are studying. A Ditto sheet may be prepared to read as follows:

	French	not French
Selection 1	○	○
Selection 2	○	○
Selection 3	○	○

8.5.1b USING RADIO BROADCASTS

The teacher uses a portable tape recorder to record snatches of foreign language broadcasts. In Spanish class the students raise their hands when the language is Spanish and keep their hands down when some other language is being played.

8.5.2 *Anticipating Sentence Completion*

Students become more involved in listening comprehension activities if they themselves are called upon to predict how the speaker will complete the sentence or what word he will use next.

The teacher plays a recorded sentence or part of a dialogue and then stops the tape before a predictable word:

Voice 1: Kennst du das Buch?
Voice 2: Ich habe es gestern gekauft, aber ich habe es noch nicht _____.

Students: gelesen, angefangen. . . .

Voice 1: Tu veux aller au cinéma ce soir?
Voice 2: Il y a un bon _____.
Students: film, western. . . .

Then the teacher rewinds the tape toward the beginning of the sentence and plays the entire sentence.

8.5.3 *Listening to Stories*

you could use a little story or fairy tale

From time to time, the teacher should give the students practice hearing stories in the foreign language. Although the students will not understand much of what they hear, they will catch a few words here and there, and they will be getting a feel for the foreign language.

8.5.3a USING VISUALS

The teacher uses a flannel board or line drawings as an aid in telling a familiar story, such as "Goldilocks and the Three Bears," in the foreign language.

8.5.3b USING AN ILLUSTRATED STORYBOOK

The teacher tells a story in the foreign language, pointing to the illustrations in a book to help the students in their comprehension of what is being said.

8.5.3c USING GESTURES

The teacher tells of an incident that happened to him over the weekend. Maybe he parked his car in a tow zone and came back to find the car missing. As he tells of his misadventures, he uses gestures and pantomime to help convey meaning.

8.5.3d READING FAMILIAR MATERIAL ALOUD

At the time of a religious holiday that is celebrated in the country where the foreign language is spoken, the teacher can read aloud the corresponding passage from the Bible.

Sometimes commercial products have labels or instructions printed in several languages. For example, in a German class, the teacher might bring in and read aloud the German instructions to a Lego construction set. A French teacher might bring in a French book on origami and explain in French how to fold a paper bird. The Spanish teacher might get a Spanish TV guide and read the write-up of a popular TV program as it appears in Spanish.

8.5.4 *Listening to Newscasts*

The teacher records the previous night's foreign language newcast (over local radio or shortwave) and brings the tape to class. Since the students are aware of current events, they can understand much of the foreign language newscast, especially when place names and the names of prominent people are mentioned.

8.6 UNDERSTANDING SHORT ORAL PASSAGES

Students at all levels of instruction need much practice in listening to short passages which recombine known vocabulary and structures with occasional unfamiliar expressions.

8.6.1 *Prepared by the Teacher*

Teachers can prepare short recorded passages similar to those suggested below. Several teachers can work together to develop and record such paragraphs for use in the classroom or in the language laboratory.

8.6.1a DEFINITIONS

After hearing the definition, the student is expected to furnish the correct answer:

(1) Je pense à un animal qui a de longues oreilles et une petite queue. Il aime beaucoup les carottes, les choux et la laitue. Qu'est-ce que c'est?

(2) Es un artículo de ropa que se lleva cuando hace frío. ¿Que es?

(3) Ich kenne ein kleines Land in Europa. Dort findet man viele hohe und schöne Gebirge. Die wichtigsten Sprachen dieses Landes sind: Deutsch, Französisch und Italienisch. In diesem Lande werden sehr gute Uhren hergestellt. Die Hauptstadt heißt Bern. Das Land heißt _____.

(4) Damit kann man über den Ozean reisen. Die Reise dauert mehrere Tage. Es gibt sehr gutes Essen. Abends kann man trinken, tanzen und singen. Wir reisen auf einem _____.

8.6.1b EAVESDROPPING

Students are expected to infer certain information from what they hear:

(1) Listen to the following comments made by teachers in a French school. On your paper, indicate which subject each one teaches:

1. Je ne sais pas pourquoi la prononciation de mes élèves est si mauvaise. J'ai pourtant de très bons disques américains que je leur fais écouter en classe.
2. Mes élèves ont mauvaise mémoire. Ils oublient toujours les dates les plus importantes.
3. Il faut que je donne à manger à mes rats. Les élèves n'ont rien mis dans leurs cages.

(2) Listen to the following statements spoken by German salesmen. Indicate on your papers what product each man is selling:

1. Wollen Sie nicht ihrer Freundin einen herrlichen Rosenstrauß kaufen?
2. Nehmen Sie zwei von den roten Tabletten, eine um acht Uhr morgens, die andere acht Uhr abends!
3. Wenn Sie einen Volkswagen kaufen, können Sie viel leichter durch den Verkehr kommen.
4. Herr Schmidt, das ist das echte Schwarzbrot, das wir hier verkaufen.
5. Frau Köhler, diese Bratwürste sind gerade angekommen. Sie sind frisch und billig.

8.6.1c PROVIDING TITLES

The teacher reads a short narrative while the students listen and try to retain the details. Then the students are asked to give possible titles to the selection. This exercise reveals their understanding of the passage:

(1) Les habitants du village se demandent s'ils ne devraient pas essayer de pénétrer dans cette maison. Voilà cinq ans que l'on ne voit personne entrer ou sortir de l'ancienne demeure des Dufour. C'était une famille qui n'aimait pas la société et qui n'invitait jamais.

Récemment un voisin a entendu des cris terrifiants qui semblaient venir de la tour.

(2) A Paris quand il n'y a plus de place dans un autobus le conducteur met sur la porte du véhicule une affiche qui porte le mot COMPLET. Cela veut dire qu'aucun voyageur n'a le droit de monter.

Un touriste américain, ignorant cette coutume, croyait que COMPLET était le nom d'une ville importante puisque tous les autobus qui y allaient étaient pleins. Alors il courait après tous les autobus qui portaient ce nom dans l'espoir de visiter cette ville importante.

Le malheureux a dû retourner en Amérique sans avoir jamais découvert COMPLET.

8.6.1d LISTENING FOR INFORMATION

Before playing the recorded passage, or before reading it aloud, the teacher tells the students what to listen for:

(1) Questions in English

You are going to hear about Juan. Find out how many people are in his family, where he lives, and what sport he enjoys:

> Hoy es domingo. Juan no va a la escuela. Después de la comida del mediodía, Juan va con sus dos hermanos a un partido de sóccer. A los jóvenes mexicanos les gusta mucho este deporte.

(2) Questions in the foreign language

Ecoutez bien ce paragraphe. Je vous demanderai combien de garçons il y a dans la famille d'Henri, où il habite, et quel sport il aime:

> C'est aujourd'hui dimanche. Le dimanche les enfants ne vont pas à l'école. Après le déjeuner, Henri et ses deux frères vont à un match de football. Les jeunes Parisiens aiment beaucoup ce sport.

8.6.2 *Commercially Recorded Passages*

Most language textbooks have some supplementary dialogues and passages which are available in recorded form. The most useful passages for teaching listening comprehension are those which the student has not had the opportunity to read in advance. If the dialogues are in the students' textbooks, have the students keep their books closed.

A fine source for listening comprehension passages are the tapes that accompany programs which were previously used in the school but which have been replaced by new materials. Students should be encouraged to guess at words and expressions they do not know. The teacher can present a few unfamiliar key words before playing the passage if he feels that this would improve the students' comprehension.

Another advantage of the commercial passages is that the teacher can usually obtain a copy of the tape script. (In previously used series, the script is the textbook.) From the script the teacher can prepare the types of activities suggested below.[1]

8.6.2a ORAL QUESTIONS

The teacher plays the tape and then asks oral questions about the content of the passage. In the Holt series, for example, the recombined conversations are accompanied by questions.[2] The teacher can also formulate his own simple questions.

If students are not able to answer all the questions, play the tape for them once more.

8.6.2b WRITING QUESTIONS ON THE BOARD

Write the questions on the board or put them on an overhead transparency. Have students read the questions aloud. Play the tape to the class. Call on students to answer the questions orally. Then play the tape a second time and have the students raise their hands when they hear the answer to the first question. When the hands go up, stop the tape. Repeat the question aloud and have students give the answer according to what they have just heard on the tape.

Variation: A writing exercise may be introduced at this point by having the class write out the correct answers.

8.6.2c TRUE-FALSE STATEMENTS

The teacher prepares a series of true-false statements on the listening passage. The following options may be used:

(1) The true-false statements are written on the board (or placed on an overhead) before the tape is played. They are read aloud in advance. Then the students listen to the passage. When the tape is finished, the students answer the questions.

(2) The true-false statements are shown after the tape has been played.

(3) The true-false statements are not written down for the students to read. The teacher reads each statement aloud once the tape has been played. Students answer by writing true or false on their papers.

After the students have answered the true-false questions, the teacher replays the tape, stopping it at appropriate points to indicate the correct answers to the quiz.

---

[1] Adapted from a talk by Frederick Bourassa, Calgary Annual Teacher's Convention, Calgary, Alberta, February 28, 1970.
[2] Dominique Côté, Sylvia Levy, and Patricia O'Connor *Ecouter et Parler* (New York: Holt, Rinehart and Winston, 1968).

The following true-false questions were prepared to accompany Conversation No. 4 in Lesson 9 of *Ecouter et Parler:*[1]

1. Pauline n'a pas de travail à faire ce matin.   oui
2. Marie veut aller à la bibliothèque.   non
3. Il fait plus chaud qu'hier aujourd'hui.   oui
4. Pauline va demander à son père si elle peut accompagner Marie. non
5. Plus tard, elles vont aller au cinéma.   non
6. Marie préfère les films d'aventure.   non
7. Elles vont se retrouver vers trois heures.   oui

8.6.2d MULTIPLE-CHOICE QUESTIONS

The teacher prepares brief multiple-choice questions on the listening passage. These may be presented to the students in one of the following ways:

(1) The teacher writes the multiple-choice questions on the board (or on an overhead transparency). He lets the students read them and then covers the questions up. He plays the tape, stops the tape, and then lets students answer the questions.

(2) The teacher writes the multiple-choice questions on the board, but lets the students see them only after they have heard the tape.

(3) The teacher writes only the answer choices on the board. He plays the tape and then reads the questions aloud while students select the appropriate options.

(4) The teacher plays the tape. Then he reads both the questions and the options. When students have answered the multiple-choice questions, he plays the tape again. He stops it at appropriate points to indicate the correct answers.

The following multiple-choice questions were prepared to accompany Conversation No. 2, Lesson 9 of the 1968 edition of *Ecouter et Parler:*[2]

1. Guillaume téléphone à _____.
   a. Richard   b. Martin   c. Robert   d. Henri
2. Guillaume lui demande _____.
   a. s'il a du travail   b. s'il doit aider son professeur
   c. s'il aime le français   d. quel travail le professeur leur a donné
3. Guillaume lui demande cela parce qu'il _____.
   a. l'a oublié   b. est libre ce soir
   c. y a de bons programmes à la télé   d. ne va pas bien
4. Un des graçons va téléphoner à _____.
   a. Lisette Bernier   b. Jeannette Benoît
   c. Paulette Renier   d. Claudette Fournier

[1] Ibid., p. 123.
[2] Ibid. p. 120.

5. Guillaume demande à son ami de lui téléphoner à _____.
   a. cinq heures moins le quart   b. six heures et quart
   c. six heures et demie   d. six heures moins le quart

8.6.2e   RECORDED QUESTIONS AND ANSWERS

If the listening passage is accompanied with recorded questions and answers, the following approach is possible:

Play the conversation. Then play the first question and stop the tape. Ask students for possible short answers to the question. Then play the answer (often longer) as given on the tape. Stop the tape again and have the entire class repeat the recorded answer. Continue in like manner for the remaining questions.

8.6.2f   DITTOED WORKSHEETS

Simple questions, true-false statements, and multiple-choice questions may be prepared in Ditto form. These Dittos may be used in the language laboratory or for individual work with tapes or cassettes in the classroom. The teacher prepares the tape to accompany the dittos in the following manner:

1. Voice on tape tells students to record the name and number of the recorded exercise.
2. Teacher plays the recorded conversation once (or twice).
3. Voice on tape tells students to answer the questions.
4. Teacher gives the correct answers.
5. Teacher plays the recording one last time.

8.7   UNDERSTANDING COLLOQUIAL SPEECH

The aim of instruction in the listening skill is to bring the student to a point where he can understand colloquial speech, with its muffled or missing sounds and its fused vowels and consonants. The true test of listening comprehension occurs when the student goes abroad and hears people all around him speaking another language.

In the classroom the teacher must go beyond textbook recordings. Most textbook recordings are not appropriate for listening practice at this colloquial level, for the speakers enunciate too clearly and speak too slowly. The best types of materials are recorded interviews, either radio broadcasts or records of conversations with famous persons. Speeches, songs, radio plays, and newscasts are also usable, even though the speech is often stylized.

8.7.1   *General Comprehension*

The teacher can check on the general comprehension of students by asking questions about the recording, by having students give titles to the passage, or by letting the students themselves ask questions about what they have heard.

In the following example the teacher prepared questions on a short-wave newscast which he had recorded at home. The questions are distributed before the newscast is played.

1. ¿Qué ciudad fué atacada?
2. ¿Qué partido salió victorioso?
3. ¿Cuánto tiempo duró la operación militar?
4. ¿Cuántos muertos hubo?
5. ¿Cómo dejaron la ciudad?
6. ¿Qué les pasó a los habitantes?

Ahora, ¡escuchen Vds.!

Las victoriosas tropas federales acaban de entrar en la ciudad de Córdoba. Después de tres días de batallas sangrientas, perdimos dos cientos soldados. Según los cálculos oficiales el número de muertos enemigos serían tres mil.

Los reporteros dicen que la mitad de la ciudad fué destrozada y que hay incendios por todas partes. Los habitantes ya empiezan a refugiarse en las montañas.

8.7.2 *Paraphrasing Rapid Speech or Regional Variants*

Eventually the student must be introduced to rapid speech and to the regional variants of the language he is learning (Austrian German, Provençal French, Castilian Spanish, Cuban Spanish).

The objective of instruction is that the student understand other types of speech, even though he is not expected to imitate them. The most appropriate comprehension check is paraphrasing the speech sample into standard speech.

8.7.2a ORAL PARAPHRASING

The student hears a sentence in rapid speech or a dialect, for example, *i'vient pas, chaps nicht*. The teacher then asks the students to give the standard equivalent of what they have heard: *Il ne vient pas. Ich habe es nicht*.

This type of exercise may be done with a full class where the teacher either imitates the rapid speech or regional variant, or where he plays recorded samples on a tape recorder and then stops the tape to let students paraphrase the sentences.

A taped exercise may be prepared on the same model to allow students to work individually. The student hears the rapid speech sentence, and in the pause that follows he tries to give the standard equivalent. Then he hears the voice on the tape confirm the standard equivalent and repeat the rapid sample once more.

8.7.2b WRITTEN PARAPHRASING

The standard speech equivalents may be prepared in written form.

(1) Overhead transparency: The teacher prepares an overhead transparency with the standard sentences. The sentences are masked. The teacher says or plays the first sentence of regional speech. The students try to give the standard equivalent and then the teacher lowers the mask to show the written form.

(2) Ditto: Students are given a Ditto to work with independently. They are told to mask the sentences with another piece of paper and to look at the written paraphrase only after they have listened to the recorded sentence and tried to understand it.

8.7.3 *Written Transcriptions*

Advanced students should be allowed to listen to a recording several times to try to understand every word that is being said. As they listen, they write out what they hear, that is, they make a written transcription of the selection.

8.7.3a TYPES OF TRANSCRIPTIONS

(1) Full transcription: The student writes down the entire selection.

(2) Partial transcription: The student is given a Ditto sheet in which difficult parts, garbled sections, and the like are written out. He fills in the remaining text.

(3) Graded transcriptions: The best students do a full transcription. Good students get a Ditto on which several very difficult parts are written out. Average students get a ditto on which all difficult parts are written out.

8.7.3b USING THE TRANSCRIPTION IN CLASS

(1) Before class, each student puts a sentence of his previously written transcription on the chalkboard. The teacher has the first student read his sentence aloud. Then he asks the others if they have any corrections or additions. As the sentences are being reviewed, the teacher may use the errors as a point of departure for brief grammar explanations. Students correct their own papers. They are told to listen to the recording once more after class. (The teacher may wish to play the recording to the entire class.)

(2) The teacher asks a student to read aloud the first sentence of his transcription. He writes on the board, or on a transparency, those parts of the sentence which are correct. He calls on other students to fill in the blanks. Gradually the entire transcription is reconstructed. Students correct their own work.

(3) The teacher brings a tape recording to class. He first plays the selection. Then he goes back to the beginning, plays the first part of the first sen-

tence, and asks students to tell him what they have heard. He writes the difficult parts on the board. If students have not understood every word, he replays that segment until they understand it.

If the teacher himself has difficulty understanding conversational French, similar transcription exercises may be done with short excerpts from recordings of plays or books. In this way, the teacher has a written copy of the recording, even though the students do not. Often record albums of foreign language songs provide copies of the lyrics. The teacher can use these texts to make Dittos for partial and graded transcriptions.

8.7.4 *Foreign Language Movies*

Students should be encouraged to go to foreign language movies as often as possible. To improve listening comprehension, the student should see the same movie at least twice. The first time, he is involved with the plot. The second time, he can visually notice cultural differences while listening to the language more attentively. He should be instructed to ignore the subtitles and listen only to the foreign language. The best test of listening comprehension is the ability to follow the dialogue with eyes closed.

CHAPTER NINE
SPEAKING

Learning to speak a second language is a lengthy process. First the student must carefully repeat models and imitate the teacher. He may memorize basic sentences to gain confidence in his ability to speak the second language. He may practice sentences and do oral drills. These activities are all preliminary to actual conversation. In a sense, these activities may be termed vocalizing.

The student is truly speaking only when he is generating his own sentences. The student who says *Répétez, s'il vous plaît* is using the new language to communicate what he wants to say.

In the classroom the teacher should try to allow for some true speaking activity, either guided conversation or, at later stages, free conversation in every unit. Foreign language is one item in the curriculum where students should be encouraged to talk a great deal in class and to express their own ideas, not simply what the teacher tells them to say.

9.1 GENERAL CONSIDERATIONS

After the basic dialogue or list of sentences is learned, and after the guided conversation or directed dialogue is practiced, the real work begins. It is at this point that true speaking activity can take place. The teacher should ask numerous questions and elicit responses from comments he makes. For example, if the dialogue sentence

160

is about buying a blue dress, ask individual girls if they own a blue dress or if they have bought one recently. If one of the basic sentences is about disliking spinach, ask individual students whether they dislike spinach and what vegetables they prefer.

As the students begin to learn to speak the foreign language, the teacher plays the role of umpire. He can tell the students whether they are pronouncing the new language accurately and whether they are using correct forms.

Gradually the teacher guides the students to a point where they can begin to judge whether they are producing the new sounds correctly and whether they are using appropriate sentence patterns. When this point is reached, the teacher's main concern is no longer primarily to correct, but rather to encourage the students to practice speaking the foreign language as frequently as possible.

Speaking a language differs from writing it in an important way. When a student can judge how accurately he spells and how well he uses the sentence patterns he has learned, he usually produces rather accurate written compositions. He has the time to reread what he has written and to correct his own work. But when the student is speaking freely, he tends to make mistakes he would not make in writing. Frequently he notices his mistakes right after he has said them, but it is too late to correct them. *Only through much free speaking practice will the student improve his command of the spoken language.*

It is the responsibility of the teacher to assume two roles. First, he must be a meticulous judge and correct mistakes in the initial language-learning stages. Second, at the more advanced stages he must be a coach who encourages and reviews performance. Most frequently he will be shifting from one role to the other.

9.2   INITIAL PRESENTATION: DIALOGUE TECHNIQUE

The elementary lessons in many foreign language courses begin with a dialogue. Traditionally, the student is expected to memorize the dialogue and to recite it fluently before practicing structure drills and doing grammar generalizations. The lesson may either contain one longer dialogue followed by the grammar presentation, or several shorter dialogues, each followed by a section of the grammar presentation.

Should the student memorize the dialogue? Memorization can lead to greater fluency and less hesitancy in speaking. The memorization of dialogue sentences helps the student acquire correct intonation patterns and offers him a model of natural, colloquial speech.

If too much class time must be spent on memorizing the dialogue, however, the activity will have a negative effect on the students. The good students will get bored and the slower learners will be frustrated by the difficulties they are experiencing. Moreover, the memorization is simply a point of departure for the teaching of grammar and vocabulary and for the development of language skills. A great deal of time spent memorizing dialogues will mean proportionately less time devoted to language-learning activities.

The teacher must judge how best to utilize the dialogues. If one class memorizes material readily and enjoys doing so, then memorization is a worthwhile activity. If another class balks at this type of rote learning, the dialogues could be used for listening comprehension or reading aloud. In either case, the teacher must go beyond simply teaching the dialogue if he expects his students to develop language skills.

The following sections contain suggestions for enlivening the learning of dialogues.

9.2.1 *Presenting the Dialogue*

Some teachers present the dialogue first in English, then in the foreign language. Others use the foreign language exclusively. The following techniques are designed to establish the meaning of the dialogue lines, either with or without the use of English.

9.2.1a CUE CARDS

The teacher places cue cards on the chalkboard ledge and points to them as he says the line (in English or in French). The class repeats the French in chorus, by groups or rows, and finally one by one.

Tu veux aller au cinéma ce soir?

Non, il faut que j'étudie.

Alors, je vais y aller avec Anne.

9.2.1b CHALKBOARD DRAWINGS

1. Wohin gehst du jetzt, Helga? [1]

2. Ich gehe nach Hause.

3. Warum fragst du?

4. Trinkst du eine Limonade mit mir?

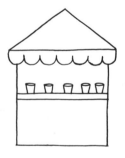

5. Dort drüben ist ein Stand.

6. Gut. Ich trinke Limonade gern.

9.2.1c FLANNEL BOARD

The teacher can use commercial figurines and flocking paper[2] or draw his own on flannel. The sentences are pronounced either by the teacher or a recording.

---

[1] *A-LM German Level One*, 2d ed. (New York: Harcourt Brace Jovanovich, Inc., 1969), p. 7.
[2] Available from Istrex: 15 W. 38th St., New York, N.Y.

1. ¿Dónde está Tomás?[1]

2. ¿Está enfermo?

3. No, se cayó en la escalera . . .

4. . . . y se rompió un diente.

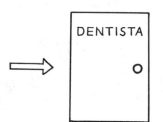

5. ¿Fué al dentista?

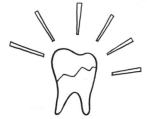

6. Sí, tuvo que ir. Le dolía mucho.

9.2.1d IDEOGRAMS

Ideograms are sets of symbols which are used to depict a sentence. Students can help make their own symbols.

[1] Gregory G. LaGrone, et al., *Entender y Hablar*, Teacher's Ed. (New York: Holt, Rinehart, and Winston, 1965), p. 278.

Où habite Jean-Michel?

Il habite près de l'église.

Et toi?

Moi, j'habite près de l'école.

9.2.2 *Drilling Dialogue Lines*

9.2.2a CUE CARDS

Cue cards can be homemade or prepared by a publisher:

(1) The teacher places cue cards on the chalkboard ledge and writes a number above each one. As he says *Quatre,* he points to a student, who answers: *Vraiment? Moi, je déteste les films de guerre.* In addition to individual responses, the teacher can use choral drills, half-class drills, boys and girls, teacher and class dialogue practices.

(2) The teacher puts cue cards in a stack and remembers which one is on top. Then he holds the stack behind him so that the students cannot see them. The students then guess which card is on top. This gives them practice in saying all the lines. (This exercise is for young junior high school students.)

9.2.2b WHO SAYS WHAT?

The teacher speaks a certain line and asks which character says it:

Teacher: ¿Quién dice, "¿Por qué no me llamaste anoche?"
Student: Pedro dice, "Por qué no me llamaste anoche?"

9.2.2c DIRECTED DIALOGUE

Directed dialogue practice is difficult for the students. It should be carefully prepared, so that the students know what to do. Both the questions and answers should be taught and drilled before this exercise begins:

Question: John, are you going to the movies tonight?
Answer: No, I am not going because I have homework to do.

The difficulty lies in the question: Paul, ask John if he is going to the movies tonight. Many pupils tend to answer: John, if he is going to the movies tonight? Much practice is necessary with this exercise:

Teacher: Carlos, pregúntele a María si va a la fiesta.
Carlos: María, ¿Vas a la fiesta?
Teacher: María, contéstele que sí, que Ud. va a la fiesta.
María: Sí, voy a la fiesta.

9.2.3   *Going beyond the Basic Dialogue*

Once the students have memorized the dialogue, the teacher can use the sentences as a basis for additional speaking practice.

9.2.3a   YES/NO QUESTIONS

The teacher puts cue cards on chalkboard ledge and asks questions to be answered by *yes* or *no* plus a statement:

Teacher: Est-ce que Guillaume téléphone à Valérie?
Student: Non, Guillaume téléphone à Sylvie.

Teacher: Ist Heinz im Garten?
Student: Nein, Heinz ist im Wohnzimmer.

9.2.3b   EITHER/OR QUESTIONS

The teacher puts magazine cutouts on the chalkboard with magnets and asks questions such as the following:

Teacher: ¿Le gusta más el café o la leche?
Student: Me gusta más la leche.

Teacher: Préférez-vous le football ou le tennis?
Student: Je préfère le football.

9.2.3c   WHY—BECAUSE QUESTIONS

Teacher: Ouvrez vos livres à la page 32. Répondez à toutes les questions avec *parce que.*

           Pourquoi est-ce que Jacques s'est cassé la jambe?

Student: Parce qu'il est tombé.

9.2.3d   WHO DOES WHAT?

The teacher puts dialogue on overhead projector and asks questions about it:

Teacher: Was macht Hans?
Student: Hans spielt Tennis.

Teacher: Que fait Bernard?
Student: Il regarde un film policier.

9.2.3e HOW (ADVERB) QUESTIONS

The teacher dramatizes each action before he asks a question about it:

Teacher: (Sings "La Cucaracha" off key.)
¿Cómo canta Isabel?
Student: Isabel canta mal.

Teacher: (Speaks rapidly.)
Comment est-ce que Claude parle?
Student: Claude parle vite.

9.2.3f VARYING DIRECT OBJECTS

The teacher puts flannel or flocking-paper objects on chalkboard ledge. He asks individual students to come forward, pick up an object, answer the question *Was bringt Fritz nach Hause?* or *¿Qué trae Paco a casa?* and put the object on the flannel board. Example: *Fritz bringt eine Katze nach Hause. Paco trae un bote a casa.*

9.2.3g VARYING INDIRECT OBJECTS

On each flash card there is a magazine cutout of a person; some represent professions: doctor, engineer, teacher, and so on. The teacher holds up the cards, and the class says: *Je dis bonjour à la dame, au professeur, au médecin, à la jeune fille.*

9.2.3h PERSONAL QUESTIONS BASED ON DIALOGUE

¿De qué color es el coche de su padre?
¿Cómo se llama la última película que vió Ud.?

Quel est votre programme préféré à la télévision?
A quelle heure avez-vous dîné hier soir?

Wie oft gehen Sie ins Kino?
Welcher Film gefällt Ihnen am besten?

9.2.3i PRACTICE USING DEPENDENT AND INDEPENDENT CLAUSES

The teacher should supply most of the information that the students are to use in their answers in his question. If the pattern is established, the student needs to furnish only the last two or three words; each of his sentences begins with *Si j'étais riche* or *Si yo fuera rico*:

Teacher: Si vous étiez riche, où iriez-vous?
Student: Si j'étais riche, j'irais à Paris.

Teacher: Si vous étiez riche, quelle voiture achèteriez-vous?
Student: Si j'étais riche, j'achèterais une Cadillac.

Teacher: Si Ud. fuera rico, ¿adónde iría Ud.?
Student: Si yo fuera rico, iría a Buenos Aires.

Teacher: Si Ud. fuera rico, ¿qué clase de coche compraría Ud.?
Student: Si yo fuera rico, compraría un Cadillac.

9.2.4 *Using Audio-Visual Programs*

Audio-visual programs provide a film or sound filmstrip to accompany the dialogue or basic presentation. Many of the techniques of presentation suggested for dialogues may also be adapted to audio-visual programs.

Moreover, the visual part of the program may be used without the sound portion to cue the lines. Individual students may be called upon to play the role of the people on the filmstrip or in the movie.

The filmstrip or the movie is a fine means of presenting parts of a lesson. But like any technique, overuse can lead to boredom. As a change in pace the teacher might wish to present one of the dialogues using posters or cue cards. Later the film can be played to reinforce what the students have already learned.

As a further change in pace, discontinue using the visual aids in drills. This will serve to check students' ability to perform without the "crutch."

9.3 INITIAL PRESENTATION: SEPARATE SENTENCES

The basic presentation of a lesson might consist of sentences which do not form a dialogue. If the sentences are in a sequence, perhaps the teacher will want them memorized. If the sentences form mainly questions and answers, perhaps the teacher will simply insist that the students learn to answer questions fluently.

9.3.1 *Physical Movement*

The basic sentences of the unit may form a Gouin series, that is, a sequence of activities which lend themselves easily to dramatization.

The teacher acts out each activity as he models the sentences. The students repeat the sentences as some of them take turns performing the actions: *J'ouvre la porte. J'entre dans la salle de classe. Je ferme la porte. Je vais au tableau noir. J'écris mon nom.*

The teacher can vary the activities by having one student do the actions, *Tu ouvres la porte*; or a pair of students, *Vous ouvrez la porte.*

9.3.2 *Question-Answer Technique*

In the question-answer presentation, the teacher, using props or visuals, teaches the basic sentence patterns of the lesson. Using questions, the teacher cues the students' responses. Students are gradually led to say sentences that they have never heard modelled.

The advantage of this type of presentation is that from the first day of instruction the students are using the language creatively to answer questions. They move from the simple repetition of new sentences to individualized responses. In the next step of instruction, which might even take place on the same day (depending on the class), the students learn to ask the questions of each other in a sort of directed dialogue.

The limitation of this technique is that not all spoken communication takes the form of questions and answers. The drill may be expanded in the following way: the initial presentation of the lesson material (basic nouns, verbs, adjectives, adverbs, prepositions) could take the form of questions and answers. Once the students control this material orally and can use it in their own sentences, they can be introduced to the lesson dialogue or reading selection. Since they have been taught the new material already, they will be able to understand most of the dialogue they hear. They can be led to infer the meaning of expletives and conversational fillers. Some students may present the dialogue as a skit. Others may prefer reading it aloud.

9.3.2a SELECTING SENTENCES TO BE TAUGHT

The question-answer technique may be used with any set of teaching materials. The teacher selects the questions and answers.

(1) The first step is to determine the basic material of the lesson, both grammar and vocabulary. Let us assume that a given French lesson teaches the verb *aller*, certain names of places, and the contractions of the definite article with *à*. The students have already learned the verb *être* and the use of the definite article.

(2) The second step is to determine the order of presentation:

1. New vocabulary: Voici le théâtre. Voici le cinéma. Voici le stade.
2. Familiar question: Où est Michel?
   Introduction of *au:* Il est au cinéma.

3. Introduction of *va:* Michel va au cinéma.
4. Introduction of *vas* and *vais:* Où vas-tu? Je vais au stade.
5. New vocabulary: Voici l'église. Voici l'école. Voici la piscine. Voici la gare.
6. The form *à l':* Il va à l'église. Il est à l'eglise.
7. Introduction of vont: Où vont-ils?
8. Introduction of *à la, allez,* and *allons:* Où allez-vous? Nous allons à la piscine.

(3) The third step is to determine the types of materials to be used. The above sentences might be taught by using line drawings on the chalkboard to designate places, stick figures on index cards, and index cards of the places to distribute to the students.

9.3.2b SAMPLE PRESENTATIONS

The question-answer technique lends itself readily to the use of visual aids. These contribute to the "realness" of the exchanges, for both teacher and student are talking about specific objects and actions.

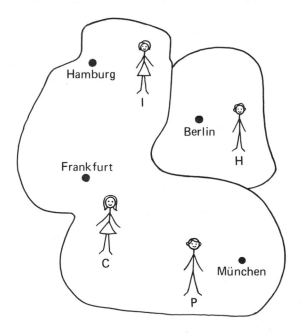

(1) The overhead projector: The teacher prepares a transparency with a line map of Germany. He adds dots for a few major cities, such as Berlin, Hamburg, München, Frankfurt. Then he places the first letter of each city next to the dot which represents it.

The teacher points to the outline of Germany and says: *Das ist Deutschland.* The class repeats. The pattern is repeated for *Das ist Berlin, Das ist Hamburg, Das ist München, Das ist Frankfurt.* The teacher then calls on the class and eventually on individuals to answer the question: *Was ist das?*

The teacher draws a stick figure of a boy on the transparency next to Berlin. He asks: *Wer ist das?* He teaches the answer: *Das ist Hans.* As the class repeats the sentence, he writes a small H under the drawing. Similarly he teaches (and adds to the transparency): *Ilse (Hamburg), Peter (München), Christl (Frankfurt).*

When the students can handle these sentences, the teacher goes around the class pointing to students and asking: *Wer ist das?* The others give the name of the student indicated.

The teacher introduces a new question: *Wo ist Hans?* and a new response: *Hans ist in Berlin.* The teacher continues with *Ilse, Peter* and *Christl.*

When the students can handle the new pattern, the teacher divides the classroom into four sections, representing the four cities. (If desired, the teacher may write the name of each city on a sheet of typing paper and give the "name" to each of the sections.) Questions and answers are now personalized, using the names of the students.

If the class responds easily, the teacher may also wish to introduce: *Wo sind Anna und Ilse? Wo bist du? Ich bin in Hamburg.*

(2) Cue cards: The teacher prepares enough cue cards for the entire class. For example, if there are twenty-four students in the class, the teacher makes six index cards with milk, six with wine, and so on. (Masculine nouns may be drawn in blue and feminine nouns in red.)

The teacher takes one of each card. He explains he is thirsty and is going to drink some coffee. He pretends to drink the coffee on the card and says: *Tomo café.* Students repeat. The teacher introduces the three other nouns: *¿Qué tomo? Tomo leche.*

Then he calls a student forward and gives him a card. He models and the class repeats: *Juanito toma leche. ¿Qué toma Juanito? Toma leche.* The student keeps his card and goes to his seat. Other students come forward and are given cards while the teacher asks questions and elicits responses. Then the remainder of the cards are distributed.

Students are taught to ask each other: *¿Qué tomas?* and to answer *Tomo....*

The pace may be enlivened by alternating types of questions and by having the students exchange cards.

If time allows, the plural forms of the verb may also be taught. Two students holding the same card stand up. The teacher asks: *Qué toman Marta y Carmen?* The students are taught the reply: *Marta y Carmen toman Coca-Cola.* Only ten or fifteen minutes should be devoted to this activity. Otherwise, this kind of exercise can become long and drawn out simply because too much time is consumed in movement and too little time is left for actual language practice.

(3) Magazine pictures: The teacher cuts out magazine pictures of nouns which the students either know or are to learn in the lesson. For masculine French nouns, the magazine pictures are mounted on blue construction paper. Pictures of feminine nouns are mounted on red construction paper. These pictures are sorted into three piles: masculine nouns beginning with a consonant sound, feminine nouns beginning with a consonant sound, both genders beginning with a vowel sound.

Teacher: (Holds up a picture of a house.) Regardez cette belle maison. C'est ma maison. Répétez. C'est ma maison.

Class: C'est ma maison.

Teacher: (Holds up another picture of a house.) Voici une autre belle maison. Qui aime cette maison? Barbara? Alors, viens ici. (Gives the house to Barbara.) C'est la maison de Barbara. C'est sa maison. Répétez. C'est sa maison.

Class: C'est sa maison.

Teacher: (Points to Barbara's house.) Est-ce que c'est ma maison? (Cues class response.) Non, c'est sa maison.

Class: Non, c'est sa maison.

Teacher: Je vais donner ma maison à quelqu'un. Alain, viens ici. Je donne ma maison à Alain. (Gives first picture to Alain.) Maintenant c'est la maison d'Alain. C'est sa maison.

The teacher uses other pictures in the same way to teach the forms of the possessive adjectives.

9.4   PRACTICING SENTENCE PATTERNS

Once the students have been presented with the basic patterns, they need ample opportunity for practice. This practice can be stimulating if techniques are varied frequently and if visual aids are introduced. For suggestions on pattern drills, see section 6.4.3.

9.4.1 *Magazine Cutouts*

The class is studying the partitive. Students bring to class as many magazine cutouts of foods as they can find. When called on, they offer them to their neighbors:

Student 1:   Voulez-vous de la viande?
Student 2:   Merci, je n'ai plus faim.
Student 3:   Voulez-vous des haricots?
Student 4:   Oui, s'il vous plaît.

9.4.2 *Sentence Practice with Reading Cues*

One card is flashed at a time:

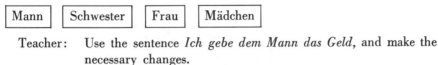

Teacher: Use the sentence *Ich gebe dem Mann das Geld*, and make the necessary changes.
Students: Ich gebe der Schwester das Geld.
           Ich gebe der Frau das Geld.
           Ich gebe dem Mädchen das Geld.

9.4.3 *Transparencies*

1. El   2. Ellos   3. Nosotros   4. Yo   5. Tú

Teacher: Yo digo, *"Cuatro."*
Uds. dicen, *"Saldré para México."*
Yo digo, *"Dos."*
Uds. dicen, *"Saldrán para México."*
¡Empiecen[*"Cinco."*
Students: Tú saldrás para México. (And so on.)

Following this drill, there are sentences like: *Hará un viaje. Pondré un telegrama. No podrán salir. Vendré mañana.*

9.4.4 *Props*

The teacher should teach the names of articles of clothing first:

Teacher: Ma chemise est blanche. De quelle couleur est votre chemise?
Student: Ma chemise est bleue.
Teacher: Marie, de quelle couleur est votre jupe?
Marie: Ma jupe est verte.
Teacher: Sylvie, de quelle couleur est votre blouse?
Sylvie: Ma blouse est blanche.

After drilling all the feminine articles, the teacher proceeds to the masculine articles.

Teacher: Mon pantalon est marron. De quelle couleur est votre pantalon?
Georges: Mon pantalon est noir.
Teacher: Anne, de quelle couleur est votre sac?
Anne: Mon sac est rouge.

After drilling all the masculine articles, he proceeds to plurals:

Teacher: De quelle couleur sont vos chaussures?
Paul: Mes chaussures sont noires.
Teacher: De quelle couleur sont vos chaussettes?
Pierre: Mes chaussettes sont bleues.

9.4.5 *Executing Commands*

Teacher: Hans, geh an die Tafel!
(Hans executes command.)
Hans, was hast du getan?
Hans: Ich bin an die Tafel gegangen.
Teacher: Hilde, was hat Hans getan?
Hilde: Hans ist an die Tafel gegangen.

9.4.6   *World Map*

Indicate with a pointer the countries and cities that Henri goes to or comes from:

Teacher: (Moves pointer from New York to Paris.)
　　　　　Où va Henri?
Student: Henri va à Paris.
Teacher: (Moves pointer from Mexico to the U.S.)
　　　　　D'où vient Henri?
Student: Henri vient du Mexique.

9.4.7   *Chalkboard Frieze*

Before class a few artistically talented students draw a series of pictures on the top section of the chalkboard around the classroom. Each picture depicts two people or objects of visibly different characteristics. This frieze is kept for several days. (In picture 1 the 1971 car is blue, and the other is green.)

Teacher: ¡Miren Uds. el cuadro uno! Alicia, ¡compare Ud. los dos coches!
Alicia: El coche verde es más viejo que el coche azul.
Teacher: Sí, ¿otra respuesta?
Juan: El coche azul es más moderno que el coche verde.
Teacher: ¡Miren Uds. el cuadro dos! Enrique, ¡compare Ud. los dos muchachos!
Enrique: El muchacho a la izquierda es menos gordo que el muchacho a la derecha.
Teacher: ¡Muy bien! ¡Miren Uds. el cuadro tres! Eduardo, ¡compare Ud. las dos casas!
Eduardo: La casa A es más grande que la casa B.

9.4.8   *Large Cards.*

Prepare large cards with the following pictures. Place the cards on the chalkboard ledge:

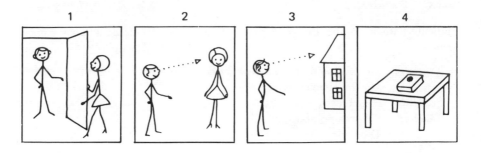

1. Jim enters first.   *Who* enters first?
2. Jim looks at Louise.   *Whom* does Jim look at?
3. Mark sees the roof.   *What* does Mark see?
4. The book is on the table. *What* is on the table?

Teacher: Regardez les images. Je vais décrire ce qu'il y a sur chaque image. Posez la question correspondante.

1. Jacques entre le premier.
   Student: Qui est-ce qui entre le premier?

2. Jacques regarde Louise.
   Student: Qui est-ce que Jacques regarde?

3. Marc voit le toit de la maison.
   Student: Qu'est-ce que Marc voit?

4. Le livre est sur la table.
   Student: Qu'est-ce qui est sur la table?

9.4.9 Game: "*¿Quién soy yo?*"

Practice using adjectives with only a few nouns permitted. The persons described are all T.V. stars. Boys will be male personalities; girls, female personalities.

One student leaves the room while the others decide who he will be. When she returns, she asks questions of one student after the other: *¿Soy joven? ¿Soy cómica? ¿Soy bonita? ¿Soy alta? ¿Soy americana? ¿Soy cantatriz? ¿Soy famosa? ¿Soy bailarina?*

9.4.10 Direct to Indirect Discourse

When the students are learning how to form indirect discourse, the teacher may place dialogues from earlier lessons on an overhead transparency for class practice. The students take turns transforming the lines of dialogue into indirect speech:

Richard: Ich will ins Kino gehen.
Student 1:   Richard sagt, daß er ins Kino gehen will.
Student 2:   Richard sagte, daß er ins Kino gehen wollte.

Patrice: Je veux aller au cinéma.
Student 1:   Patrice dit qu'il veut aller au cinéma.
Student 2:   Patrice a dit qu'il voulait aller au cinéma.

9.4.11   *Paired Speaking Drills*

If the teacher prepares Ditto sheets for speaking practice, the students can work in pairs (see section 3.2.6). One student of the pair has a Ditto sheet and initiates the exercise. He also prompts his classmate if he has trouble responding. When the exercise has been completed, the students exchange papers and run through it once more. This time the roles are reversed. The advantage of this type of speaking practice is that all the students are actively engaged in listening and speaking. Furthermore, the teacher is free to walk around and help individual students.

(1) The first student takes the Ditto sheet and the second student opens his text to a map of the French-speaking world:

Student 1:   (Reads.)
             Montrez-moi Québec.
Student 2:   (Points to Quebec.)
             Voici Québec.
Student 1:   (Reads *Voici Québec* on his Ditto sheet, and acknowledges that the answer was correct by continuing with the next sentence.)
             Montrez-moi Fort-de-France.
Student 2:   Voici Fort-de-France.

(2) The first student reads the description of the scene:

You don't like your younger sister. Each time I say something nice about her, you say that the opposite is true.

Student 1:   Ta soeur est jolie.
Student 2:   Mais non, elle est moche.
Student 1:   (Reads.)
             Elle est gentille.
Student 2:   Mais non, elle est insupportable.

9.5   GUIDED CONVERSATION

In dialogue presentations and sentence practice, the student is required to respond according to a fixed pattern. This groundwork is essential to the development of the speaking skill. However, conversation by its very nature means that the student himself decides what he wants to say. In guided conversation, the student is given a framework within which to build his sentences, but the actual choice of what he will say is left up to him.

Some work in guided conversation should be provided even for beginning students. Only in expressing their own thoughts will they realize that the foreign language is a viable means of communication.

9.5.1   *Mini-Conversations*   *good for warm ups*

A mini-conversation is an exchange of at least four lines. All too frequently the teacher asks a student a single question and then goes on to another student without developing the conversation. A conversation is a longer exchange between two people.

9.5.1a   IMPROMPTU ORAL QUESTIONS

In a mini-conversation the teacher asks two or more related questions of the same person: 1. *Hast du einen Bruder? Wie heißt er? Ist er älter oder jünger als du? Hast du ihn gern?*   2. *Quel sport préfères-tu? Avec qui joues-tu au——? Où jouez-vous?*   3. *¿Qué clases tiene Usted este semestre? ¿Cuál le gusta más? ¿Y menos?*

Variation: To maintain pace, the teacher might ask several students one question each and ask the next student three consecutive questions which are related to one another. Information questions are more effective than yes/no questions.

9.5.1b   PREPARED QUESTIONS

The teacher distributes Dittoed sheets of a one-sided conversation. He leaves blanks for the other person's part. He should give students a few minutes to think of what they will say when called on.

Situación: Ud. ha perdido algo importante y tiene miedo de contárselo a sus padres:

Yo: ¡Roberto! ¿Por qué ese cara tan triste?
Ud.: _____
Yo: ¿Dónde lo has perdido?
Ud.: _____
Yo: ¿Cuánto vale?
Ud.: _____
Yo: ¿Por qué no compraste otro?
Ud.: _____
Yo: ¿A quién vas a contar lo que ha pasado, a tu mamá o a tu papá?
Ud.: _____

Yo:	¿Porqué?
Ud.:	_____
Yo:	¿Tus padres te darán el dinero que necesitas?
Ud.:	_____
Yo:	Entonces, ¿qué vas a hacer?
Ud.:	_____

9.5.2   *Role Playing*

Two or more students come before the class to act out an impromptu conversation. (Note: this activity may be correlated with the study of culture patterns; see section 12.3.6.) If the class is large, the students may be divided into three or four groups, each carrying out their own role-playing activities in a corner of the room.

9.5.2a   PREPARING THE STUDENTS

The success of role-playing activities depends on careful preparation. The students must have learned the needed sentence patterns and vocabulary in advance. The situation should be carefully described so that even an unimaginative student has something to say. At the same time, leeway must be allowed for the creative student to express himself in unexpected ways.

(1) SHOPPING
    ¿Cuánto vale ese vestido?
    ¿Cuánto vale esa camisa?
    ¿Cuánto valen esos zapatos?
    Se lo dejo por diez pesos.
    Se la dejo por doce pesos.
    Se los dejo por veinte pesos.

(2) DOCTOR'S VISIT
    Où est-ce que vous avez mal?
    J'ai mal à la tête.
    J'ai mal à l'estomac.
    Qu'est-ce que vous avez mangé hier soir?
    Montrez-moi votre langue.

(3) TELEPHONING: AN INVITATION
    Invitations
    Veux-tu aller au cinéma avec moi dimanche après-midi?
    Je t'invite à aller à la piscine avec moi.
    Tu veux prendre un Coca-Cola demain après l'école? C'est moi qui paie.

    Acceptances
    Volontiers! A quelle heure est-ce qu'on se rencontre?

Avec plaisir! Tu viens me chercher? On y va dans ta voiture ou en autobus?

Chic alors! Où est-ce qu'on se rencontre?

Refusals

Merci, Paul. Malheureusement j'ai des devoirs à faire.

Merci, Marc. Mais je n'ai pas de maillot.

Je regrette, Claude. Maman veut que je rentre tout de suite après l'école. Nous avons des invités.

9.5.2b CREATING THE SITUATION

Students must be given cues as to what they are to say and how they are to react.

(1) Guided role playing: One or both students draw a slip of paper telling them how they are to react. Slips for the different roles are in separate envelopes:

DOCTOR'S VISIT

(Patient):   You have a sore throat.

(Doctor):   You discover appendicitis and send him to the hospital.

ORDERING FOOD

(Client):   Choose whatever you like.

(Girlfriend): You like everything your friend suggests, except the dessert. Choose something else.

(Waiter):   You are out of one of the dishes the client orders.

(2) Bartering: The class is divided into two teams: the salesmen and clients. The salesmen draw a slip of paper naming the object they are to sell and giving a suggested minimum retail price. The winner is the one who gets the highest price for the object.

Variation: The clients are told to buy the object. Whoever gets it for the lowest price is the winner.

Variation: The class is divided into pairs of a salesman and a client and are told that all negotiations must be carried out in the foreign language. When they have come to an agreement, the pair comes to the teacher and announces the price they have decided on.

If bartering becomes too serious, a time limit may have to be set.

9.5.3 *Oral Descriptions*

Oral descriptions are most effective if the rest of the class is actively encouraged to listen to their classmates. The following techniques involve both speaking and listening.

9.5.3a MAGAZINE CUTOUTS

For homework, each student finds a magazine cutout and prepares four sentences about it. Only known vocabulary and expressions may be used. One or more of the sentences may be inaccurate. When the class hears an inaccurate sentence, they raise their hands.

Variation: A member of the class may be called upon to correct the inaccuracies.

9.5.3b VERBAL DESCRIPTIONS

For homework, the student prepares six statements about some object for which the foreign language equivalent is known. In class the student says the first sentence. One classmate is chosen to guess which object is being described. If he guesses right, another student gives his description. If he guesses wrong, the first student reads the next sentence of his description. Again one more guess is allowed. If no one has guessed the object at the end of the description, the student gives the correct answer.

9.5.3c WALL CHARTS AND OTHER ILLUSTRATIONS

The teacher puts up a wall chart with four or more drawings. These are labeled (a), (b), (c), (d). A student comes to the front of the class and draws a letter from a hat. Without using gestures, he must describe the drawing which corresponds to the letter he drew. When he has finished, the class votes which one they think he described. The teacher asks, for example, "How many think it was (a)? Raise your hands."

This exercise may be made more difficult by using more complex pictures. For example, if the textbook has a colored illustration with many people, a student could be told to describe one of the people. The teacher then holds up his book, pointing to the people one by one. The class indicates which person they think was being described.

Drawings on the overhead projector may also be used for this type of speaking activity.

9.5.3d TWENTY QUESTIONS

One student leaves the room while the others decide on an object in the classroom. The student comes back and has twenty questions to discover what the object is.

9.5.3e WHAT'S MY LINE?

A student draws a slip of paper naming a profession, or he thinks up a profession and writes it down for the teacher. The class asks questions to guess what the profession is.

9.5.3f SLIDES

The teacher shows a few selected slides from his trip to Mexico. As he projects them on the screen he makes a statement about each slide, using the first person:

1. En esta diapositiva estoy bajando del camión.
2. Quiero comprar un sarape.
   Ahora estoy regateando.
3. Estoy pagando.
4. Ahora estoy comiendo un taco.
5. En esta diapositiva estoy subiendo la Pirámide del Sol.
6. Ahora estoy en la cima. Caramba! Empieza a llover!

Later he shows the same slides and asks students to tell the story in the third person.

9.5.3g SUPPLEMENTARY FILM STRIPS

(1) The teacher first shows several sections of film strip No. 5 (*Deux rivières se rencontrent*) [1] and plays the accompanying tape. This is repeated as many times as necessary.

(2) The teacher shows the frames again without tape. He asks questions about each slide:

1. Comment s'appellent les deux fleuves qui traversent Lyon?
2. Quels animaux voyez-vous dans le parc?
3. Qui est-ce vous voyez sur la péniche?

(3) The teacher shows the filmstrip again without tape and calls on individual students to describe what they see.

9.5.4 *Prepared Talks*

The student is given a topic or a choice of topics for a prepared talk. He writes out what he plans to say. (This written form is handed to the teacher for correction. Its main purpose is to encourage thoughtful preparation. Its secondary purpose is to afford practice in writing.) In class the student gives his talk. He can memorize what he has written or speak extemporaneously. He is not, however, allowed to use notes.

Prepared talks are most effective with intermediate and advanced classes. At the beginning of a school year, for example, each student could prepare a short talk introducing himself (if there are new students in the class) or he might talk about what he did during the summer.

---

[1] Peter Buckley, *A Year in France* (New York: Holt, Rinehart and Winston, 1964).

Variation: With weaker students, the teacher might require that the written form be submitted two days in advance, so that he can correct and hand back the text the day before the oral talk is due. If the student intends to memorize certain sections of his talk, he will be memorizing correct French, Spanish, or German.

9.5.5 *Skits*

In intermediate and advanced classes, groups of five to eight students can get together to prepare a skit. The students will probably have their own ideas, but if not, the teacher can offer suggestions. When the skits are ready, they can be presented to other members of the class. The preparation of the skit might be an activity stretching over a week or two, with a quarter hour allotted for rehearsal at the end of each class period. The skits might be presented to other foreign language classes or to the language club.

In dividing the class into groups for skits, the teacher should try to put some good students with each group. They may serve as scribes in taking down the script accurately.

9.5.6 *Stories*

The teacher begins a story which the class finishes orally. This type of activity may be done with smaller groups also. Each student in turn adds a line to the plot.

Il fait nuit. Un homme grimpe à un balcon et entre à pas de loup dans une chambre à coucher. Il allume son briquet. Il voit un collier de perles sur une commode.

Finissez l'histoire.

9.6 FREE CONVERSATION

In free conversation the students assume the initiative for guiding the speaking activities. The teacher's primary task is to stay in the background and act as an informational resource. Generally it is easier for the teacher to encourage the students to talk than it is to keep quiet himself.

9.6.1 *Discussion Groups*

Discussion initiated by students requires a point of departure. The most usual is a reading selection, even though a play, film, a visit to a museum, and so on, can also serve as a springboard.

9.6.1a   PREPARATION

Each student prepares two or three questions on the reading selection for homework. These may be directly related to the text: *Why did the main character not notice that. . . ?* Discussion is more animated if opinions are solicited: *On page. . . , the author says that. . . . Do you agree?* or personal reactions asked for: *What would you have done in a similar situation?*

When discussions are first initiated, the teacher might give a short lecture on what types of questions can be derived from a reading passage. Even advanced students often need a review about how questions are formed.

9.6.1b   WHOLE-CLASS CONVERSATION

In class the first few discussions might be carried out in a single group. Chairs are arranged in a large circle. The teacher joins the group and asks one student to begin the discussion with a question. That student may direct his question to anyone who wants to answer it. The greater the number of participants, the better. When the topic seems exhausted, the teacher calls on another student to ask a question. If some students are quiet, they might be singled out to give questions. Toward the end of the time allotted for conversation, the teacher should be sure to include those who have not yet said anything.

Except for encouraging participation, the teacher makes no comments or corrections during the discussion. He may take notes and reserve five or ten minutes at the end of the conversation to review the errors that were made.

9.6.1c   SMALL-GROUP CONVERSATION

Once the students understand how the discussion is carried out, the teacher can divide the class into groups of three to five. The students take turns asking questions and giving opinions. The teacher moves from group to group, taking notes on mistakes that are being made, but saying nothing unless asked a direct question.

When time is called, the teacher briefly gives corrections to the class as a whole.

The small-group conversation technique involves all the students. It is hard to be silent in a group of three or four. Even the timid students do not mind trying to express themselves, especially if the teacher is working with another group at the time. At any given moment, the various groups might be discussing entirely different topics, even though one reading furnished the point of departure. This diversity is fine, for the aim of the conversation is self-expression, and the choice of topics is secondary.

The teacher should shift the composition of the groups from time to time, perhaps by listing the groups for the week on the class bulletin board. Conversation develops more readily if groups contain students of mixed ability and mixed interests.

9.6.2 *Debates*

9.6.2a TOPICS

Class debates are most effective if the topics are of interest to the students. This means that students are most fluent in discussing topics they know about, such as aspects of American cultural and political life. Debates about aspects of foreign life are usually less lively.

Ask the students to write out subjects they would like to debate, and select debate topics accordingly. Some possibilities are:

Grades in high school should be abolished.
All students should be required to study a foreign language.
A high school dress code should be maintained.

The debate topic should be strongly worded so that it is possible to take a definite affirmative or negative stand.

9.6.2b FORMING TEAMS

Although students may be allowed to choose sides, this often results in uneven teams. It is simpler to divide the class into two sides (with students of mixed abilities on each team) and then flip a coin to see which team has first choice at selecting the affirmative or negative position.

In a French class students might be told that a Frenchman is willing to debate either side of a topic, for fluency of expression is more important than sincerity of position.

9.6.2c PREPARATION

The teacher may hand out a Ditto containing key words and expressions which relate to the topic. As homework, students jot down notes about what they might say. If teams are assigned in advance, students prepare only one side of the question. It is also possible to have students prepare both sides of the question and to divide the class into teams on the day of the debate.

9.6.2d RUNNING THE DEBATE

The class is divided into two teams. Each team meets in a "huddle" to elect a captain and to plan strategy. A point to defend is assigned to each member. The captain sees that all the members of his team are called on to make statements. This "huddle" may last fifteen minutes. Both teams are required to discuss strategy in the foreign language.

The debate begins with the affirmative team. Its members elaborate their position and then the negative team is allowed to reply. The only role of the teacher is to see that all students are given a chance to participate.

The teacher makes notes of persistent errors. These are corrected during ten minutes at the end of the debate.

Many students prefer not to have an arbiter; the fun of debating is reason enough for this activity. If, however, a class wishes to appoint a judge or a jury, this should be decided before the teams are organized. The teacher may or may not be chosen to judge the debate.

9.6.3 *Panel Discussions*

Students may be asked to prepare panel discussions on subjects relating to the foreign culture. The teacher divides the class into committees according to interests. Each group does research on its topic and later presents its findings to the class using overhead and opaque projectors.

9.6.3a THE TEACHER'S PREPARATION

Before sending a class to the library or resource center, the teacher himself must research the topic. Then he can either give the students titles of books and periodicals where they can find necessary data, or he can hand them the materials to read. If this preparation is not done, much class time will be wasted.

9.6.3b CLASS ORGANIZATION

One committee may work on a topic for one week, and another committee take up another topic the next week. If this system is used, the committee-of-the-week can work at the back of the classroom while the teacher works with the rest of the class. Then the class is given a written assignment while the teacher confers with the committee. The students will need guidance in selecting appropriate articles, summarizing them, and pronouncing new words.

The entire class may be divided into four or five committees. The committees work in various corners of the classroom. The teacher goes from group to group offering guidance.

9.6.3c SAMPLE BIBLIOGRAPHY

The teacher may wish to prepare a short bibliography on a given topic. He can find excellent articles in the Spanish Scholastic Series *¿Qué tal?*, *Hoy Día*, and *El Sol*. Others are in weekly Latin American periodicals:

Mexico: *Hoy, Tiempo, Revista Mañana*
Argentina: *Planeta, Panorama*
Venezuela: *Momento, Semana*
Colombia: *Cromos*

School texts are another rich source.

Here is a sample bibliography on recreation in Latin America—*Diversiones y Deportes en Latinoaméria.*

(1) El Esquí en Chile

"El Esquí" by Dora Salazar, *Hablar y Leer*, La Grone, McHenry and O'Connor (New York: Holt, Rinehart and Winston, 1962), p. 295.

(2) La Corrida de Toros

Hablar y Leer, op. cit., pp. 160–67

A Los Toros, Vol. 2
an encyclopedia of the bull and the bullfighter
one LP record with text: GMS—Disc 7110
Wible Language Institute

La Corrida de Toros
MX 30; 16 color slides
Wible Language Institute

Plaza de Toros, La Fiesta Brava, Vol. 2
a recording made in Mexico: ASFD—58 17 Stereo
Wible Language Institute

"Juan Belmonte se elevó a la cumbre con solo un capote, una muleta y el corazón," *Leer, Hablar y Escribir*, Keesee, La Grone, and O'Connor. (New York: Holt, Rinehart and Winston, 1963), pp. 145–47.

(3) El Fútbol

"Rumbo al Mundial de Chile," *Hablar, Leer y Escribir*, op. cit., pp. 10–13.
"Brasil se Adjudicó el Campeonato Mundial de Fútbol," ibid., p. 44.

(4) El Béisbol

"Temporada de Béisbol: Tigres y Monterrey Inician la Campaña en el Parque del SS," ibid., p. 218.

"Tigres Ganó en 10 Entradas," ibid., p. 242.

"Los Tigres Ganaron el Juego 10-9, y la Serie," ibid., p. 276.

(5) La Fiesta

"Fiestas Nacionales de México," Elida Wills, *Español que Funciona, Libro Cuarto México y Otros Vecinos, Edición Revisada* (Dallas: Banks Upshaw and Company, 1960), pp. 101–13.

"El mercado y la fiesta," John A. Crow, *Spanish American Life*, rev. ed., (New York: Holt, Rinehart and Winston, 1963), pp. 84–91.

Fiesta Mexicana
Javier de Leon's Panorama of Mexico
one LP record: MF-472 Mono; MFS-472 Stereo
Wible Language Institute

Fiesta Ranchera (Mariachis)
one LP record: ST 10465
Wible Language Institute

(6)   El Baile

Bailes Regionales
by Mariachi Vargas de Tacalitlan
one LP record: MKL 1448
Wible Language Institute

Argentine Tangos
one LP record: accordian and orchestra
AFSD 5869 Stereo
Wible Language Institute

CHAPTER TEN
READING
COMPREHENSION

do thy ? ,

For many students, reading is the one skill they may occasionally use when they have left the classroom. It is also the skill which is retained the longest.

Reading is more than just assigning foreign language sounds to the written words; it requires the comprehension of what is written. Students differ in their ability to read English, and these same differences reappear in their ability to read the foreign language. Reading skills in one language are not necessarily transferred to another language and may be inhibitory when they do. A student who reads English easily may have difficulty reading the foreign language. But the student who reads English with difficulty will surely have problems reading stories in the foreign language. The teacher must take these differences into account when teaching the reading skill.

10.1 GENERAL CONSIDERATIONS

Reading is a developmental process. The first stage is learning sound-symbol correspondences, either directly or by reading aloud sentences and words which have been mastered orally. Then the student learns to read these same words and sentence patterns in new combinations.

From the reading of sentences, the student progresses to the reading of paragraphs and short passages. The teacher helps the student develop techniques for inferring the meanings of new words, reading for information, and increasing comprehension of structural signals.

As the number of reading experiences increases, the differences in reading rate and comprehension among the students become very apparent. It is desirable, at this point, to organize the students into reading groups; each group could then read at its level of proficiency, from very easy to advanced readings. Another approach, especially valuable in advanced classes or upper level intermediate classes, is to provide a reading program for each individual student.

Literature may be introduced as early as the first year of language instruction, if the selections are accessible to the students. Often poetry is introduced first, followed by short stories, plays, and then longer prose works. The aim of literature study is not that the student learn about authors and periods, but rather that he develop personal techniques for approaching a literary work.

The following sections of this chapter suggest ways of introducing the student to the printed word and gradually bringing him to a point where he can study longer works.

10.2   INITIAL STEPS

It is possible to teach a student to read a second language aloud by beginning with sound-symbol correspondences, that is, by teaching which spellings represent which sounds. In most language courses, however, students first engage in listening and speaking activities before they are introduced to the printed word. The time elapsing between audio-lingual practice and reading aloud may range between the extremes of thirty minutes and several months. Students are taught to read entire sentences and then later are presented with sound-symbol correspondences.

The following sections offer techniques for teaching reading to students who have had prior listening and speaking practice. (For techniques of teaching sound-symbol correspondences, see Chapter 4.)

10.2.1   *Reading Memorized Sentences*

10.2.1a   OVERHEAD TRANSPARENCIES

Print on a transparency the dialogue sentences out of order. Number each one. The class repeats them after the teacher. This technique prevents the students from merely parroting the dialogue without looking at the spelling:

1. Allez, ne discute pas tout le temps.

2. Pas question. Il y a beaucoup à faire.
3. Bon, Anne prépare le dessert, moi, je goûte.
4. Mais nous manquons toujours la fin.[1]

10.2.1b DITTOED SHEETS

Sentences appear on the sheet with a number above each word. Students repeat the whole sentence after the teacher models it. Then the teacher says a number, and an individual student reads the word under the number:

1	2	3	4	5	6
Pedro	vive	en	una	casa	pequeña.

good idea

Teacher: Cinco, Julia.
Julia: Casa.

Note: In preparing similar exercises in French, word groups linked by liaison should be numbered as one word. For example, *les amis* or *j'habite* would be grouped as one *word*.

10.2.1c CUE CARDS

The teacher places cue cards for each line of the dialogue on the chalkboard ledge. Above each card he writes the dialogue line. The teacher reads each line and asks students to repeat. Then he calls on individuals to read. Finally the visuals are removed and students read the lines without the help of the visuals:

Wo ist die Bibliothek? | Nicht weit. Nur über die Straße. | Gut! Ich bin sehr müde, und diese Bücher sind schwer.

---

[1] *A-LM, Level One*, op. cit., p. 9.

10.2.1d FLANNEL BOARD

Each word of the sentence is written on a card backed with flocking paper or flannel. The cards are scattered on the flannel board. Individual students come forward and arrange them into sentences:

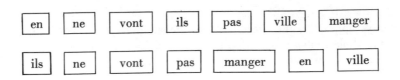

10.2.2 *New Sentences with Familiar Words*

Once students can read familiar sentences readily, they may be given the opportunity to read new sentences formed with words that they already know.

10.2.2a FLANNEL BOARD

The teacher begins by forming a sentence with just a few cards. He then asks who can read it. Little by little the sentences are expanded by adding additional cards (usually adjectives) and the students are asked who can read the longer sentences:

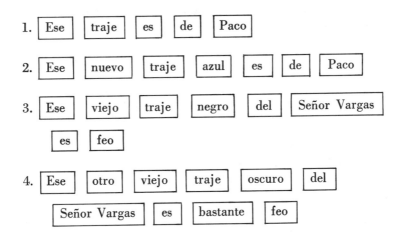

10.2.2b CUE CARDS

The teacher places along one section of the chalkboard ledge several cards with a word on each. The cards are not in correct order. He forms one sentence to use as a model, for example, *Heute bringt Karl einen Freund nach*

Hause. Then he puts the cards back on the ledge. One by one students are called on to form other sentences:

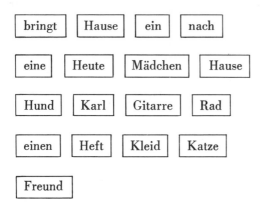

| bringt | Hause | ein | nach |

| eine | Heute | Mädchen | Hause |

| Hund | Karl | Gitarre | Rad |

| einen | Heft | Kleid | Katze |

| Freund |

10.2.2.c POCKET CHART

The teacher prepares cards for the pocket chart which contain words familiar to the students. On the first ledge of the pocket chart, the teacher forms a question:

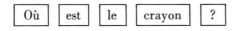

| Où | est | le | crayon | ? |

The second ledge contains cards with which plausible answers to the question may be formed:

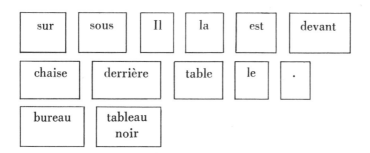

| sur | sous | Il | la | est | devant |

| chaise | derrière | table | le | . |

| bureau | tableau noir |

Students choose cards from this collection and place them on the third ledge in order to form an answer to the question:

| Il | est | sur | la | table | . |

Variation: The teacher puts various props in different positions in the room. He asks questions about them orally. Students form sentences on the pocket chart:

Teacher: Où est le cahier?
Student: (Places cards.)
          Il est sous le bureau.

10.2.3 *Understanding Sentences*

The teacher writes sentences on the chalkboard for the students to read.

10.2.3a COMMANDS

The teacher writes a command on the board and then calls on a student to execute it. *Geh an die Tafel und schreib deinen Namen, or Va à la fenêtre, ouvre-la, et retourne à ta place.*

10.2.3b QUESTIONS

The teacher writes questions on the board. The students answer them orally: *Quel temps fait-il? Où habitez-vous?*

10.2.4 *Reading Aloud in the Language Laboratory*

The teacher can prepare exercises for oral reading to be used in the language laboratory or individually—with cassette recorders or a tape recorder in the classroom.

A Ditto worksheet is prepared containing the selection to be read aloud. Each pause is marked by a slash line (/). The teacher records a tape on the following model:

Lisez / Hier soir à minuit /
Lisez / Quand je suis rentré chez moi / . . .

In Spanish each line would be preceded by ¡*Lea Ud.!* In German each line would be preceded by *Lesen Sie!*

The student takes his worksheet to the lab. When he hears the command *lisez*, he reads the first sentence during the first pause. Then he hears the sentence read by the teacher and has another pause in which to read it once more himself. He hears the next *lisez* and reads the next sentence.

Students must be encouraged to read the sentence aloud *before* they hear the confirmation on the tape.

10.3 GUIDED READING TECHNIQUES

When the student can read aloud, guided reading activities begin. Beginning, intermediate, and advanced classes all spend a certain portion of their time on guided reading. The level of the reading material grows more difficult, but the basic classroom procedures remain the same. Passages are generally not more than one typewritten page in length.

10.3.1 *Locating Suitable Materials*

Most teachers use the reading materials provided in the textbook for guided reading practice. If the basic program does not offer sufficient materials, additional selections must be located.

10.3.1a HOMEMADE RECOMBINED NARRATIVES

The teacher should select vocabulary and structures from several chapters or units. He can write a short story (seven or eight sentences) using this material. This is a good technique for reviewing old lessons and for diagnosing the students' progress, especially at the beginning of the second year of language study. Here is a sample of such a story:

> Este muchacho se llama Juan. Tiene quince años. Vive en la Avenida Lane, número veinte. No vive cerca de la escuela. Vive lejos de la escuela. Juan sale de casa a las ocho. Toma el autobús a las ocho y cuarto. Llega a la escuela a las ocho y media.

It is recommended that such recombination narratives be written by native speakers only. It is extremely easy for a nonnative to use words and expressions that native speakers find unnatural.

The American teacher might agree to grade a set of test papers or prepare a bulletin board for the native teacher in exchange for some recombination narratives.

10.3.1b BORROWING FROM OTHER TEXTBOOKS

If the department library has copies of other textbooks, of old editions of the current textbook, or of readers, the teacher will be able to find a variety of readings. Perhaps the text might have to be slightly revised or simplified, but this is a much simpler process than writing a new passage oneself.

10.3.1c PERIODICALS

For intermediate and advanced classes, suitable selections may be found in periodicals. These may be edited to suit the needs of the class.

10.3.2 *Format and Presentation*

Guided reading means that the teacher, either directly or indirectly, is guiding the students' reading activities and focusing his attention on specific aspects of the reading.

10.3.2a ACTIVITIES LED BY THE TEACHER

Activities led by the teacher may be engaged in by the entire class or by a group at a time. The material read may be in one of three formats:

(1) Overhead transparency: The teacher types the reading selection and has it transferred to a transparency. The advantage of this presentation is that the teacher has close control over what the students are reading. He can watch their eye movements and tell when they have finished a selection. He can mask certain parts of the reading and control the rate of presentation. He can point out certain words and phrases and know that the students are reading precisely what he wants them to read.

(2) Commercial materials: The teacher may guide the students in reading a paragraph or two from a textbook, reader, magazine, or other printed source. Discussion of the material is simplified if the lines are numbered. With these types of materials it is harder for the teacher to guide the class: some students may not have found the right place, while others may quickly be reading something else on the same page.

(3) Dittoed sheets: The teacher prepares a Ditto of a text to be closely read. The teacher can underline certain words and expressions and perhaps number these parts for easy reference. Lines should be numbered also. The Ditto sheet has the advantage that students can take notes directly on the handout; sufficient margins should be left for this purpose. If desired, questions may be placed at the bottom of the page.

10.3.2b ACTIVITIES LED BY STUDENTS

Students may engage in guided reading individually, in pairs, or in small groups led by students. For this type of instruction, the readings are most manageable if prepared on Dittos. Another possibility is the preparation of a Dittoed worksheet with questions and a list of activities to accompany a reading selection in the textbook.

Another Ditto may contain the answers to the questions on the worksheets. This way the students can check themselves when they have finished.

10.3.3 *Sample Reading Exercises*

The following types of reading exercises may either be performed orally, with the teacher leading the discussion, or independently, by the students. If a group of students is working together, one acts as scribe and writes down the group's answers.

In work led by the teacher, the teacher immediately corrects the students. When students lead activities, they correct their own work once they have finished the exercise. If the entire class is engaged in independent reading activities, the teacher is free to circulate and to answer questions as they arise.

10.3.3a READING FOR STRUCTURE SIGNALS

Students tend to read the foreign language for content words rather than for structure signals. The students' attention may be focused on written grammar signals by questions of the type:

Is the author talking about one person or about several people?
  How do you know?
Has the action already taken place? How do you know?
Are the people definitely planning to do. . . ? Or are they just considering
  it as a possibility? How do you know?
Look at the pronoun *lo* in the fifth line. What does it refer to?
What is the antecedent of *qui* in line 10?
Does *lequel* in line 11 refer to *le garçon* or *la chemise?* How do you know?
What is the direct object of the verb *kaufen* in line 6?
Why did the speaker in the third paragraph use the subjunctive rather
  than the indicative?

Student should recognize endings of verbes

10.3.3b TECHNIQUES OF INFERENCE

Students should be taught how to infer meanings from paragraph context. Let us assume that the students do not know the word *maussade* (cheerless). If they read simply *Le temps était maussade,* they cannot guess what kind of weather it is. But if they read *Le temps était triste et maussade en cette saison. Il pleuvait tous les jours,* they can tell that *maussade* has a negative sense and is vaguely synonomous with *triste* (sad). For more on techniques of inference, see section 7.5.3.

The students should also be guided in inferring meanings of words which are related to each other or to English. For techniques in teaching word families and recognition of cognates, see Chapter 7.

3rd level ALM has examples of lessons on this topics

10.3.3c PARAPHRASING

If a sentence or part of a selection seems too difficult, many students will simply skip it, hoping that they are not missing anything essential. Paraphrasing techniques make students try to grasp the meaning of a selection in its entirety.

(1) Providing paraphrases for the students: Difficult words and expressions may be glossed in the foreign language. An effective language laboratory reading exercise may be prepared as follows:

The teacher prepares a Ditto of the reading, underlining the difficult words and expressions. He then prepares a tape script in which the difficult words are replaced by easier ones. As the student reads his Ditto selection in the laboratory, he hears the simplified glosses instead of the underlined expressions.

Text: El viaje que hice fue doblemente agradable para mí <u>por el hecho</u> <u>de que</u> un amigo mío, Emilio Quintani, de La Paz, quiso acompañarme <u>de vuelto para</u> su casa. Los dos <u>experimentamos</u> la misma sensación al descubrir <u>de nuevo</u> cosas y costumbres conocidas.[1]

Voice: El viaje que hice fue doblemente agradable para mí porque un amigo mío, Emilio Quintani, de La Paz, quiso acompañarme cuando volvió a su casa. Los dos sintimos la misma sensación al descubrir otra vez cosas y costumbres conocidas.

Note: Many textbooks and readers have foreign language glosses. The teacher types up the reading and then inserts the glosses in the recorded version of the selection.

(2) Asking for paraphrases: The teacher can ask students to paraphrase difficult passages. These paraphrases are usually done in the foreign language. Occasionally it might be necessary to request an English paraphrase, but the English should simply give the gist of the text. Word-for-word translating should be discouraged.

10.3.3d METAPHRASING

Metaphrasing is a technique developed by Waldo E. Sweet for teaching students to read Latin.[2] It is equally effective with modern inflected languages such as German and Russian. In metaphrasing the student shows both the lexical and structural meanings of words as they occur in the sentence:

Wir . . .	*We* are doing something.
Wir werden . . .	We are *going to* do something.
Wir werden das Buch . . .	We are going to do something *to the book.*
Wir werden das Buch später . . .	We are going to do something to the book *later.*
Wir werden das Buch später lesen.	We are going to *read* the book later.

10.3.3e READING FOR INFORMATION

A widely used reading technique, which should be used in conjunction with the techniques described above and not to their exclusion, is reading for information.

(1) Beginning level—simple questions: At the beginning levels the recombined readings also offer practice in both speaking (oral responses) and

---

[1] *Hablar y Leer*, op. cit., p. 249.
[2] See Lorraine A. Strasheim, *Teaching the Latin Student to Translate*, ERIC Focus Report No. 17 (1970). Available from MAL/ACTFL Materials Center, 62 Fifth Avenue, New York, N.Y. 10011, for twenty-five cents.

writing (written responses). Questions require a simple restatement of the text.

Ce garçon s'appelle Jean. Il habite rue Brun. Son père, Monsieur Dupont, est professeur de français. Jean a deux soeurs et un frère. Les quatre enfants vont à une école près de leur maison.

Procedure 1:   Répondez aux questions en français:

Comment s'appelle ce garçon?
Où habite-t-il?
Qui est professeur de français?
Combien de soeurs Jean a-t-il?
Où est l'école?

Procedure 2:   Corrigez les phrases suivantes:

Ce garçon s'appelle Marc.
Il habite Rue Buffon.
Son père est professeur d'anglais.
Jean a deux frères et une soeur.
Les quatre enfants ne vont pas à l'école.

(2) Intermediate and advanced level—content questions: As students progress in their reading skills, the teacher can ask questions that require the students to demonstrate their understanding of the entire selection. These questions are often asked before the student reads the passage.

The teacher distributes the reading or places it on the overhead projector. He says: *Je vais vous montrer (donner) une petite histoire. Lisez-la et soyez prêts à répondre aux questions suivantes: 1. Qui pleure? 2. Pourquoi cette personne pleure-t-elle? 3. Pleure-t-elle à la fin de l'histoire? Pourquoi ou pourquoi pas? Vous avez trois minutes!*

C'est aujourd'hui l'anniversaire de mariage des Duclos. Monsieur Duclos est stupéfait! Il avait complètement oublié que c'était l'anniversaire de son mariage.

Madame Duclos commence à pleurer. A ce moment-là, Monsieur Duclos a une idée. Il voit une belle robe dans le journal. Il donne le journal à sa femme et lui dit, "Voici ton cadeau."

Madame Duclos crie, "Un journal! Quel cadeau!"

Monsieur Duclos lui dit, "Ce n'est pas le journal, c'est la robe que je vais t'acheter." Madame Duclos embrasse son mari et lui dit, "Que tu es gentil, mon chéri!"

The teacher may also wish to continue by asking more precise questions which can be answered by a simple rewording of the text. For example: *4. Qu'est-ce que Monsieur Duclos voit dans le journal? 5. Quand Monsieur*

Duclos donne le journal à sa femme, que dit-il? 6. Que dit Madame Duclos quand elle embrasse son mari?

(3) All levels—questions initiated by students: Students can be taught to formulate their own questions before they have read the entire passage. For example, the teacher might show only the first three sentences of the story about Monsieur and Madame Duclos on the overhead: the students learn that Monsieur Duclos has forgotten his wedding anniversary. Then they are encouraged to formulate their own questions. They might wonder what the wife's reaction will be or what Monsieur Duclos will do about his oversight. Thus the following questions might be formulated by the class and written on the board: *Quelle sera la réaction de sa femme? Qu'est-ce que Monsieur Duclos va faire?*

The whole passage is then revealed on the overhead or distributed to the students. When they have finished reading, they provide the answers to their own questions.

(4) All levels—finding a title: An excellent technique for encouraging students to consider the reading passage as a whole is asking them to suggest a good title. The various suggestions are written on the chalkboard, and their merits and drawbacks are discussed. The class might want to vote on which is the best title.

10.3.4 *Preparing for Standardized Tests*

The teacher can use reading passages and items from the booklets which describe standardized tests to teach reading skills and at the same time to prepare students for tests they might be taking. The printed text of listening comprehension items can also be transformed into reading materials.

The text is put on an overhead transparency if it is short. Otherwise it is typed or reproduced on a Ditto master. A transparency is prepared with the questions alone. A second overlay contains the multiple-choice responses.

Zu Beginn des neuen Schuljahres bestellte Herr Braun, der Direktor einer deutschen Mittelschule, alle Lehrer zu einer Konferenz und sagte zu ihnen: "Wir haben uns heute versammelt, um unsern neuen Kollegen, Herrn William Macy, willkommen zu heißen. Herr Macy hat in den letzten zehn Jahren in New York Deutsch und Französisch unterrichtet und wird jetzt an unserer Schule den englischen Unterricht übernehmen. Unsere Schüler erwarten mit Ungeduld ihre erste Stunde bei Herrn Macy. Sie haben allerlei über die amerikanischen Unterrichtsmethoden gehört, die so ganz anders als unsere deutschen sein sollen. Es wird unserem Kollegen nicht schwer fallen, die Begeisterung seiner Schüler zu wecken. Wir werden hoffentlich des öfteren Gelegenheit haben, mit Herrn Macy über seine Beobachtungen zu sprechen. Auch unsere Schüler sollen sich an solchen Diskussionen beteiligen. Das wird für uns alle von großem Nutzen sein. Vor allem aber hoffe ich, daß die Zusammenarbeit mit unserem amerikanischen Kollegen zu einem Gefühl von gegenseitigem Vertrauen und echter Freundschaft führen wird. Und ich nehme an, wir werden am Ende dieses Schuljahres finden, daß wir nicht so verschieden sind, wie wir geglaubt hatten." [1]

Transparency 1	Overlay
1. *Was ist der Zweck dieser Zusammenkunft?*	(A) Die Schüler mit Herrn Macy bekanntzumachen.
	(B) Herrn Macy über deutsche Methoden zu informieren.
	(C) Das Interesse der Schüler zu wecken.
	(D) Herrn Macy seinen neuen Kollegen vorzustellen.
2. *Mit welchen Gefühlen erwarten die Schüler ihren amerikanischen Lehrer?*	(A) Mit Mißtrauen.
	(B) Mit Neugier.
	(C) Mit Furcht.
	(D) Mit Bewunderung.
3. *Was denkt der Direktor über den Unterschied zwischen Deutschen und Amerikanern?*	(A) Daß die Amerikaner praktischer sind als die Deutschen.
	(B) Daß die deutsche Jugend mehr Interesse am Lernen hat.
	(C) Daß der Unterschied geringer ist als man gewöhnlich glaubt.
	(D) Daß der Unterschied ein gegenseitiges Verstehen unmöglich macht.
4. *Was erhofft der Direktor am meisten von der Zusammenarbeit aller Lehrer?*	(A) Daß sie zu dauernden Freundschaften führen wird.
	(B) Daß die Schüler englische Diskussionen führen werden.
	(C) Daß Herr Macy deutsche Methoden lernen wird.
	(D) Daß deutsche Lehrer nach Amerika gehen werden.

The students read the text. Then the teacher places the first transparency on the overhead. The questions are asked and possible answers are discussed orally in German. When the students have answered the questions, the overlay is placed on the overhead projector. The students read the options aloud and decide which one most closely parallels the answer they themselves had given the question.

10.3.5 *Building Reading Speed*

The teacher prepares a reading passage on an overhead transparency. The selection should be one that most of the students can read readily.

---

[1] College Entrance Examination Board, *A Description of the College Board Achievement Tests* (Princeton, New Jersey: ETS, 1962), pp. 81–82.

The presentation of reading is timed by the teacher in one of the following ways: (1) The entire reading is exposed for a limited amount of time only. (2) A mask reveals one line after the other. (3) Two masks, or a mask with a slot the width and breadth of a line of type, reveal only one line at a time.

After the students have quickly seen the reading, the teacher turns off the projector and asks one or two content questions.

10.4 READING LONGER SELECTIONS

When students have mastered the basic techniques of reading, they should read longer selections in addition to shorter passages used for guided reading. In fact, even the passages for guided reading will often be taken from longer articles and stories.

10.4.1 Types of Materials

There are many types of reading materials. The teacher must look at available selections to check whether the contents are appropriate for the age and maturity of the students. If possible, students should be offered a choice of readings so that they may select topics which interest them.

10.4.1a STUDENT PERIODICALS

Periodicals designed for language students have articles, written in rather simple style, which cover a wide range of topics. Each student receives his own copy.

The Scholastic foreign language magazines have different magazines for the different levels of learning:

	Level I	Level II	Level III	Levels IV & Up
French	Bonjour Ça va	Ça va	Chez Nous	Loisirs
Spanish	Que tal El Sol	El Sol	Hoy día	
German	Das Rad	Schuss	Der Roller	Der Roller
Russian	Kometa	Kometa		

The McGraw-Hill Book Company distributes *Passe-Partout* and *Lazarillo*. Each issue contains articles that range in difficulty from simple to more difficult. Two issues a year are accompanied by records.

10.4.1b READERS DESIGNED FOR SPECIFIC READING LEVELS

Some readers are written for students who have attained a specific level in their study of the foreign language. New words above the given level are glossed, usually in the foreign language. Some examples of readers of this type are:

Valette and Valette, *Lisons* (New York: McGraw-Hill, 1968)
The first part is based on the present tense and 250 words.
The second part is based on the *passé composé* and 250 additional words.

Scherer, ed., *Reading for Meaning* (New York: Harcourt Brace Jovanovich, Inc., 1966)
Stories are based on structure and vocabulary taught in the first twenty-three units of A-LM, first edition. Available in French, German, Spanish, Russian, Italian.

Textes en Français Facile (Paris: Hachette, 1962, 1963, 1964, 1965, 1966)
and *Collection Lire et Savoir* (Paris: Didier, 1962).
Readings are based on vocabularies of 750 words and 1300 words.

10.4.1c GRADED READERS

These readers gradually progress from easy selections to more difficult ones. New vocabulary is gradually introduced, so that the comprehension of each story depends on that of the previous one.

D.C. Heath has several series of this sort in the commonly taught languages. Houghton Mifflin publishes the Bauer-Campell series in French (Boston: Houghton Mifflin Co., 1966).

10.4.1d READERS WITH GLOSSES AND END VOCABULARIES

These are the standard type of readers. Most publishers offer a wide selection of readers. These typically have glosses in English or the foreign language and a comprehensive end vocabulary.

10.4.1e READERS WITH INTERLINEAR GLOSSES

Interlinear readers have glosses printed above the line of text. A special grid is used which hides the glosses so that the students can see only the text. The grid is moved when necessary to reveal the glosses.[1]

10.4.1f BILINGUAL READERS

In bilingual readers the foreign language is on one page or column and English is on the other. The advantage of these books is that the student need not thumb through an end vocabulary. It is essential, however, that all class-

---

[1] Joseph P. Ebacher, *Programmed Reading French Series* (Englewood Cliffs, N.J.: Prentice-Hall, Inc., 1965, 1966, 1967).

work be conducted in the foreign language so that students are obliged to read the foreign language text.

10.4.2 *Integrating Reading and the Other Aspects of the Language Program*

The teaching of reading, especially the reading of longer selections, offers a wide range of possibilities for bringing in other aspects of the foreign language program.

10.4.2a READING AND CULTURE

Almost all readings contain some cultural content. If places are mentioned, the teacher can point them out on the map. Slides and photographs might be appropriate. If the reading is going to take several days, a few students might prepare a short presentation on the region where the action takes place.

If a composer or a piece of music is mentioned, an appropriate record should be played.

If an artist or work of art is mentioned, some of the works should be shown. Works of art should also be used to depict the region or the historical events under discussion (Goya's paintings and the Napoleonic wars).

If a holiday is mentioned, the traditions should be explained.

If dates or historical events or figures are mentioned, these should be briefly presented.

If social customs are part of the story, their significance should be discussed.

Individualized reading programs should contain materials from as many fields as possible: science, history, political science, architecture, mechanics, and so on. There are many possibilities in the foreign language other than literature—both in the language classroom and later in life for business or recreation.

10.4.2b READING AND WRITING

Reading and writing activities can be easily coordinated. The answering of questions and the writing of resumes are obvious examples of written work. Who, what, where, and when questions may serve as the basis of a brief synopsis of a story: 1. *¿Quién es el hombre en este cuento?* 2. *¿Qué está haciendo?* 3. *¿Dónde está?* 4. *¿Cuándo ocurre este incidente?* Other types of writing assignments may grow out of reading selections.

As a grammar exercise, a paragraph from the selection may be changed from one tense to another. Direct speech may be turned into indirect discourse, and vice versa.

Elementary and intermediate students might rewrite the opening of the story by simply changing some of the nouns and adjectives. The sentence structure stays the same, but the plot is transformed. More advanced students may write about the same incident from the point of view of another character in the story.

A story with action and dialogue might be rewritten as a skit by a group of students. They could then present their version to the others in the class.

A student could rewrite the story as if it were a brief newspaper item. He would furnish headlines and a summary of what occurred. A longer story might be rewritten as a series of newspaper clippings, which might be arranged in a bulletin board display.

10.4.2c READING AND THE SPOKEN SKILLS

Reading selections can be used for oral practice in several ways. Traditionally this means that the teacher reads the questions in the book and the students respond. As a variation, each student might be told to write out two or three questions about the story, which he can address to various classmates. The teacher tries to remain in the background, unless it is necessary to encourage the more reticent members of the class to participate.

Sentences from the reading which contain difficult grammatical patterns may become models for rapid pattern drills with the teacher giving the cues.

In more advanced classes a group of students might prepare a synopsis of the reading in the form of a radio newscast. The students take turns recording the individual "news items," and the resulting tape is played to the class.

If the character in the story faces a difficult dilemma, a short debate might be organized on the pros and cons of the alternatives he has.

10.4.3 *Reading Groups*

Not long after students begin their foreign language study, and certainly by the time they reach Level II, their individual differences, both in rate of learning and in interest, are usually very great. Some students are quite advanced, others are able to handle textbook materials at their grade level, and a few have difficulty understanding the simplest texts. Some students can look at a new word and see how it is derived; others see no relationship between one word and another. The use of reading groups enables the teacher to work with students on their own level. There are a number of different procedures which can be followed with reading groups.

(1) The teacher divides the class into groups on the basis of their demonstrated ability in reading (usually three groups for most efficient management—group A containing the strongest students; group B, the average ones; and group C, the weakest). He gives each group a different reading selection.

To Groups A and B the teacher distributes Dittoed sheets with either background material on the story or a partial synopsis (without the ending). Then he distributes a few guiding questions.

The teacher sits down with Group C and introduces the story orally; he reads the first paragraph aloud and asks questions in either English or the foreign language. Then he distributes Dittoed sheets with guiding questions for the following paragraphs or pages.

By this time Group A is ready to answer the questions on their reading. The teacher sits down with them and leads a discussion. He distributes the next set of questions and then goes on to Group B and checks their work.

Variation: The teacher can give the written answers to the questions to one of the members of the group, who will lead the discussion in his place.

Group work requires much preparation on the part of the teacher. On certain days the teacher may be able to meet with only one group. When this is the case he should supply the other groups with as many aids as possible: vocabulary cues, word study, grammatical explanations, and guided questions.

In curriculums that use modular scheduling, team teaching, or differentiated staff, there might be interns, student teachers, or teacher aides[1] to work with smaller groups.

(2) The teacher divides the class into ability groups and gives each one the same reading material. Each group proceeds at its own rate. (See (1) for the other techniques.)

(3) The teacher allows the students to choose their own group members or a partner to work with. (See (1) for the other techniques.)

10.4.4 *Individualized Reading*

In individualized reading, students are given freedom to select what they wish to read. Generally some teacher guidance is needed.

10.4.4a THE TEACHER-FILE SYSTEM

The teacher compiles a list of readings in categories from very easy to very advanced. He prepares a synopsis of each reading on index cards.

After the student reads the synopses he makes a selection and checks his choice with the teacher. If the teacher thinks it is at the appropriate level of difficulty, he gives his approval. If not, he suggests another reading.

In his file the teacher has two sets of material to accompany each text the students read: one is a series of worksheets to guide the students through their reading, the other is a quiz to evaluate their progress.

10.4.4b THE "CHECKER" SYSTEM

Each student keeps a notebook. At the beginning of the individualized period, students are allowed to choose what they would like to read from a

---

[1] The term "intern" usually refers to a person who holds a college degree, but is not yet certified to teach; he spends a year doing part-time teaching. A teacher's aide is usually a nonprofessional person without a college degree. A student teacher is a college student who is in a teacher training program.

list of available readings. When a student has finished a selection, he makes note of this in his notebook.

The teacher calls on students one at a time after they have finished a selection. He asks some content questions in the foreign language and checks off that selection in the student's notebook. If the student shows that he has understood the selection, he is named "checker" for that selection.

On the bulletin board is kept a list of students and the selections for which they are "checker." When another student finishes a selection for which a "checker" is listed, he may go to him rather than to the teacher. The "checker" asks some content questions in the foreign language and is allowed to check off the selection in the student's notebook.

Variation: The "checker" must write out the questions he intends to ask. The teacher has to approve the questions before the "checker" is allowed to ask them.

10.5 LITERATURE IN THE CLASSROOM

Simple poems and proverbs are often introduced early in language instruction, usually to teach the sound system or to give a sampling of foreign culture. Later in the language program, longer and more difficult literary works are introduced. This section deals with selections chosen primarily for their literary value.

10.5.1 *Aims in Teaching Literature*

Before introducing a literary work to the class, the teacher must decide what his aims are. What does he expect the students to get from this particular work? Why introduce literature at all?

The primary aim is to show students many different techniques for reading and interpreting a work of literature. If the student develops various approaches to literature, perhaps later he will enjoy reading literary works on his own. The aim should not be to cram his head full of facts: names of authors, centuries, titles of works, literary movements, and the like; he can always look these things up in an encyclopedia when he needs the information. But the encyclopedia cannot teach him to read—this is the role of the teacher.

The secondary aim is to reinforce certain points of grammar and items of vocabulary. In studying a work of literature the student will simultaneously be developing his command of the second language. Vocabulary lists might be derived from the work. Some lines of poetry could be memorized, not only for their poetic value, but also because they contain examples of grammatical patterns (such as the use of the *passé composé* in Prévert's *"Le Déjeuner du Matin*)." To meet this secondary aim, the teacher would do well to select contemporary works, because their structures and vocabulary will more closely parallel the type of language the student has been learning.

10.5.2 *Presentation of the Work*

Usually the students will need to be introduced to a literary work before they can appreciate it. They may need to learn the historical background of a novel, the social conditions which the author is trying to portray in a play, the geographical setting of a story. Sometimes a short presentation of the author's life helps the student better understand a lyric poem or a semi-autobiographical piece.

The following examples briefly indicate how literary works might be presented in class:

(1) *Pensativa,* by Jesús Goytortuá: The necessary background is an understanding of the causes and outcome of the Mexican Revolution of 1910 and of the status of the Church before and after the Revolution. A good source is the series *The Struggle of the Mexican People for Their Liberty.*[1] The complete teaching kit includes slides, text with tape, and tests. It contains the following titles:

The Epoch of Porfirio Díaz
Madero
Toward the Present Constitution
The Victory of the Constitutionalists

(2) *Le Petit Prince,* by Antoine de Saint Exupéry: The author's life is an interesting background.

Il était pilote. Il a eu une panne dans le désert "à mille milles de toute région habitée." Il avait perdu son petit frère (la mort du petit prince). Il aimait sa rose (sa femme).

The teacher could try to find photos of Saint Exupéry as a child and as an adult (pilot) and show them with an opaque projector.[2] He could also show the film *Saint Exupéry*[3] for glimpses of his life and career and the sound of his voice.

(3) *El Sombrero de Tres Picos,* by Pedro Antonio de Alarcón: To create atmosphere the teacher can play excerpts of the recording *España*[4] containing The Three Cornered Hat Suite, by Falla.

(4) *Le Bourgeois Gentilhomme,* by Molière: The necessary background is an understanding of the life of seventeenth-century bourgeois and aristocrats and of the humor in Molière's comedies. From the film *Une Journée à la Comédie Française,* the teacher can show the last scene, *"La Leçon de Phonétique,"* narrated by Louis Seigner.[5]

---

[1] Wible Language Institute, 24 South Eighth Street, Allentown, Pa. 18105.
[2] Technique demonstrated by Alfred N. Smith in film, *Teaching French Literature in the Secondary School,* College of Education, Ohio State University.
[3] FACSEA, 972 Fifth Avenue, New York, N.Y.
[4] *España,* 6186, Lorraine Music Co., 23-80 48th Street, Long Island City, N.Y. 11103.
[5] New York: McGraw-Hill, Inc.

(5) *"Der Augsburger Kreidekreis,"* by Bertolt Brecht: The necessary historical background is the Thirty Years' War. The teacher can use the slide series 330.2/1 which treats the Thirty Years' War.[1]

10.5.3 *Teaching Poetry*

Poetry is introduced early in the student's language learning career.[2] At first, it is primarily used as a device for improving his pronunciation. Poems memorized in the first year may be reintroduced later for literary analysis.

10.5.3a SCANNING

Students may be taught the rules of traditional prosody in the language they are studying. They should be given the opportunity to apply this knowledge to the scanning of simple unfamiliar poems. Advanced students might be encouraged to try writing poetry of their own within the traditional patterns of the literature under study.

10.5.3b UNDERSTANDING THE SURFACE MEANING

Teachers often wrongly assume that students have grasped the surface meaning of the poem, that they understand the "story," or that they mentally envision the scene; they begin by lecturing on poetic images, themes, and so on. Actually, many students dislike poetry because they have never been taught to see the picture or pictures which the poet has depicted. Time spent clarifying the "story" is invaluable in bringing the students to an appreciation of poetry.

Before teaching Rilke's poem about the panther, find photographs of caged cats: tigers, lions, panthers. Let the students talk about how they would feel if they had once roamed a jungle and were obliged to spend the rest of their lives behind bars. What kind of view of life would they have? Then let the students read Rilke's poem, and they will be in a better position to grasp the meaning of the work.

Ronsard's *"Ode à Cassandre"* often seems uninteresting to students because they see in it merely a poet talking about roses. A lecture on "carpe diem" does not add to their appreciation of the work. It is more effective to put the setting in modern terms. A boy has his eye on a girl, but she is always with other people; his first objective is to get her away from the crowd. How might he do this? After students have given their suggestions for ways of handling

---

[1] Available from Teaching Aid Project, NCSA/AATG Service Center, 339 Walnut Street, Philadelphia, Pa. 19106. There is no charge to AATG members, except the cost of postage and insurance. A catalogue of other slides, film strips, and tapes is available.

[2] See also G. Bording Mathieu, *Poems in Early Foreign Language Instruction*, ERIC Focus Report No. 15 (1970). Available from MLA/ACTFL Materials Center, 62 Fifth Avenue, New York, N.Y. 10011, for twenty-five cents.

the problem, the teacher might point out that in the sixteenth century, a good place for privacy was a remote corner of the garden. The trick was to ask the girl to come look at a special rose growing there. The boy's next problem (second verse) is to get the girl in the proper mood for what he plans to propose. He simply points out how quickly the beautiful flower wilts in the hot sun and loses its charm. It's nature's fault that we get old so quickly. In the final verse he makes the analogy explicit: How about it? How about us? We're young . . . let's make love before it's too late. Once the students understand what the poet is saying, they will be more willing to examine the poem to see how the effect was accomplished.

10.5.3c FIGURES OF SPEECH

Poems make frequent use of figures of speech. An analysis of these figures should be postponed until the students understand the poem itself. Many students have done some work in picking out such figures in their English courses, and they can apply what they know to the foreign language.

Goethe's poem *"Erlkönig"* lends itself well to a study of the technique of personification.

Students could be asked to identify the passage in which Death is speaking, the nature of its message, references that are made to it (pronouns, for example), and its physical characteristics. For example, in this part of the ballad Death is trying to woo a small boy from the arms of his father with the following words:

Willst, feiner Knabe, du mit mir gehn?
Meine Töchter sollen dich warten schön;
Meine Töchter führen den nächtlichen Reihn
Und wiegen und tanzen und singen dich ein.

10.5.3d USE OF VOCABULARY AND STRUCTURE

The teacher may use a simplified "explication de texte" technique to help the students see how the poet's choice of words and use of tenses create a desired effect.

In teaching Prévert's *"Barbara,"* for example, the teacher would first create the two scenes: the happy prewar scene and the wartime bombings of Brest. The students would locate the poet's strong antiwar statement and its central position in the poem.

The following is a brief sample of how the teacher might focus the students' attention on the choice of adjectives, verbs, and verb tenses:[1]

(1) Le professeur aide les élèves à chercher les adjectifs et les verbes importants à la compréhension du poème.

---

[1] Adapted from B. J. Gilliam, *Teaching French Poetry in the American Secondary School.* Unpublished Ph.D. dissertation, Ohio State University, 1969, pp. 192–207.

Professeur:	Le titre du poème est *Barbara*. Qu'est-ce que nous savons de cette jeune femme à part son nom? Cherchons les mots qui la décrivent...
Elèves:	Souriante... épanouie... ravie... ruisselante... visage heureux.
Professeur:	Excellent. Ce sont des adjectifs qui font partie d'un portrait. Cherchons maintenant les mots qui expriment ce qu'elle fait, les verbes...
Elèves:	Tu souriais... tu as couru vers lui... tu t'es jetée dans ses bras... tu marchais souriante...

(2) Le professeur pose des questions sur certains thèmes contrastés (substantifs).

Professeur:	Plus tard vous voyez le thème de la guerre—"sous cette pluie de deuil terrible et désolée." Alors on trouve des thèmes contrastés, n'est-ce pas? Qu'est-ce qui contraste avec l'amour, la beauté, la jeunesse, la tendresse, la joie?
Elèves:	La violence... la haine... l'horreur... la destruction... le désespoir...

(3) Le professeur pose des questions sur la grammaire.

Professeur:	Je vous ai dit que M. Prévert écrit des scénarios de film. Ce poème est un peu comme un film. Les événements du *passé* servent d'arrière plan à un *présent* qui se déroule sous nos yeux. Quels temps utilise-t-on pour exprimer des actions passées? L'imparfait et le passé composé. Qui peut nous expliquer la différence entre ces deux temps?
Elève:	On emploie l'imparfait pour les actions de durée imprécise.
Professeur:	Bien. L'imparfait est utilisé pour décrire aussi la condition, l'état, le temps, les faits accessoires à l'action principale. Et le passé composé?
Elève:	On utilise le passé composé pour exprimer un fait précis qui a lieu à un moment donné.
Professeur:	Excellent. Maintenant, cette moitié de la classe va dresser une liste de tous les verbes qui se trouvent à l'imparfait dans ce poème. L'autre moitié va chercher tous les verbs qui sont au passé composé.

10.5.3e ORAL INTERPRETATION

The teacher should try to find two or more dramatic interpretations of the poem being studied. Usually the best-known poems in a language have been recorded by leading actors and speakers. Musical versions are often available. The teacher prepares a tape made up of several interpretations. Students listen to the tape independently, or in the laboratory, and write a short essay stating which version they prefer and why. They might also say that they do not like any of the interpretations and try reading the poem themselves the way they think it should sound.

10.5.4 *Teaching Fiction*

Stories, novellas, and short novels are often introduced in high school language classes. In teaching fiction, the teacher often tends to focus entirely on the plot and to neglect literary considerations. There are a number of easy techniques which help the student to develop some skill in literary analysis once he has understood the story.

10.5.4a FINDING RECURRING THEMES

Students become more aware of recurring themes if they are actively engaged in looking for passages where these themes are expressed. The simplest way to focus students' attention on themes is to have them count references to a particular theme.

For example, in reading Camus' *L'Etranger*, the students would be asked to note all words which refer to sun, heat, and light. By the time the students reach the scene where Meursault kills the Arab, they will be aware of the effect of the sunlight reflected off the Arab's knife: La lumière a giclé sur l'acier comme une longue langue étincelante qui m'atteignait au front.

10.5.4b POINT OF VIEW

The teacher can ask the students to uncover the point of view of a work. It may be narrated in the third person, and yet all of the scenes may be depicted as they appear to only one of the characters. Maybe the narrator plays "God" and goes inside many of his characters.

As a written exercise, the students may try to rewrite a scene from another character's point of view.

10.5.4c THE ROLE OF DESCRIPTION

Some works are heavily descriptive throughout, while others are more action-oriented. Some works begin with descriptive passages and then move to scenes with much movement and dialogue.

To help the students become aware of the role of description, have them go through the story marking descriptive passages. Quantitative results may be given:

Story A:	5 pages description	10 pages action and dialogue
Story B:	2 pages description	16 pages action and dialogue
Story C:	7 pages description	3 pages action and dialogue

The students could then list their impressions of the three stories and compare these to the quantitative analyses. Students usually prefer stories with a low proportion of descriptive passages.

The teacher could have the students look at one story again and ask them how it would read if all the description were eliminated. Would it still make sense? What role does the description play? Are parts essential, while other parts could be cut? Which could be cut?

A similar study might be done with chapters of a longer work.

10.5.4d PLOT DIAGRAMS

Students in small groups can try to diagram the development of the story. Does the story begin with the chronological end of events and then go back to the chronological beginning and follow through consecutively? Does the story begin at the middle, with some flashbacks? Does the first half of the story cover ten months of time, and the last half cover four hours? Do conflicting interests build up and meet near the end of the work?

The diagrams may take the forms of lines and arrows. They may be shown as a time line to which are attached the various scenes or chapters. The number of pages devoted to particular episodes may be noted. Once the students are told to find a way to represent the story in a graphic fashion, they will probably come up with a variety of interpretations.

10.5.5 *Teaching Drama*

Plays are often introduced in advanced language classes because they can be relatively short and because they contain much dialogue, which the students are expected to find easy to understand. Actually, many students fail to enjoy plays because they cannot visualize the story.

10.5.5a VISUALIZING THE ACTION

The first concern of the teacher who is presenting a play to the class must be to bring the work to life. An excellent device is the flannel board. The students read the description of the setting and design their own stage. The layout of the first scene is placed on the flannel board.

Then the students make figures to represent each character. One student may be assigned to handle the exits, entrances, and stage movements of each felt figure. If there are more students than characters, the remaining students can be put in charge of scenery and props.

Variation: The stage and characters may be drawn on acetate. The teacher moves the figures around on the overhead projector.

10.5.5b FIGURES OF SPEECH

The text of the play may also be used as the basis of a study of figures of speech. The following examples are drawn from *La Dama del Alba* by Alejandro Casona.[1] The students are to search for metaphors and similes.

Trae un cansancio alegre arrollado a la cintura. (Act I, p. 24)
(He wears a roll of happy lassitude tucked in his belt.)

(A Snowstorm)
Parecía una aldea de enanos, con caperuzas blancas en las chimeneas y barbas de hielo colgando en los tejados. (Act I, p. 25)
(It looked like a village of dwarfs, with large white caps on the chimneys and beards of ice hanging from the roofs.)

(Laughter)
Es un temblor alegre que corre por dentro, como las ardillas por un árbol hueco. (Act I, p. 35)
(It is a tremor that runs through my being, like squirrels through a hollow tree.)

Assignment: In the first half of Act II look for metaphors and similes about death.

(Death by drowning)
Es como una venda de agua en el alma. (Act II, p. 56)
(It's like a bandage of water on the soul.)

10.5.5c PLOT DEVELOPMENT

Most plays have a careful plot development, which lends itself readily to diagramming. Students can pick out the key scenes and show how other earlier scenes led up to them.

In studying French classical theater, the students can also draw several clocks to accompany the scenes of the play, in order to show that the action takes less than twenty-four hours.

10.5.5d THEMES

Drama also lends itself well to a study of themes. Students can be told to look for recurring themes and make note of them while they are reading. The teacher can ask for themes and write them on the board or on the overhead. Students can discuss the suggestions and try to decide which are most important to the play.

---

[1] New York: Charles Scribner's Sons, 1947.

10.5.5e CHARACTERIZATION

Students can make lists of adjectives which the characters use to describe one another. Do the other persons see a main character the way he really is, or does this character, in monologues and actions, show that he is trying to deceive the others?

The students may then make lists of adjectives which they themselves would use to describe the main characters in the play. Do the students' lists resemble or differ from the list derived from the play itself?

10.5.5f RECORDINGS

Recordings of plays are often available. Listening to the recording should not be a substitute for analyzing the structure of the play. However, once the play has been studied, it is often interesting to play the recording of a particular scene and to evaluate the performance of the actors.

Recordings may also be used for individual work in the laboratory. The students read the play as they listen to the recording. Often the actor's interpretation of a speech helps the student understand what is meant.

CHAPTER ELEVEN
WRITING

Writing may well be considered the most difficult of the language skills. People are flattered when a foreigner tries to speak their language, and they tend to tolerate a light accent and occasional awkward expressions with good grace. The speaker's personality makes a greater impression than the accuracy of his spoken language. But a letter is judged more severely on its purely linguistic merits. Errors in spelling and grammar are not easily excused, even if the meaning is clear and the handwriting is attractive and legible.

Writing has been equated with formal education. Persons who write are expected to write correctly. In France especially, where the French language is central to the school curriculum, students are taught not only to write correct French, but to develop an individual literary style.

Obviously it takes many many years of intensive study to write a second language fluently. Even most American language teachers who read with facility the language they teach do not feel qualified to express themselves in writing with the same ease as in English. Although students will not attain a high level of proficiency after only a few years of language training, they can learn how to write brief stories and how to write informal letters or short business letters.

216

11.1 GENERAL CONSIDERATIONS

Skill in writing begins with simple copying and ranges to free self-expression. As the student progresses in his development of the writing skill, he will require guidance from the teacher.

Ability to write well grows out of prior experience in listening, speaking, and reading. If a student knows what the sentence he wishes to write sounds like, he is well advanced on his way toward fluent written expression. He may make some spelling mistakes, but the foreign national will understand what he is trying to say. Spelling mistakes must be continually checked and corrected, if the student is to express himself accurately. He does not see his own mistakes readily, only the teacher does.

The most serious writing problems arise when the student tries to transform an English sentence word for word into a foreign language equivalent. At the early levels the teacher can combat this tendency by providing leading questions and cues in the foreign language. Assigning a written resume or a free composition before students are ready to handle it can lead to frustration and negative learning.

The techniques that follow are samples of writing experiences from early to advanced levels.

11.2 COPYING

The first step in learning to write is copying written models. Since copying is not a very challenging activity, students become careless and make mistakes. Yet accuracy is an important feature in writing, and students should not be permitted to make mistakes which go uncorrected.

The following techniques suggest ways of maintaining students' interest in activities that require copying. After each activity, it is wise to correct the work immediately. Students exchange papers and the correct answers are placed on the overhead. If no overhead is available, the teacher may have the sentences on the chalkboard, covered with a map or chart.

11.2.1 *Fill in the Blanks*

The students fill in the blanks by copying model sentences in their book or on a Ditto:

Model: Bonjour, Jeanne. Comment vas-tu?
B__ __jour, Jea__ __e. Co__ __ent va__-tu?

Model: ¿Cómo está Usted?
¿__om__ e__ __á __s__ed?

Model: Was machst du heute?
W__ __ ma__ __ __t d__ h__ __t__?

11.2.2   *Noticing Capitals*

As the student copies the foreign sentence in each pair, he underlines both those letters which are capitalized in English and not capitalized in the foreign language, and those letters which are capitalized in the foreign language and not capitalized in English.[1]

There are many Mexicans who do not speak Spanish.
Hay muchos mexicanos que no hablan español.

I shall arrive on Monday, March 29th.
J'arriverai le lundi, 29 mars.

The teacher sends the letter and the card.
Der Lehrer schickt den Brief und die Karte.

11.2.3   *Scrambled Sentences*

Sentences from the dialogue are presented with the words in random order. The student rewrites the correct sentences:

la balle joue Marie avec.
inglés no María practicar quiere.
die kenne Frau ich nicht.

11.2.4   *Putting Dialogue Sentences in Correct Order*

The students rewrite a set of sentences, putting them in the correct order:

Ich gehe in die Stadt.
Darf ich mitkommen?
Wohin gehst du, Ilse?

11.2.5   *Answering Questions on the Dialogue*

Stimulus: Qui dit, "Ah, tu fais du français!"
Students write: Marc dit, "Ah, tu fais du français!"

Stimulus: Quien dice, "No puedo. Tengo que ir a la tienda."
Students write: Ana dice, "No puedo. Tengo que ir a la tienda."

11.2.6   *Line Drawings*

The teacher distributes a Ditto sheet containing line drawings which match the basic sentences of the lesson. Students match the sentences with the appropriate pictures:

[1] Thomas W. Jackson, *Developing the Writing Skill in Spanish for Native Speakers of English.* Unpublished Ph.D. dissertation, Ohio State University, 1968.

L'appartement est au quatrième étage.
Sa voiture est à côté de la maison.
Si on allait au cinéma ce soir!

1.

Write: _____

2.

Write: _____

3.

Write: _____

11.2.7 *Magazine Pictures*   *good idea to use for writing a story*

Students bring to class magazine pictures corresponding to the basic sentences of the lesson.

(1) Students exchange pictures and write the lines of dialogue on separate pieces of paper. Then they pass pictures to other classmates.

(2) Teacher puts pictures in opaque projector. Students write corresponding lines of dialogue.

11.2.8   *Copying the Question and the Correct Rejoinder*

The students copy the question and follow it with the appropriate reply:

¿Tienes un lápiz azul?

a. No, tengo una pluma.
b. Sí, una pequeña.
c. No, tengo un lápiz blanco.

Was ißt Rolf?

a. Er ist mein Freund.
b. Er hat Apfelmus.
c. Er ißt Kuchen.

11.2.9   *Matching Questions and Answers*

The students copy questions and the appropriate replies:

¿Adónde van?	Tengo quince años.
¿Cómo estás?	Tengo cuatro hermanos.
¿Cuántos años tienes?	Muy bien, gracias.
¿Cuántos hermanos tienes?	A casa.

11.2.10   *Correcting Sentences*

The students change the sentences to make sense, using items from the column on the right:

Je vais à l'école en avion.	en bateau
Je vais en France à bicyclette.	le dimanche
Je vais à l'école le dimanche.	en autobus
Je vais à l'église le mardi.	à pied
	le lundi

11.2.11   *Crossword Puzzles*

Students fill in crossword puzzles with given words:

Die Monate des Jahres heißen: Januar, Februar, März, April, Mai, Juni, Juli, August, September, Oktober, November, Dezember.

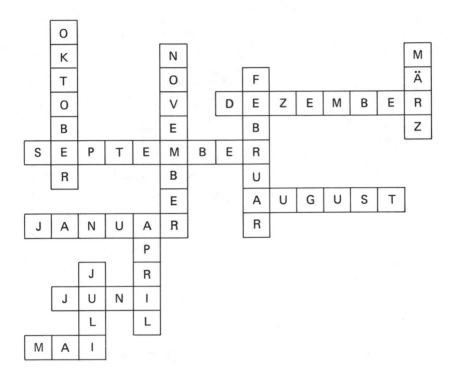

Les chiffres sont: un, deux, trois, quatre, cinq, six, sept, huit, neuf, dix.[1]

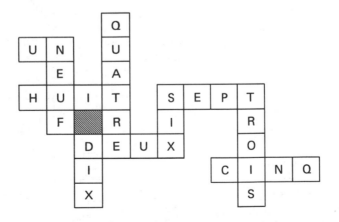

---

[1] Technique developed by Professor Alfred N. Smith, Department of Foreign Languages, Utah State University, for his course on the teaching of French (unpublished papers).

Los días de la semana son:

Horizontal

1. domingo
4. miércoles
5. jueves
6. viernes

Vertical

2. lunes
3. martes
7. sábado

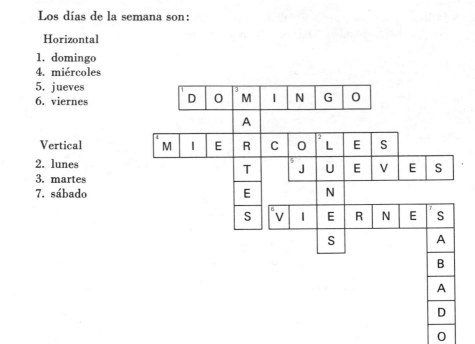

11.2.12   *Sentence Builders*

The sentence builder is a chart that allows the student to select the component parts of the sentence and to create a sentence which may be different from those of his classmates.

11.2.12a   ONLY CORRECT FORMS POSSIBLE

As the student uses the sentence builder in this form, he will be able to choose only correct combinations:

Marie Mademoiselle Brault	est	partie	à midi
			hier
Paul Monsieur Duroc		parti	dimanche
les garçons Paul et Monique	sont	partis	cet été
			à Noël
Monique et Marie les amies de Paul		parties	vers une heure

Qu'est-ce que tu vas prendre comme . . .	Je vais prendre . . .		
viande ?	du bifteck du poulet		des côtelettes
légume ?			des carottes des tomates
boisson ?	du vin	de la bière	
dessert ?	du gâteau	de la glace	des fruits

11.2.12b STUDENT SELECTS CORRECT FORMS

The student is asked to write ten sentences using the sentence builder. He must select the forms which may correctly be used together:

Je Jean Il Elles Paul et moi Georges et Louis	sont sommes est suis	à l'école. dans le salon. au musée. au café. à l'église.

Yo Juan El Ellos Pablo y Ana Tú María y yo	habl tom estudi compr	é amos ó aste aron	español. leche. francés. álgebra. los boletos. café. inglés. té. un coche.

11.3 WRITING FROM DICTATION

In writing from dictation, the student is closely guided by the model he hears. At a beginning level, the student is already familiar with the sentences he hears dictated; his problem is one of spelling and punctuation.

11.3.1 *Spot Dictation: Individual Symbols*

Spot dictation allows the teacher to focus on specific points. In the following examples, the teacher is concerned with punctuation marks and accents.

11.3.1a MIMEOGRAPHED SHEETS

The teacher writes on the board:

¿————————————————? ¡————————————————!

Students have a mimeographed sheet with sentences, but no punctuation.
As teacher reads, students fill in the marks:

__ Cuidado __   (¡ !)
__ Viene un camion __   (¡ !)
__ Vive Juan en Madrid __   (¿ ?)
__ La maestra es bonita __   (¿ ?)

A second mimeographed sheet with answers is then distributed to the class.[1]

11.3.1b OVERHEAD PROJECTOR

The teacher projects a list of words on the screen. In each word, one letter
is missing. The students write the entire word as they hear it pronounced by
the teacher:

Complete with é or e:		Complete with ó or o:	
cant__	(canté)	habl__	(habló)
habl__	(hable)	compr__	(compro)
llam__	(llamé)	cant__	(canto)
compr__	(compré)	contest__	(contestó)
contest__	(conteste)	escuch__	(escuchó)
escuch__	(escuche)	llam__	(llamo)

The teacher then projects an overlay with the missing letters filled in.

11.3.1c TAPE RECORDING

(1) The teacher writes on the board: é. The students have a Dittoed sheet
with a list of words. They complete each word with é as they hear it pronounced:

caf__   C__cile
pr__sent   t__l__vision
côt__   pr__pare

(2) The teacher writes on the board: è. The students fill in the blanks as
they hear the words read on the tape:

S__vres   compl__tement
l__ve-toi   s__che
m__ne   p__se

[1] Jackson, op. cit., p. 46.

(3) The teacher writes on the board: *é è*. The students fill in the blanks as they hear the words:

H__l__ne   mis__re
t__l__graphe   pr__f__re
Th__r__se   d__sordre

11.3.1d DITTO SHEETS AND BOARD

Students have a Dittoed sheet with minimal pairs; the vowel is left out in each word. The teacher writes the vowels on the board, pronounces them, and then asks the class to repeat both the long and the short varieties of these sounds: *u—ü, a—ä, o—ö*.

As each word is read, the students fill in the missing vowel:

m__chte   m__chte
  o   ö
sch__n   sch__n
  ö   o
h__tte   h__tte
  ä   a
L__ge   L__ge
  a   ä
Br__der   Br__der
  u   ü
M__tter   M__tter
  ü   u

11.3.2 *Spot Dictation: Words*

11.3.2a WALL CHART

The teacher prepares the following wall chart.[1]

cómo	(how?)	como	(as)
cuál	(which?)	cual	(which, as)
cuánto	(how much?)	cuanto	(as much)
cuándo	(when?)	cuando	(when)
dónde	(where?)	donde	(where)
qué	(what?)	que	(that, which)
quién	(who?)	quien	(who, whom)

The teacher then distributes a sheet with missing words. The students look at the wall chart and fill in the words as the teacher reads the sentences:

Parece _____ no hace nada.

---

[1] Jackson, *op. cit.*, p. 43.

_____ llega el tren?
_____ robó el dinero?

11.3.2b OVERHEAD TRANSPARENCY

One student writes the dictation on the transparency in front of the class (the projector is off). The remainder of the class write at their seats.

As each sentence is completed, the teacher checks the transparency and turns the projector on. In an exercise on the agreement of past participle with preceding direct object, for example, the following sentences might be dictated:

Voilà les fleurs que j'ai achetées.
Voilà la voiture que j'ai vendue.
Voilà les romans que j'ai lus.
Voilà les lettres que j'ai reçues.

11.3.2c DITTO SHEETS

Paragraph completion dictation: The teacher prepares and distributes a short mimeographed selection in which certain words have been left out. As the teacher dictates, the students fill in the blanks. (In the following examples, the verbs have been left out.)

Claude et Georges _____ à la balle. Georges _____ la balle. La
                        jouent   jette
balle _____ sur la maison. Claude _____ "Que tu es stupide! Tu
            tombe   crie
_____ la balle sur la maison! Va _____ avec les enfants!"
   as jeté   jouer

Anoche _____ a casa a las once. _____ un cigarrillo de mi bol-
              llegué   Saqué
sillo y _____ a fumar. De repente, mi perro _____ un ruido
            empecé   hizo
infernal, _____ mi sombrero y _____
               cogió   se huyó

11.3.3 _Full Dictation_

The teacher dictates sentences, which the students write out in their entirety. This exercise is particularly difficult in French, where there are many silent letters.

11.3.3a DICTATION WITH BEGINNING STUDENTS

Half the class is at the board, the others are at their seats. The first three steps precede writing:

(1) The teacher reads the short paragraph in its entirety.

(2) He begins again and reads only one line.

(3) Then he reads short segments with backward buildup. Students repeat chorally and individually:

Teacher	Students
al cine	al cine
a las tiendas o al cine	a las tiendas o al cine
¿Quiere ir Manuel?	¿Quiere ir Manuel?
¿Quiere ir Manuel a las tiendas o al cine?	¿Quiere ir Manuel a las tiendas o al cine?

(4) Students write the sentence.

(5) The teacher asks the class to look at a sentence on the board that is accurately written. Next, he asks students to make corrections.

(6) After all sentences are corrected, the teacher goes on to the next sentence and follows the same procedures.

11.3.3b DICTATION WITH MORE ADVANCED STUDENTS

The teacher reads through the entire paragraph. Then he dictates each sentence slowly, pausing after word groups. The selection is read slowly a second time. Then the teacher reads the paragraph at normal speed as students read over their work. The teacher should *not* heed any requests to read sections over again. This merely leads to repeated requests for rereading and a waste of class time.

At the end of the final reading students exchange papers and put the corrected form of the dictation on the overhead. The teacher may wish to use a mask and show portions of the dictation at a time. Students correct each others' work.

11.4   PRACTICING SENTENCE PATTERNS

When the student practices sentence patterns, he himself must select and write the appropriate forms. There is no written or spoken model to guide him.

11.4.1   *Sentence Completion*

The teacher distributes a Dittoed sheet with words missing. Students fill in the blanks. Then the teacher distributes an answer sheet.

In a program of individualized instruction, the students do the exercise and then get the answer sheet when they are finished. They place their corrected sheets in a folder where the teacher can check on their progress.

(1) Write the correct form in the blanks below:

Qu'est-ce que, Qu'est-ce qui, Qui est-ce que, Qui est-ce qui

1. Marc achète une montre.
   _____Marc achète?

2. Marie voit son ami.
   _____ Marie voit?

3. Monsieur Duclos entre le premier dans le bureau.
   _____ entre le premier?

4. Notre école est loin du centre.
   _____ est loin du centre?

(2) Using the list of interrogatives, complete each telephone conversation with the correct form:

adónde, qué, dónde, por qué, cuándo[1]

1. Julio: ¿Está María Elena?
   Luis: No, no está.
   Julio: Entonces, ¿_____ está?

2. Gloria: ¿No vienes porque es tarde?
   Susana: No, porque es tarde no.
   Gloria: Entonces, ¿_____ no vienes?

3. Mario: ¿Llega mañana Josefina?
   Pedro: No, mañana no.
   Mario: Entonces, ¿_____ llega?

11.4.2 *Written Pattern Drills*

Most pattern drills lend themselves to written exercises. The teacher may read the cues aloud, or the students may work from the written cues.

11.4.2a SPOKEN CUES

The teacher places half the class at the chalkboard. The others work at their seats:

Teacher's voice	Students write
Il est beau.	Il est beau.
Elle	Elle est belle.
Ils (pluriel)	Ils sont beaux.
Elles (pluriel)	Elles sont belles.

---

[1] *Writing Modern Spanish*, a student manual for *Modern Spanish*, 2d. ed., a project of the Modern Language Association (New York: Harcourt Brace Jovanovich, Inc., 1966), pp. 10–11.

Es un muchacho guapo.   Es un muchacho guapo.
muchacha   Es una muchacha guapa.
muchachos   Son unos muchachos guapos.
muchachas   Son unas muchachas guapas.

All sentences are corrected.

11.4.2b WRITTEN CUES

Half the class is sent to the board. The others remain at their seats to write. The teacher raises a map under which is a model sentence and a list of cues. Students write complete sentences:

Modèle: Paul / au cinéma. Paul est allé au cinéma.

Maman / en ville
Monique et Thérèse / au concert
mes deux frères / au match de football

11.4.3   *Use of World Map and Pointer*

The teacher points to a country and asks a question. Students write the reply:

Teacher: (Points to France.)
               Où allons-nous?
Students: Nous allons en France.
Teacher: (Points to Canada.)
               D'où venons-nous?
Students: Nous venons du Canada.

Variation: If students are unsure of the gender of the countries, the teacher can word his questions as follows: *Voici la Suisse. Où sommes nous?*

11.4.4   *Flash Cards*

The teacher prepares flash cards as follows:

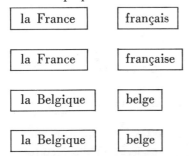

The teacher shows the country and the stick figure. The students write a sentence on the model: *Il est français.* Then the teacher turns the card over and students check their work.

The teacher can also show the nationality side of the card and ask: *Paul est français. Où habite-t-il?* Students write: *Il habite la France.*

11.4.5 *Overhead Transparency*

The teacher prepares a transparency with sets of paired sentences. The correct response is written on the line below the cues. Using a masking device, the teacher shows the model and the first set of sentences to be rewritten. When students have finished, he slides down the mask to show the correct response. Then he lowers the mask to expose the next row of sentences.

11.4.5a RELATIVE PRONOUNS

Modèle: Voilà le garçon. Il est français.
　　　　 Voilà le garçon qui est français.

1. Voilà l'autobus. Je le prends.
   Voilà l'autobus que je prends.

2. Voilà le roman. Vous m'en avez parlé.
   Voilà le roman dont vous m'avez parlé.

11.4.5b INDIRECT DISCOURSE

Model: Herr Benz sagte: „Der Volkswagen ist der billigste Wagen."
　　　　 Herr Benze sagte, der VW wäre der billigste Wagen.

1. Meine Mutter sagte: „Wir haben keine Zeit."
   Meine Mutter sagte, wir hätten keine Zeit.

2. Der Mann sagte: „Sie sprechen nur Deutsch."
   Der Mann sagte, sie sprächen nur Deutsch.

3. Seine Freundin sagte: „Es geht uns hier sehr gut."
   Seine Freundin sagte, es ginge uns hier sehr gut.

4. Er sagte: „Wir sind fertig."
   Er sagte, wir wären fertig.

11.4.6 *Magazine Cutouts* *Use this for comparison*

Students bring to class magazine pictures containing two or more persons or objects which can be easily compared.

The teacher puts several pictures on the board with magnets. Students come forward to write comparative sentences underneath the pictures:

Le monsieur à gauche est plus âgé que le monsieur à droite.
La voiture bleue est moins grande que la voiture verte.

La chica a la izquierda es más bonita que la chica a la derecha.
El coche negro es menos grande que el coche verde.

11.4.7 *English Equivalents*

The teacher passes out Dittoed sheets with short English sentences. The students write the answers. Then the teacher passes out a second sheet with answers:

I like ice cream.	Me gusta el helado.
I just arrived.	Acabo de llegar.
We've got to have a record player.	Il nous faut un pickup.
I'm thinking of my friend.	Je pense à mon ami.
He doesn't like the car.	Der Wagen gefällt ihm nicht.
Does she feel warm?	Ist ihr warm?

The paired sentences may also be placed on an overhead transparency, as in section 11.4.5. The teacher may wish to read the English sentences and have the students write down the foreign language equivalents.

The sentences should be kept fairly short. Translation of paragraphs and longer selections is an art that requires specialized training.

11.4.8 *Using Ideograms*

Ideograms are simple line drawings used to represent entire sentences. Students may be asked to help develop ideograms for the basic sentences in their textbook. Through participation they become more interested in generating foreign language sentences, and they feel proud of the code they have invented.

Le garçon est très gentil.
Der Junge ist sehr nett.
El chico es muy bueno.

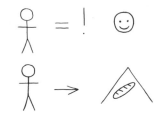

Robert va à la boulangerie.
Robert geht zur Bäckerei.
Roberto va a la panadería

11.4.9 *Game: Matching Clauses*

The teacher writes a sentence on the chalkboard: *Si vous prépariez le dîner, je ne le mangerais pas* or *Si Ud. cocinara, yo no comería.*

He then asks each student to take several small scraps of paper. The students on one side of the room write *if* clauses starting with *vous* or *Ud.*; those on the other side write independent clauses starting with *je* or *yo.* Each piece of paper contains only one clause.

The teacher puts the scraps into two hats (one for *if* clauses, the other for independent clauses). He sends several students to the board. Each student takes a scrap from both hats and writes the results on the board. Many hilarious sentences will appear!

Note: The same game may be played with relative clauses: *Je déteste les hommes . . . qui travaillent beaucoup.*; coordinate clauses: *Je reste à la maison . . . parce que je dois travailler*; dependent clauses: *Je vais chez Pierre . . . pour qu'il m'aide avec mes devoirs*; infinitive clauses: *On peut toujours réussir . . . sans travailler.*

11.4.10 *Dehydrated Sentences*

The teacher hands out Ditto sheets containing a series of model sentences. Under each sentence are segments which are to be used in forming other sentences. Students may work in pairs if desired. When they are finished they come to the teacher's desk to pick up a Ditto with the correct answers and check their work:

Modelo: Roberto ha buscado el libro.
muchachos / comprar / televisión
Los muchachos han comprado la televisión.

1. Yo me lavé la cara.
   Ella / quitarse / guantes

2. Ha venido para que yo lo ayude.
   llegar / sin que / tú / la / llamar

Model: Mein Bruder wohnt in Berlin.
Dein / Schwester / fahren / Hamburg
Deine Schwester fährt nach Hamburg.

1. Seine Mutter kauft sich einen neuen Mantel.
   Er / sich erkälten / jeder / Winter

2. Sie steht immer früh auf.
   Der Zug / abfahren / um sieben Uhr

3. Ich muss heute abend in die Stadt fahren.
   Ilse / dürfen / gehen / ins Kino

11.5   GUIDED COMPOSITION

In a guided composition, the students write a series of connected sentences. The composition may be highly structured, as in the first examples given below. In these cases, most students will be writing exactly the same composition. When less guidance is given, the student is free to introduce an element of originality into what he is writing, but he still uses known vocabulary and structures.

11.5.1 *Changing a Narrative to a Dialogue*

The teacher distributes a Dittoed sheet. One group of students writes the dialogue on the board, the other at their seats. The teacher circulates to give assistance.

Jacques demande à Nicolas ce qu'il va faire après ses cours. Nicolas répond qu'il ne sait pas et demande à Jacques ce qu'il a l'intention de faire. Jacques dit qu'il doit aller au magasin. Il demande à Nicolas s'il veut l'accompagner. Nicolas répond qu'il est trop fatigué.

Ecrivez la conversation entre Jacques et Nicolas:

Jacques: _____

Nicolas: _____

Jacques: _____

Nicolas: _____

11.5.2 *Changing a Dialogue into a Narrative*

This exercise involves the same procedure as above. The teacher distributes a Dittoed sheet; one group of students goes to the board while the rest write at their seats:

Begin each sentence with either *José pregunta si* . . . or *Pedro contesta que.* . . .

José: ¿Qué vas a hacer después de la escuela?
Pedro: No sé, ¿y tú?
José: Tengo que ir al centro. ¿Quieres acompañarme?
Pedro: No, gracias. Estoy muy cansado.

11.5.3 *Changing the Point of View*   *good idea*

The student retells a story from another person's point of view:

Le Facteur

M. Lebrun arrive chez Madame Fournier tous les matins à onze heures et demie. Il a toujours des lettres pour M. Boisseau. Quand il ne voit pas la concierge, il commence à crier. Madame le trouve pénible. Mais elle lui fait toujours une tasse de café.

Vous êtes le facteur. Vous racontez cette histoire:

J'arrive. . . .

11.5.4   *Changing the Time*

Passages may be rewritten to indicate past time, present time, future time:

(1) Change from the present tense to the *passé composé:*

J'invite Jean à venir chez moi. Il apporte ses nouveaux disques. On écoute tous les disques. Après, nous dînons ensemble.

(2) Change from the past tense to the future:

Gestern bin ich in die Stadt gefahren. Ich habe mir ein Paar Schuhe gekauft. Um zwei Uhr habe ich Erika getroffen. Wir haben ein Eis gegessen. Dann sind wir ins Kino gegangen.

11.5.5   *Cued Dialogue*

Brief cues are suggested for a dialogue. Students write out the complete conversational exchange:

AU RESTAURANT

Create a restaurant scene

Garçon:	Désirez?
Client:	Spécialité?
Garçon:	Biftek.
Client:	Alors.
Garçon:	Vin?
Client:	Rouge.

11.5.6   *Cued Narration*

11.5.6a   DESCRIPTION BASED ON QUESTIONS

Beschreiben Sie Inge! Sie ist Schülerin auf einem Gymnasium. Beantworten Sie folgende Fragen!

1. Wie alt ist sie?
2. Hat sie braunes Haar oder blondes?
3. Welchen Sport treibt sie gern?
4. Hört sie gern Schallplatten?
5. Was für Musik gefällt ihr?
6. Welche Fremdsprachen lernt sie?
7. Möchte sie nach Amerika reisen?

11.5.6b   DESCRIPTION BASED ON INSTRUCTIONS

Pensez à un voyage que vous avez fait. Ecrivez où vous êtes allé, qui vous a accompagné, comment vous avez fait le voyage, combien de temps le voyage a pris, si vous connaissiez des gens dans la région, ce que vous avez fait pendant votre séjour, combien de temps votre séjour a duré, si vous aimeriez retourner dans cette région.

11.5.6c RESUME OF AN ORAL PASSAGE

Students listen to a passage on the tape recorder. The passage is played twice. Then the students write a paragraph of not more than eight sentences re-creating the passage.

The teacher may want to give the first sentence and suggest additional words and phrases which might be used:

Hier après-midi Anne et Marc ont décidé d'aller au théâtre.

avoir l'occasion	s'installer
autobus	pièce
faire la queue	applaudir

11.5.7   *Writing Paragraphs*

Most students need guidance in writing paragraphs. The following techniques suggest steps by which the teacher can bring the students to an awareness of what constitutes a paragraph.

11.5.7a SCRAMBLED SENTENCES

The teacher selects a well-organized paragraph from a reader or textbook. He writes the individual sentences on a transparency and then cuts the transparency into strips, one sentence per strip. (Note: The sentences can also be typed in a large type on a sheet of white paper and then a transparency may be made with a Thermofax machine.)

These strips of acetate are placed on the overhead in random order. The students read the sentences. Some of them might be read aloud. Then he asks the students to identify the opening sentence. This sentence is placed at the top of the overhead, and the remaining sentences moved down. Gradually the students tell the teacher how to reconstitute the paragraph.

11.5.7b SEPARATING PASSAGES INTO PARAGRAPHS

The teacher selects a passage in the foreign language which is divided into a number of clearly organized paragraphs. This passage is typed in run-on fashion onto a Ditto master. The teacher then numbers the lines (5, 10, 15, etc.) down the margin to make class discussion easier.

In class Dittos are distributed to the students. The students, working as a whole class, in groups, in pairs, or individually, divide the passage into paragraphs. The results are compared and discussed.

11.5.7c WRITING TOPIC SENTENCES TO GIVEN PARAGRAPHS

The teacher selects two or three well organized paragraphs in which the opening sentence is clearly the topic sentence. He Dittoes the paragraphs, leaving out the opening sentence. In class the students try to write appropriate opening sentences. The best suggestions are written on a transparency and discussed. Finally the teacher writes the author's opening sentence on the transparency.

11.5.7d WRITING TOPIC SENTENCES ON A GIVEN SUBJECT

The teacher suggests a subject, and the students write opening topic sentences. These are discussed. Sentences may be put on the board or on the overhead. The class selects two or three opening sentences (either from the ones suggested or by combining ideas). Students finish the paragraph for homework for the next day.

11.6 WRITING LETTERS

Writing letters can become a very meaningful classroom activity, especially if the letters are sent and answers received (see section 12.5.2).

11.6.1 *Teaching Salutations*

The teacher uses the opaque projector and letter formats. He shows several types of documents: business letters, formal invitations, friendly notes, announcements of weddings, births, baptisms, and funerals.

As each is shown, he points out the different salutations, the layout of the document (position of addresses and salutations, indentations of paragraphs), and the closings.

He then shuffles the items and shows them again, covering up the salutations. The students write the salutation, and then check what they have written when the teacher uncovers the original.

11.6.2 *A Collective Letter*

Using a letter that one of the students has received from a pen pal, the teacher reads it twice to the class. Then he composes an answer on the board with the help of the class. The student who received the letter makes a copy at his seat:

Querido Carlos,

Muchas gracias por tu carta del 22 de noviembre. La descripción de tu vida escolar me fascinó.

Me pediste describir la mía. Entonces, acquí está:

The teacher gives oral cues:

¿Cuántos alumnos hay en nuestra escuela?

¿Qué cursos toma Carlos?

¿Cuáles son los deportes que juegan los alumnos?

¿Tenemos un buen equipo de fútbol o no?

¿Cuáles son los pasatiempos de los alumnos?

¿Quiénes son los cantantes favoritos de los alumnos?

¿A qué edad terminan los alumnos sus estudios?

¿Qué porcentaje de los alumnos de nuestra escuela van a la Universidad?

11.6.3   *Guided Individual Letters*

(1) The teacher distributes mimeographed sheets with blanks to be filled in by students:

1. Ich heiße _____
2. Ich wohne _____
3. Ich bin _____ Jahre alt.
4. Ich besuche die _____ (Schule) in der _____(Straße).
5. Ich lerne _____
6. Mein Lieblingsfach ist _____
7. Ich spiele gern _____

(2) Dites à Jean que 1. vous avez été très content de recevoir sa lettre, 2. les jolis timbres vous ont beaucoup plu, 3. vous avez été navré d'apprendre son accident d'automobile, mais 4. vous êtes content qu'il n'ait pas été blessé, 5. l'équipe de football de votre école a gagné son dernier match, 6. il y aura encore un match avant la fin de la saison, 7. le prochain match sera le plus dur, et 8. que vous le décrirez dans la prochaine lettre.

11.6.4   *Requesting Sample Products*

The teacher prepares a model business letter: Have students choose a foreign company and write away for descriptive material and perhaps for sample products. Plan this project early in the year to allow for slow international surface mail.

Letters may also be sent to foreign tourist offices requesting material about regions and cities. (See further suggestions in section 12.3.3f.)

11.6.5   *"Adopting" a Child*

The Spanish Club may wish to "adopt" a Spanish-speaking child through an international organization, such as Save the Children Federation. Dues and money-raising projects, together with contributions, can pay the fifteen dollars or so a month which these agencies request. It is possible to request an older child, who will be able to exchange letters with the members of the club. Spanish classes may join in the reading of the letters and the writing of replies.

It is important that the Club make provisions to continue aid over the summer months. A lump sum may be sent in June, and monthly payments resumed in September.

11.7 FREE COMPOSITION

Writing whole selections in a clear, interesting manner with no mistakes in spelling or grammar is a very complex activity. Most high school teachers consider it an unrealistic objective. Nevertheless, some aspects of free composition can be successfully achieved. If, for example, the teacher is willing to sacrifice perfection in a few of the mechanical details of writing, he can succeed in getting his students to express their thoughts and opinions.

Nothing is more discouraging to a student than to find his paper covered with red marks. Before grading a paper, the teacher needs to restate in his own mind the purpose of the exercise. If the goal of the composition was self-expression, the teacher should base the grade primarily on the content and secondarily on the form.

One way to help students get ready for free composition is to diagnose individual problems. Bob is told to concentrate on agreement of adjectives; Mary is asked to check the subjunctive with *croire* and *penser*; Sue is given a review on the position of direct and indirect pronoun objects. Each student's individual problem is recorded and regularly observed. By the end of a given marking period, the specific errors should disappear.

The teacher must do all he can to inspire students to write. Topics must be exciting and within their realm of experience.

11.7.1 *Creating Situations with Verbal Cues*

The teacher provides brief written guidelines for the composition:

(1) Breaking a Date: Write what you would say over the telephone to a girl with whom you wished to break a date.

Expliquez que vous avez complètement oublié la visite de vos parents ce soir-là, que vous ne les avez pas vus depuis longtemps, que vous aviez l'intention de demander de l'argent à votre père, que vous espérez qu'elle vous pardonnerait, et que vous voulez la revoir un autre jour.

Maintenant, inventez vos propres excuses!

(2) English Cues: Write a description in Spanish of how you and your brothers and sisters spent a rainy Saturday. Put every verb in the imperfect tense: Who was listening to records? writing letters? watching television? playing cards? washing the dog? Finally, the last sentence is in the preterite: some dreadful catastrophe occurred.

(3) Planning an Outing: Look at the topic sentence. What words and expressions do you need to describe your proposed activity?

Esta tarde vamos al lago.

la merienda	pescar
el traje de baño	los avíos de pesca
nadar	el bote
la guitarra	el termo
la cámara	

11.7.2   *Creating Situations with Props*

The teacher shows a toy pistol, a handkerchief, and a whistle. Students write a composition in which these objects play a role.

11.7.3   *Creating Situations with Visual Cues*

11.7.3a   SANS PAROLES

The teacher distributes mimeographed sheets with a comic strip format. Students supply the narrative:

C'est un incident dans la vie de Paul (P), Sylvie (S), et Marc (M).

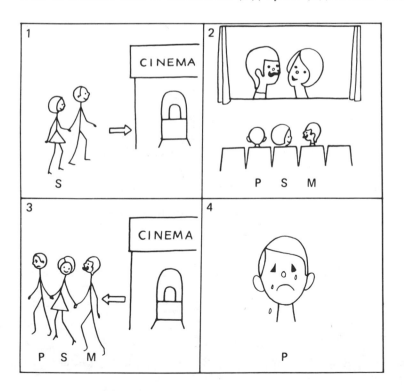

11.7.3b COMIC STRIP CUTOUTS

Cut out a comic strip and put it on a transparency. Blacken or remove the dialogue. Students fill in the conversation on their papers.

11.7.3c BABY PHOTOS

Students exchange baby pictures and write imaginary comments to express the baby's attitudes. These are fastened with paper clips to the pictures and put in the opaque projector:

Yawning: ¡Qué aburrida está la fiesta!
Astonished: ¡No, hija! ¡No me digas! ¡Qué barbaridad!
Crying: ¡Nunca me dejas salir con mi novia!

11.7.4 *Writing a Collective Story*

The teacher writes the beginning of the story on the board. Then, through guided questioning, he gets the students to dictate all but the ending.

For homework each student completes the story. The next day all share their versions of how it ended.

AUSFLUG OHNE BADEANZUG

Morgen ist Sonntag. Einige Schüler machen einen Ausflug nach dem schönen Starnberger See.

1. Was möchten sie dort machen?	7. Wo treffen sie sich?
2. Wer möchte mit?	8. Was vergißt einer?
3. Was soll jeder mitnehmen?	9. Wann erfährt er es?
4. Wie kommen sie dorthin?	10. Was sagt er?
5. Wie lange dauert die Fahrt?	11. Was möchte er jetzt tun?
6. Um wieviel Uhr fahren sie ab?	12. Was muß er nun machen?

11.7.5 *What then? Extending a Story*

Students read a story and extend it beyond the author's ending.

LA PARURE
Guy de Maupassant

Madame Loisel a raconté à Madame Forestier la vie horrible qu'elle menait depuis la perte de la parure.

Madame Forestier lui a dit, "Oh! ma pauvre Mathilde! Mais la mienne était fausse. Elle valait au plus cinq cent francs."[1]

Et puis . . .

---

[1] Camille Bauer, et al, *Lire Parler et Ecrire* (New York: Holt, Rinehart and Winston, 1964), pp. 153–57.

11.7.6 *Writing a Story from Another Character's Point of View*

Students read a story about a crime. The storyteller thinks he knows who did it and how it happened. However, there are other points of view. Students are asked to tell the story from the point of view of the accused.

LA VERDAD ES UN MISTERIO[1]

Apareció en el periódico un reportaje de un accidente de avión que hubo en Guatemala hacía unos meses; era un avión pequeño en que murieron tres américanos, dos hombres y una mujer.

Del agua sacaron los restos del avión y los cuerpos destrozados de la mujer y uno de los hombres, pero el cuerpo del dueño del avión despareció.

Según los informes ese hombre estaba vivo; fué visto en un balcón del Hotel Victoria.

Se sabe que era un hombre muy rico pero que estaba lleno de deudas. Como tenía seguros de vida que alcanzaban a un total de más de dos millones de dólares, una compañía de seguros mandó un detective a Guatemala para buscar a ese hombre.

Usted es el fugitivo. Cuente Ud. lo que ha pasado.

[1] Frederick Richard, "La Verdad es un Misterio," in *Spanish—Reading for Meaning* (New York: Harcourt Brace Jovanovich, Inc., 1966), pp. 109–14.

PART FOUR
BEYOND
LANGUAGE

CHAPTER TWELVE
TEACHING
CULTURE

The word *culture* may be defined in two different ways. In one sense it is the sum total of a people's achievements and contributions to civilization: art, music, literature, architecture, technology, scientific discoveries, and politics. The second meaning includes the behavioral patterns or life styles of the people: when and what they eat, how they make a living, the way they organize their society, the attitudes they express toward friends and members of their families, how they act in different situations, which expressions they use to show approval and disapproval, the traditions they must observe, and so on. In recent years the attention of language teachers has been focused on the second definition, usually called an anthropological approach or "culture with a small *c*." Both types of culture are treated in this chapter.

12.1 GENERAL CONSIDERATIONS

While most foreign language teachers agree that culture should be taught as part of a foreign language course, not all of these teachers agree about what should be taught and how it should be introduced.

What constitutes culture? If we wish to teach French culture with a small *c*, then we focus on contemporary patterns of culture. These patterns reflect the value system of the people. It soon becomes evident from looking at the school curriculum, the popular magazines and comic books, TV programs, and transcribed interviews and conversations that the French are proud of their history, proud of their literature, proud of their language. In this sense, then, the American student must develop an awareness of French history and French literature in order to understand contemporary French attitudes.

A study of contemporary German culture, on the other hand, reveals a people much more concerned with the present and the future than with the past. A knowledge of German geography is therefore necessary if the American student wishes to understand the Germans' concern over a divided country. An awareness of German music and opera is also necessary if the American student is to understand why the people of Dresden, a city bombed out during the Second World War, rebuilt the opera house and revitalized the opera company, which played nightly to full houses, while rubble still lay in the streets and a single streetcar line provided the only transportation.

Once the content of the cultural portion of the language course has been established, the language of instruction must be determined. Should culture be postponed until the student can study it in the foreign language? The disadvantage of waiting until the third year before introducing culture is that only about ten percent of those students who begin a foreign language ever reach that level. Culture can be taught in English from the very beginning, and it can be an integral part of all instruction rather than an added frill.

One of the concepts which students should develop in their study of a second culture is that people in various cultures respond to life's needs in a variety of different ways. The American way is not the only way, nor is it the best way. It is simply the way that works best for Americans. Other ways work best for other peoples.

Perhaps the greatest risk in teaching culture is the tendency on the part of the teacher and the students to generalize from too little data. It is essential, therefore, to discuss the way people live in big cities as well as in small country villages, the reactions of young people and those of their elders, the points of view of different ethnic groups, the attitudes of people in different socio-economic strata and in different regions.

The following sections suggest some techniques for introducing culture into the foreign language classroom.[1]

12.2   EVIDENCE OF THE FOREIGN CULTURE TO BE FOUND IN THE UNITED STATES

There are many evidences of the influence of various foreign cultures in this country. History books tell of Spanish, French, and Italian explorers, early

[1] Teachers of Spanish may wish to see H. Ned Seelye, ed., *Perspectives for Teachers of Latin American Culture* (Springfield, Illinois: Department of Public Instruction, 1970).

French and Spanish settlements, Dutch and German immigrants. The history of the United States is frequently intertwined with the history of Europe, of Africa, of Asia, of Latin America.

At the present time our country imports a variety of goods from all parts of the world. Frankfurters and sauerkraut, spaghetti, pizza, French fries, chili beans—all have become American foods. American movie houses show foreign films; museums hang works by foreign artists; concert halls and radio stations play music by foreign composers and orchestras; department stores sell imported goods; supermarkets carry imported foods, and so on. Signs of foreign culture are everywhere.

The role of the language teacher is to open the students' eyes to the impact foreign culture has had on American culture and to make them aware of the diversity that exists around them.

12.2.1 *The American Heritage*

Indications of the diverse origins of the people who settled this country may be easily discovered.

12.2.1a WALL MAP

Using a large wall map of the United States, the teacher points to a few cities with foreign names and shows how to determine their origin.

Spanish: Names starting with San or Santa (Saint): many were religious missions founded in the seventeenth century, such as San José, Santa Clara.

Names starting with definite articles: Los Angeles, Las Vegas.

French: Names representing natural phenomena: Eau Claire, Fond du Lac, Presque-Isle. French names of cities: Detroit, Des Moines. Names ending in *-ier*, and *-mont:* Beaumont, Montpelier.

German: Names ending in *-heim, -burg, -fort:* Anaheim, Harrisburg, Frankfort.

The teacher can have the students bring a gas station map into class and make a list of all the French, Spanish, or German place names they can find.

12.2.1b TWIN MAPS: GAME

The teacher puts up a wall map of the United States and a wall map of France or Germany. The class is divided into two teams. Team A sends a member to the map of the United States. Team B sends a member to the map of a European country. The teacher announces the name of a city, such as Frankfort or Montpelier. The student who finds the city first makes a point for his team. The players go to the end of the line, and the next two players go to the opposite map: Team A sends a player to the European map and Team B sends a player to the United States map. The game continues until everyone has had a turn at the map.

Variation: If a player finds the city on his map, he scores a point. If he then finds the same city on the other map before his opponent does, he gets a second point.

12.2.1c DRAWING A MAP

Using a large piece of cardboard, students draw the outline of the United States, including the state boundaries, and hang it on the wall. Students color the sections where people from the foreign countries under study have settled.

12.2.1d REPORTS

Students give reports on historical events or historical figures which link the United States to the country whose language they are studying: Ponce de León, Général de Rochambeau, Pennsylvania Dutch settlers. These reports might be correlated with units in a world history or an American history course.

12.2.2 *The Arts*

12.2.2a MUSIC

(1) School orchestra: If some students are in the school orchestra, the teacher can ask to see the pieces they are working on. Perhaps they are playing something by a composer from the foreign country under study; if so, he asks for some volunteers to prepare a bulletin board display on the composer and his times.

(2) Choir: A similar project might be assigned if the choir is singing a song in the foreign language or a song composed by a composer from the country under study.

(3) Current records: If the teacher goes abroad in the summer, he can buy some of the current hits. (Or, he can ask someone who is going abroad to buy them for him.) He can then play the records to the students and ask them to compare the songs to current American favorites.

(4) Transcription of lyrics: In more advanced classes, the teacher might make available records of folk songs, traditional songs, and hit tunes. During time given to independent work, students would be encouraged to find a favorite song and try to transcribe the lyrics for the rest of the class. This project might be done in pairs or in groups of three or four. (If the classroom has only a tape recorder and no record player, the records can be duplicated on tape.)

12.2.2b PAINTING

The local museum might have paintings by artists who are natives of the country under study or who resided there. To prepare students for a trip to the museum, the teacher should first go there himself and decide which paintings the class will see. He should also talk to a guide; museums often offer guided tours, lectures, and the like, free of charge. The art teacher might be willing to give a lecture with slides. The teacher could also ask the librarian for a list of books about the lives of the artists and display the book jackets on the bulletin board.

12.2.2c DANCE

If one or more students in the French class have studied or are studying ballet, the teacher can ask them to prepare a wall chart with the French terms. Perhaps a student will be willing to demonstrate some of the steps.

12.2.3 *The Culinary Arts*

12.2.3a VISIT TO THE SUPERMARKET

Students take a trip to a supermarket or a gourmet shop and make a list of the imported foods: Spanish olives, chorizo, and wines; French cheeses, wines, vinegar, bread, and Dijon mustard; German sausage, mustard, wines.

12.2.3b COOKING PROJECTS

Students read cookbooks: *La Cuisine est un Jeu d'Enfants, Eating European,* and *The French Chef Cookbook.*

For language club activities they prepare: *coq au vin, une omelette aux fines herbes, une bûche de Noël,* or a continental breakfast; or *arroz con pollo, tacos, enchiladas,* Mexican wedding cookies, or hot chocolate with cinnamon sticks; or sauerbraten with potato pancakes and red cabbage.

This is a good money-making activity!

12.2.4 *Imports and Exports*

12.2.4a VISIT TO THE DEPARTMENT STORE

Students take a trip to a department store and make a list of all the imported items with their prices.

Germany: cameras, Hummel figurines, Steif toys from Nuremberg.
Spain and Mexico: mantillas, sarapes, sombreros, Maja soap, cutlery from Toledo.

France: perfume, silk scarves and ties, lace gloves, fine leather goods, and china from Limoges.

Students who own some of these articles can make a showcase display.

12.2.4b   AUTOMOBILE MANUALS

The teacher can let interested students read manuals for European cars and encourage them to take a trip to the local dealers to examine the cars.

12.2.4c   ADVERTISEMENTS IN FOREIGN JOURNALS

Students cut out advertisements from foreign magazines, promoting either American products or their own products. They then make a bulletin board display with American products abroad at the top and foreign products popular in the United States at the bottom.

12.3   LEARNING ABOUT THE FOREIGN CULTURE

In order to gain as much knowledge as possible about a foreign culture, students need both a historical and geographical perspective and an awareness of contemporary behavioral patterns. Moreover, great changes are taking place in patterns of daily life throughout Europe. Thus, it is essential that the teacher keep informed by subscribing to such journals as *Parents, Echo de la Mode, Der Spiegel, El Mundo Español, Hoy, Mañana.*

12.3.1   *Construction Projects*

12.3.1a   CASA ESPAÑOLA

The teacher places shoe boxes in a square or rectangle to represent the walls and rooms of a house. He staples them together and pastes construction paper around the sides. Doors and windows can be cut in the walls facing the patio, or the sides of the boxes can be removed and furniture placed in each room.

The vocabulary for the rooms is taught as well as some information about the Roman origin of this architecture.

12.3.1b   THE BRANDENBURG GATE

Using a photo as a model, the teacher can build a wooden gate in the school shop and paint and decorate it according to the picture. It could be large (4′ × 7′), affixed to a piece of plywood, and nailed to the back of the German classroom.[1]

12.3.1c PHYSICAL MAP OF FRANCE

Students can make a map of France out of flour, salt, and water. This is an excellent way to learn the names and locations of the mountain ranges *les Alpes, les Pyrénées, le Massif Central, le Jura,* and *les Vosges.*

12.3.2 *Classroom Decorations*

Classroom decorations afford an unobtrusive way of initiating students to the foreign culture. The teacher should try to use all the available space for posters and displays and change the decoration every few weeks. Students will notice a change in their classroom environment. During those moments when the student's mind wanders, his eyes will encounter street scenes of Berlin and castles on the Rhine. He will unconsciously be developing mental images of the country he is studying about.

12.3.2a THE CLASSROOM CLOCK

Have an inventive student figure out a way to put the numbers 13 to 24 around the outside of the clock. Even the clockwatchers in the class will be learning something about the twenty-four-hour clock as they wonder when the period will end. The clock will be useful in teaching official time. A German radio announcer will say: *Sechzehn Uhr zehn.* A Mexican railroad employee will say: *El tren sale a las trece y media.* A French ticket agent will say: *Le spectacle commence à vingt heures.*

12.3.2b THE CLASS CALENDAR

On the class calendar, mark the foreign holidays, birthdays of important historical figures, and important historical events. The class calendar may provide the opportunity for introducing some cultural material briefly at the beginning of a period otherwise devoted primarily to language-learning activities.

12.3.2c POSTERS

Posters may often be obtained from travel agents and airline offices. Often the consulates of the smaller countries are more willing than those of large countries to provide posters. For posters in French, the teacher can try

---

[1] Runhild E. Wessell, *Die Unterrichtspraxis* (1968), No. 1, pp. 57–60.

Belgium, Switzerland, or Quebec. For posters in Spanish, he can try some of the South American countries. The German Government is usually very generous in providing classroom materials.

If the teacher goes abroad himself, he can buy posters there. He can also ask his friends who go abroad to bring back posters. Students might have posters they would be willing to put up in the classroom during a three- or four-week period.

12.3.2d   THE CLASS TIMELINE

Get two colors of ribbon and fasten a double time line around the classroom walls. Measure the length of the lines and divide by twenty-five. This gives you the length of each century, if you begin at 500 B.C. In a French class you might begin with the Greeks at Nice and add subsequent important events like Caesar's conquest of Gaul, and so on. One color is the United States time line. There is little activity there until around 1200 A.D. and the Pueblo civilizations, such as those at Mesa Verde. Different groups of students can be assigned different sections of the time line. If the classroom is used by several classes, each class might be given a section to decorate.

12.3.2e   THE CLASS BULLETIN BOARD

Different groups of students may be assigned the preparation of a bulletin board display which is changed weekly. Students should be encouraged to develop their interests: stamps, coins, art, sports, racing, and so on. Especially good displays might be put in hall display cases.

12.3.3   *Incorporating Culture in Language Learning Activities*

12.3.3a   USING VISUALS

(1) The twenty-four-hour clock may be used for those exercises in which it is necessary to tell time.

(2) Magazine pictures and drawings: To teach about breakfast in France and in the United States, the teacher cuts out pictures of foods from magazines or draws them. A typical breakfast in France consists of *deux croissants, un bol de café au lait, du beurre et de la confiture;* breakfast in the United States, of *des oeufs sur le plat, du bacon, un jus d'orange, des toasts, du beurre, de la confiture, et un verre de lait.* The teacher asks: *Qu'est-ce qu'on mange au petit déjeuner en France? Aux Etats-Unis?*

(3) Poster: The teacher prepares the following illustration, which he uses in discussing Spanish dating customs.

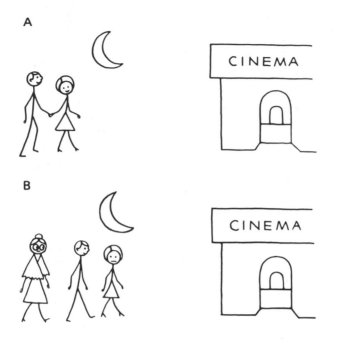

Teacher: ¡Miren Uds. el cuadro A! En los Estados Unidos, ¿se permite que un joven y su amiga salgan solos de noche?
Jorge: Sí, Señorita.
Teacher: ¿Es así en España? ¡Miren Uds. el cuadro B!
María: No, Señorita.
Teacher: Pues, en España, generalmente, una tía, un hermano, o algún amigo acompaña a la pareja.

(4) Class schedule card from the foreign country: Pen pals may be asked to send a description of their schedule of courses. The teacher can place the card on an opaque projector or copy it on a Ditto master. Students can compare, in the foreign language, a foreign student's schedule with their own.

12.3.3b USING THE MAP

Students sit in a semicircle in front of a large map of Germany. As the teacher asks questions, he hands the pointer to individual students. They in turn come forward, answer the question, and point to the places they name:[1]

Teacher: Wir sind jetzt alle in München. Wir wollen eine Reise machen. Wohin würden Sie gerne reisen, Herr Smith.
Herr Smith: Ich würde gerne nach Salzburg reisen.

[1] Eberhard Reichmann, "The Map for Pattern Practice," in *German Quarterly*, Vol. 38 (May 1965), pp. 345–50.

Other questions might be: What cities would you go through if you traveled from Bonn to Berlin? What rivers would you cross? What mountains would you see?

12.3.3c USING RADIO BROADCASTS

tape it and bring it in

The teacher makes a tape recording of a foreign radio program including commercial advertisements. The program might be a game of soccer, Jai-alai, or baseball. He plays all or part of the program to the class and then teaches essential vocabulary and difficult grammatical structures. After hearing the tape several times, the students' comprehension increases along with their knowledge of the country.

12.3.3d USING THE OVERHEAD PROJECTOR

The transparency below contains generally true statements about the working hours and eating times of the French and the Americans. Each statement is covered with a paper tab. As the teacher presents each statement, he lifts up the corresponding tab, first for the United States, then for France:[1]

AUX ETATS-UNIS

1. Dans un bureau, on travaille de 9 heures à midi.

   Dans un magasin, on travaille de 9 heures à midi.

2. Les employés de bureau déjeunent entre midi et 1 heure.

   Les employés de magasin n'ont pas d'heure fixe pour déjeuner.

3. Les bureaux sont fermés de midi à 1 heure.

   Les magasins ne ferment pas à l'heure du déjeuner.

4. Dans un bureau, on travaille jusqu'à 5 heures du soir.

   Dans un magasin, on travaille jusqu'à 5 heures du soir.

5. Les bureaux ferment à 5 heures du soir.

   Les magasins ferment à 5 heures du soir.

   Quelques grands magasins sont ouverts jusqu'à 9 heures ou 10 heures du soir.

---

[1] Techniques developed by Reid Baker, methods instructor, The Ohio State University.

6. On dîne généralement   [vers 6 heures]   du soir.

EN FRANCE

1. Dans un bureau, on travaille de [9 heures] à [midi.]

   Dans un magasin, on travaille de [9 heures] à [midi.]

2. Les employés de bureau déjeunent [entre midi] et [2 heures.]

   Les employés de magasin déjeunent [entre midi] et [2 heures.]

3. Les bureaux sont fermés [entre midi] et [2 heures.]

   Les magasins sont fermés [entre midi] et [2 heures.]

4. Dans un bureau, on travaille [jusqu'à 6 heures] du soir.

   Dans un magasin, on travaille [jusqu'à 7 heures] du soir.

5. Les bureaux ferment à [6 heures.]

   Les magasins ferment à [7 heures,] même les grands magasins.

6. On dîne généralement [vers 7 heures et demie ou 8 heures.]

Then the class is divided into two groups, one Frenchmen, the other Americans. Some questions such as these may be asked of both Frenchmen and Americans:

Vous travaillez dans un grand magasin.
A quelle heure allez-vous au travail?
Est-ce que le magasin ferme à midi?

The teacher can ask the Americans:

Pourquoi est-ce que les bureaux et les grands magasins ferment à midi en France?
Quel est le repas principal en France?

He can then ask the Frenchmen:

Pourquoi est-ce que les grands magasins ne ferment pas à midi aux Etats-Unis?
Est-ce que le déjeuner est le repas principal aux Etats-Unis?

12.3.3e DITTO HANDOUTS

Individual students, or pairs of students, are assigned as travel agents to a specific region or country where the foreign language is spoken. They prepare brief presentations accompanied by Dittoed handouts, describing their area, its main features, attractions, and annual events. They try to convince their classmates to visit the area.

At the end of the presentations the teacher distributes a ballot listing the regions. Each student marks the three he thinks he wants to visit. The best travel agents are those who attracted the most tourists.

12.3.3f SENDING FOR PRODUCTS OR MATERIALS

At the beginning of a school year an intermediate or advanced class might be given a lesson on business letters. As part of their written assignment, each student prepares a letter which he sends abroad. The letters may be sent either to a foreign company, asking for brochures and perhaps a sample product, or to various chambers of commerce, asking for illustrated descriptive material. (In France write to the *Syndicat d'Initiative* of the town. In Germany write to the *Fremdenverkehrsbüro*.)

Later in the year, when students begin getting responses, the material received may be used for reading and speaking activity as well as for cultural enrichment.

12.3.4 *Celebrating Foreign Holidays*

The teacher may wish to celebrate some foreign holidays in the classroom. *Fasching*, *Mardi Gras*, and *Carnaval* give students the opportunity to wear masks in spring.

Breaking the *piñata* may be an interesting project for a Spanish Club. To make a piñata: Blow up a balloon and cover it with papier-mâché. When the papier-mâché hardens, pierce the balloon and pull it out. Then decorate the shell with crepe paper, ribbons, or funny faces of people and animals. Fill it with hard candy and seal up the opening. Hang it at about eye-level. As individual students come forward, they are blindfolded and given a club. Each tries to hit the piñata and break it. If possible, put the piñata on a pulley or over a beam so that it can be moved while each person swings at it. As it breaks all dive for the candies that fall to the floor.

12.3.5 *Folksongs and Dances*

Folksongs and folkdances capture the spirit of a people. As the students learn the traditional lyrics and tunes, as they dance the traditional steps, they are participating in the cultural heritage of the people they are studying.

12.3.5a FOLKSONGS

(1) The Burgundian song and dramatization *"Plantons la Vigne"* illustrates the importance of wine in French life:

Seven students form a line, each holding a facsimile of an implement used for making wine. The rest of the class comprises the chorus. As each of the seven soloists sings a verse, he holds up an implement mentioned in it: first a paper grapevine, then a bunch of plastic grapes, a winepress (potato ricer), a *cuve* (kettle), a pitcher, a glass, and finally the mouth. *Bouchi, bouchons, bouchons le vin. La voilà la jolie bouche au vin (bis).*

(2) The German folksong *"Das Wandern ist des Müllers Lust"* might be used to illustrate the Germans' love for the outdoors and for hiking.

Many folksongs have grown around common experiences. The teacher can ask students to try to discover what types of activity might have given rise to a particular folksong. For example, if the class has sung *"Alouette,"* the teacher might ask: What is the action of the song? (The person is plucking a lark.) Why are birds plucked? (To be eaten.) What kinds of birds are eaten in the United States? The teacher would then explain that the French appreciate game and that many more game birds are eaten in France than in the United States. Even though larks are no longer hunted, the French do hunt quail, partridge, pheasant, and duck.

12.3.5b FOLKDANCES

The teacher who enjoys music and dancing might want to teach a folkdance to his language students.[1] The dance might be performed for the Foreign Language Club, a school assembly, or a P.T.A. meeting.

The American square dance is of French origin. Students are often surprised to discover that *do-see-do* is really *dos-à-dos*, *al-a-mand left* is *à la main gauche*, and *promenade* is the French *promenade*.

12.3.6 *Role Playing*

The teacher can create situations in the classroom that provide opportunities for students to take the roles of Frenchmen, Spaniards, Germans, Russians,

---

[1] The following sources contain many suggestions for dances and music:

Alford, Violet, *Dances of France III The Pyrenees* (New York: Crown Publishers, 1952).

Allen, Edward D., *Some Contributions of Foreign Folklore to the Secondary School Curriculum*. Unpublished Ph.D. thesis. The Ohio State University, 1954.

Duggan, Anne S., *Folk Dances of the U.S. and Mexico* (New York: A. S. Barnes, 1948).

Goldsmith's Music Shop, Inc., Language Department, 301 East Shore Road, Great Neck, N.Y. 11023.

Lawson, Joan, *European Folk Dance* (London: Pitman Publishers, 1970). (Contains dances of Spain and costume designing in Brittany.)

Lorraine Music Co., Inc., 23–80 48th Street, Long Island City, New York, N.Y. 11103.

and so on. Putting themselves in the shoes of a foreign person can be a valuable learning experience and a great deal of fun.

Careful preparation for such activities is indispensable. The teacher must determine whether the class knows enough vocabulary, sentence structure, and dialogue lines to be able to perform the assigned roles.

In the early stages of language development it is wise for the teacher to work with the class as a whole when creating dialogues for various situations. Individual members of the class dictate possible lines of dialogue and the teacher writes them on the board, making corrections when necessary or casting the utterances into a more colloquial style.

Even after the class achieves a fair degree of fluency, the teacher needs to provide an orientation session in which he supplies essential linguistic information on verb forms, nouns, idiomatic expressions, and pronunciation.

In addition to stressing role playing, the techniques below include the use of gestures and kinesics. There is a progression from elementary to intermediate to advanced language class activities.

Kids love it

12.3.6a   GREETINGS

The teacher draws a series of large buildings on the board and labels them *Le Centre de la Ville.* She then motions for a student to approach her and says (in French or English): *I am Madame Bertrand. You are Marie Dumont. Your mother is a close friend of mine. We meet by chance downtown.*

Mme Bertrand:	(Shakes hands with Marie.)
	Bonjour, Marie.
Marie:	Bonjour, Madame.
Mme Bertrand:	Comment vas-tu?
Marie:	Très bien, merci. Et vous?
Mme Bertrand:	Très bien, merci. Comment va ta mère?
Marie:	Bien, merci.
Mme Bertrand:	Au revoir, Marie.
Marie:	Au revoir, Madame.

The teacher then says: *Jeannette and Sylvie are good friends. They meet downtown and greet each other.*

Jeannette:	Bonjour, Sylvie.
	(Shakes hands with Sylvie.)
Sylvie:	Bonjour, Jeannette. Ça va?
Jeannette:	Bien, merci. Et toi? Ça va bien?
Sylvie:	Pas mal.
Jeannette:	Au revoir, Sylvie.
Sylvie:	Au revoir, Jeannette.

Successive roles include two teenage boys, two men, a man and a woman, and so on.

GENERALIZATION

Teacher:	When two French people meet, what do they usually do?
Student:	Shake hands.
Teacher:	Do American teenagers generally shake hands when they meet?
Student:	No.
Teacher:	When do American men shake hands?
Student 1:	When they are introduced.
Student 2:	When they haven't seen each other for a long time.
Teacher:	Do American women generally shake hands?
Student:	No.
Teacher:	What do you think a French person's reaction would be if you met him in the street and didn't shake his hand?
Student:	He would wonder if he had done something to offend you.
Teacher:	Yes. Now, look at the printed copies of typical conversations. Are *bonjour* and *au revoir* ever used alone?
Student:	No.
Teacher:	What are they always used with?
Student:	The first name of a person, Monsieur, Mademoiselle, or Madame.
Teacher:	Yes. And what is the difference between addressing an adult and one of your buddies?
Student:	For adults, *vous;* for friends your own age, *tu.*

12.3.6b INITIAL DATING CUSTOM (EL PASEO)

The teacher explains that girls and boys date later in Spanish-speaking countries than in the United States. Most schools are not mixed; there is a boys' school and a girls' school in most towns and cities. So, one of the best ways to see one another is on the evening or Sunday afternoon walk around the town square. The girls walk in one direction and the boys in the other; they often stare at one another and sometimes flirt. People of all ages participate and walk for hours. There are always spectators in cafés or on sidewalk benches.

The teacher "transforms" the classroom into a "plaza" and draws some buildings on the chalkboards to indicate sides of the square. Then he chooses a few students to serve as spectators (these are seated on the sides of the plaza). Spanish or Latin-American music played on a record player would help create atmosphere.

The boys in groups of two or more walk in one direction while groups of girls pass them in the opposite direction. All comments must be in Spanish, for example, ¡Qué guapa es!, ¡Qué ojos estupendos! ¡Qué pelo más lindo!

12.3.6c TABLE MANNERS

The teacher brings paper plates, silverware, and several pieces of bread to class. He pretends the slices of bread are pieces of meat and shows the class how Europeans and Latin Americans eat it. He keeps the fork in his left hand at all times and cuts the meat with his right hand. His left hand is always kept on the table. Then he calls on various students to do the same.

In French class, he brings a *porte-couteau* and a *rond de serviette*.

Students might also be asked, as a supplementary activity, to observe table manners in foreign movies.

12.3.6d BUYING A TRAIN TICKET

Students can learn a dialogue about purchasing tickets:

AM SCHALTER IM HAUPTBAHNHOF
(At the Ticket Window at Central Station)

Herr Müller:	Zwei Karten nach Hamburg, bitte. (Two tickets to Hamburg, please.)
Beamter:	Einfache oder Rückfahrkarten? (One-way or return tickets?)
Herr Müller:	Einfache, erster Klasse. (One-way, first class.)
Beamter:	Das macht sechzig Mark neunzig. (That will be DM 60, 90.)
Herr Müller:	Wann geht der nächste Fernschnellzug? (When does the next long-distance express train leave?)
Beamter:	Um zwanzig Uhr zehn auf Gleis acht. (At 20:10 on track eight.)

Variation: On a trip abroad the teacher can pick up sample train and bus schedules at train stations or tourist information centers. (A friend traveling abroad could get these for him also.) The actual schedules can be photostatted and transformed into Ditto masters or placed on an opaque projector. Students can then play roles asking when trains leave, when they arrive, and so on. A third student can point out the cities on a wall map.

12.3.6e GESTURES AND BODY MOVEMENTS

Two people conversing in France and Spanish-speaking countries stand much closer to each other than do Americans. When students act out dialogues in front of the class, their behavior is much more authentic if they get closer to each other and imitate the gestures their teacher has taught them.

The most natural gestures are those the teacher has acquired in the foreign country. Some of the more picturesque gestures, such as signs indicating eating and drinking, have a distinctly lower-class connotation.[1]

The teacher should also try to see foreign films as frequently as possible. In observing the gestures used in the films and in correlating these with the

---

[1] Two references on gestures are Gerard J. Brault, "Kinesics in the Classroom" in *French Review*, Vol. 36 (February 1963), and Jerald Green, *A Gesture Inventory for the Teaching of Spanish* (Philadelphia: Chilton, 1968).

social class of the speakers, the teacher will develop a greater sensitivity of the kinesics of the foreign people.

Some common general gestures are listed below:

(1) Refusal or reprimand (French and Spanish): Wag the index finger of your right hand vigorously to the left and right: *Non, non! Pas de ça!*

(2) Forecasting trouble or embarrassment (French and Spanish): Jiggle vigorously your right hand in front of your chest as though you were burned by a hot iron, suck in air rapidly or make a whistling sound: *Oh, là là! Qu'est-ce que je vais prendre!*   *¡Diós mío! ¿Qué va a ser de mí?*

12.3.6f ORDERING FOODS IN A RESTAURANT

Cut out magazine pictures of foods and paste them on individual cards. If possible, use foreign periodicals such as *Paris-Match, Parents, Arts-Ménagers, Hoy, Mañana,* and others.

After teaching the vocabulary words, the teacher asks individual students what food they would like. As each student responds, the teacher gives him the picture card representing that item:

Teacher:	Qu'est-ce que vous prendrez, Monsieur?
Jean:	Je voudrais de la salade.
Paul:	Je voudrais des pommes de terre.
Teacher:	(Shows picture card of beverages.)
	Et comme boisson?
Sylvie:	Je voudrais du lait.
Pierre:	Je voudrais du vin.
Antoine:	Je voudrais un Coca-Cola.
Thérèse:	Un café, s'il vous plaît.
Teacher:	(Shows picture of desserts.)
Marc:	Je voudrais une glace.
André	Je voudrais une tarte.
Valérie:	Je voudrais un gâteau.
Dominique:	Je voudrais du fromage.

The cards are all collected, and individual students take the teacher's place.

When everyone knows how to order the foods, the teacher creates a restaurant scene in front of the room. Two or three students become customers while the teacher takes the role of the waiter. Later, the students become waiters too.

Variation: Instead of pictures, the teacher may wish to use foreign menus. Many of the airlines and ship lines are cooperative in sending old menus to teachers who request them. Small conversation groups may work with the actual menus. For whole-class work, the teacher can Xerox the menu and make a photostatic Ditto master, or he can put the menu on the opaque projector.

12.3.6g GOING SHOPPING

The teacher makes artificial peso notes (1, 5, 10, 50 pesos) and cardboard centavo coins (5, 10, 25, 50) and gives each student these items. On the chalkboard he writes the sign *Comestibles*.

On a table in front of the room, the teacher places empty crackerboxes and tin cans on which he has pasted imported labels (or labels he has made). He teaches solid and liquid measure: *un kilo = mil gramos, medio kilo = quinientos gramos*. The teacher then explains that a *kilo* is a little more than two pounds. *Un litro* is slightly over a quart. He can present a dialogue such as the following:

El Dependiente:	Buenos días, señorita.
Alicia:	Buenos días, señor.
El Dependiente:	¿En qué puedo servirle?
Alicia:	¿Me da un kilo de azúcar, por favor?
El Dependiente:	Aquí está, señorita.
	(Hands it to her.)
Alicia:	¿Cuánto vale?
El Dependiente:	Veinte pesos con diez centavos.
Alicia:	Aquí los tiene Ud..
El Dependiente:	Muchas gracias.
Alicia:	No hay de qué.
El Dependiente:	Adiós, señorita.
Alicia:	Adiós, señor.

One by one, the students come forward and buy one or two items, paying with their artificial money. (The price is always payable with one or more of the coins or bills that each student holds.)

12.3.6h USING FILMS

Films like *Quelle Chance*[1] can be excellent preparation for role playing. The film should first be shown in its entirety. Then the dialogue is taught and distributed to the class.

The students learn the items sold in a café and how to ask for them:

Garçon, une glace au chocolat, s'il vous plaît.

Garçon, je voudrais un vin blanc.

Garçon, un paquet de Gauloises, s'il vous plaît.

Garçon, l'addition, s'il vous plaît.

Then the teacher creates a café scene in front of the class. Students take various roles.

This film shows people at their different tables in a French café. Each group orders something different. Humorous incidents follow.

[1] Chicago International Film Bureau, No. 1757, 1953.

12.4   ANALYZING AND UNDERSTANDING
THE FOREIGN CULTURE

While students are often quick to notice the existence of differences between American and foreign cultures, it is usually the teacher who must help the students see the reasons behind these differences. This section suggests ways of guiding students in an analysis of another culture.

12.4.1   *The "Socratic" Method*

Photos, films, radio and T.V. programs, and selected readings can be used for discussion. Through carefully planned questioning, the teacher leads the student to an understanding of the values held by the people of a foreign culture.

12.4.1a   CLASSROOM FILMS

(1) Family ties: In the film *Emilio en España*[1] Emilio meets his cousin, Paco, in a hotel lobby. The men embrace.

Teacher: What do you think of this custom?
Student: Wierd.
Teacher: Do you think the Spaniards consider it wierd?
Student: I suppose not.
Teacher: Does this scene tell you anything about the way Spaniards feel toward their relatives? What would Spaniards think of the way American fathers and sons greet each other?

(2) Gauging economic status: In one film of *Parlons Français*,[2] a middle-class family lives in an eighteenth-century house.

Pupil: They must be poor! Such an old house!
Teacher: Does anyone know when the White House was built in Washington?
Pupil: About the beginning of the nineteenth century.
Teacher: Then it is old, isn't it?
Pupils: Yes.
Teacher: Does it look poor to you?
Pupils: No.
Teacher: The house that this family lives in was built in the eighteenth century. The French are proud of their history; they want to preserve their monuments and buildings from the past. Are there places in the United States that are being preserved or restored? What about Williamsburg? Georgetown? Greenfield

---

[1] John Oller and Angel González, Chicago Encyclopedia Britannica Films, 1965.
[2] Heath de Rochemont Corp., Boston, 1961.

Village? In general, do Americans tear down old houses or try to preserve them?

12.4.1b COMMERCIAL FILMS

Foreign movies make the foreign culture accessible to students who have never traveled abroad. If you live in a big city, read the film section of the newspaper to see which movies are being shown. See the movie first before recommending it to your students. If you live in a smaller town, ask the local theaters for advance listings of the films and shorts they plan to run. Local colleges and universities often show a few foreign films every year.

If the foreign film is shown in the original version with subtitles, the students will have an opportunity to hear the language spoken. But even if a dubbed version is shown, the foreign film usually is valuable in presenting a view of the foreign culture.

Before sending the students to the film, tell them to look for certain cultural signs: status symbols, behavior at table, attitude toward children, relations between young people and adults. At the next class period, allow for a short discussion of what the students noticed.

12.4.1c READINGS IN ENGLISH

Impressions of the United States, by Sophie S. Hollander,[1] is a collection of letters from native speaking Spanish students during their year in the United States.

(1) In "Pilar Attends School with the Teen-agers," Pilar is shocked that fourteen-year-old girls date. In her hometown, Córdoba, Spain, girls do not start dating before the age of eighteen.

(2) In "Margot from Colombia Takes a Job," Margot tries to emulate her classmates by getting a part-time job. She quits after the first day because she suddenly realizes that girls of her social class in Colombia do not do manual labor.

The teacher can ask the girls in the class: *Would you have taken the job? Kept it? Why not?*

12.4.1d TEXTBOOK READINGS IN THE FOREIGN LANGUAGE

Often a textbook lesson presents a narrative or dialogue that reveals much information about the value system of a particular country.[2]

---

[1] Sophie S. Hollander, *Impressions of the United States* (New York: Holt, Rinehart and Winston, 1964).
[2] Langellier, Alice and Sylvia N. Levy, *Chez les Français* (New York: Holt, Rinehart and Winston, 1969), pp. 76–77.

(1) Georges and François are upset about arriving late for lunch at their home. Their father expects to have all his family around him when he comes home for lunch.

François: Tes excuses n'arrangent rien. Nous serons en retard pour déjeuner. Et tu connais Papa, le plus juste et le plus sévère des pères. On se met à table à midi. Tant pis pour les retardataires.

Georges: Eh bien, la famille aura commencé à déjeuner. Papa dira, "Pas de hors d'oeuvres pour les retardataires." La belle affaire!

Following the reading of this passage, the teacher leads a discussion on differences between the role of the father in France and in the United States, the importance of dining, and the custom of returning home for lunch.

(2) "Toda una señora" from *Por Esas Españas*[1] is a vignette about an elderly widow living in genteel poverty. She does not travel because she cannot afford first-class accommodations. A rich American couple invites her on a trip. She accepts and is in her glory; she now feels she is where she belongs.

El día de su salida. . . . Doña Cipriana apareció a la puerta. Estaba vestida de negro, con guantes de seda negra, un hermoso abanico . . . y un sombrero parecido a los que llevaba la reina Victoria de Inglaterra. Pasó por entre aquella gente con toda la dignidad de una reina, saludando a derecha e izquierda. . . .

12.4.2 *Culture Capsules* Nelson Brooks language + language learning

Culture capsules are short essays which discuss one characteristic difference between the foreign culture and American culture. At Level One the culture capsule will probably be written in English. At Level Two it may be written in simple sentences in the foreign language.

The culture capsule may be accompanied with photographs or magazine pictures. A prop, such as a metro ticket, a doll in bullfighter dress, or a pair of *Lederhosen*, may also be utilized in the presentation of the culture capsule.

12.4.2a PRESENTING HOLIDAY CUSTOMS

(1) Noël en France et aux Etats-Unis:

Nous sommes en France. C'est le vingt-quatre décembre. Dans le salon il y a une crèche et des santons. Les santons sont de petites figurines qui représentent Marie, Joseph, Jésus, les bergers, une vache et un mouton.

Les enfants français mettent leurs souliers devant la cheminée. Pendant la nuit le Père Noël arrive et met des cadeaux dans chaque soulier.

Dans les maisons américaines il y a un grand arbre de Noël. Les enfants américains mettent leurs bas devant la cheminée. Pendant la nuit Santa Claus descend par la cheminée et met des cadeaux dans chaque bas.

[1] Pedro Villa Fernandez, "Toda una Señora," in *Por Esas Españas* (New York: Holt, Rinehart and Winston, 1965), p. 87.

Visuals: Slide of French children's shoes with presents in them.
           Slide of American fireplace with stockings hanging in front of it.
Props: A French nativity scene (une crèche avec des santons).

(2) La Navidad en Mexico y en los Estados-Unidos

La celebración de la Navidad es una fiesta muy importante en Mexico y en los otros países de habla española. El dieciséis de diciembre empiezan las posadas. Las personas invitadas a una fiesta se dividen en dos grupos. Uno está delante de la puerta y el otro detrás. Los dos grupos cantan los tradicionales villancicos. El grupo que está afuera pide posada al grupo de adentro.

En la sala hay una representación en figuras de barro del Nacimiento. Las figuras representan a José, María, el niño Jesús, los tres reyes Magos, una vaca, y una oveja.

También hay una piñata llena de dulces. La piñata se rompe y los niños comen los dulces.

El veinticuatro de diciembre, a medianoche, todos van a la iglesia. Cuando regresan a su casa toman la cena de Nochebuena.

Los niños no reciben sus regalos hasta el seis de enero, día en que los tres Reyes Magos llegaron a Belén y vieron al Niño Jesús.

En los Estados Unidos las casas están decoradas con muchas luces brillantes. En la sala hay un árbol de Navidad que está cubierto de luces y de toda clase de decoraciones.

Los niños cuelgan sus medias delante de la chimenea. Durante la Nochebuena un hombre bastante viejo que se llama Santa Claus baja la chimenea y llena las medias de regalos y dulces. También pone otros regalos debajo del árbol.

El veinticinco de diciembre, en la mañana, todos corren a la sala, abren sus regalos y se ponen muy contentos.

Visuals: Slide of a Mexican living room with a *piñata* hanging from the
           ceiling.
           Slide of an American living room with a Christmas tree.
Props: A Spanish nativity scene (un nacimiento con las figuras de barro).

12.4.2b   PRESENTING CULTURAL VALUES

(1) The importance of bread in French life:

LE BON PAIN FRANÇAIS[1]

Les Français achètent leur pain chaque jour. Il y a même des Français qui traversent la ville pour acheter le meilleur pain. Les boulangers font du pain frais chaque jour. Le proverbe français affirme "Repas sans pain, repas de rien."

Pendant la Révolution française, la foule parisienne criait "Du pain et la Constitution." A Lyon, on criait "Le pain et l'égalité."

Les Américains disent: "He is as good as gold." Les Français disent: "Il est bon comme le bon pain." Voilà des valeurs très différentes!

---

[1] Henrietta Lendt, unpublished papers, The Ohio State University, 1970.

After reading the story, the teacher can ask questions: *Quelle sorte de pain est-ce que les Américains mangent? Est-ce que les Américains en mangent avec tous leurs repas? Quels proverbes français montrent l'importance du pain dans la vie française?*

(2) Concept of time (Spanish-speaking countries):

El señor Jones, hombre de negocios en Nueva York, quiere venderle su producto a una fábrica en Lima, Perú. El director de la fábrica le da cita para las diez de la mañana.

El señor Jones llega a las diez en punto. La secretaria lo saluda cortésmente y le dice que se siente.

Después de una hora el director llega. El señor Jones, muy irritado, le dice al director que lo había esperado una hora.

El director, muy sorprendido por la reacción del señor Jones, no quiere comprar su producto.

El pobre señor Jones no sabía que era costumbre llegar tarde en los países de habla española.

When the class has read the story, the teacher asks questions: *¿Por qué está irritado el señor Jones? ¿Qué costumbre ignora el señor Jones? Si lo hubiera saludado cortésmente el señor Jones al director, ¿qué habría pasado? ¿Qué habría hecho Ud.?*

12.4.3 *Proverbs and Stories*

12.4.3a PROVERBS

The proverbs can be lettered by students taking art. The posters can then be hung around the foreign language classroom:[1]

(1) To show the French emphasis on individualism:

Chacun pour soi, Dieu pour tous.
Mal prie qui s'oublie.
Chacun mouche son nez.
Chacun prêche pour son saint.
Charité bien ordonnée commence par soi-même.

(2) To show the French feeling of *méfiance:*

La méfiance est la mère de la sûreté.
Quand le renard se met à prêcher, fais attention à ta poule.
Chat échaudé craint l'eau froide.
Le temps est tantôt une mère, tantôt une marâtre.
Bon nageur, bon noyeur.

[1] See Genelle Grant Morain, *French Culture: The Folklore Facet,* ERIC Focus Report No. 9 (1969). Available from MLA/ACTFL Materials Center, 62 Fifth Avenue, New York, N.Y. 10011, for twenty-five cents.

12.4.3b DICHOS Y REFRANES

Spanish speakers feel they can pass judgement on any situation by reciting a pithy saying:[1]

Vale más una onza de práctica que una libra de gramática.

De tal palo, tal astilla.

Dime con quién andas y te diré quién eres.

El que da y quita, con el Diablo se desquita.

12.4.3c ANECDOTES

Northern German efficiency versus Southern German laxness is illustrated in the story of the Bavarian workers in Berlin:[2]

They worked all morning trying to uproot a tree. A Berliner who had been watching them walked over to the tree and pushed it over. Whereupon the Bavarians shouted, "Tjö, mit Gewalt!"

12.4.4 *The Foreign Press*

The teacher selects current articles from *Express, Paris-Match, Mañana, Der Spiegel,* and other magazines and finds the same subjects treated in *Time, Life,* or other American magazines.

12.4.4a COMPARING POINTS OF VIEW

The class is divided into small groups, and each group is given a pair of articles. They list the differences in points of view and try to analyze the reason behind these differences. Each group presents its findings orally to the rest of the class.

12.4.4b CLASS DEBATES

The students use the magazine articles to prepare for class debates. First they decide on a topic; then they make a list of key words and idioms from the articles. One student writes these on a Ditto master so that it may be distributed to everyone in the class. The class is divided into teams, and each member prepares some arguments. The next day, the first half of the period is devoted to organizing the presentation: the teams meet separately, choose a captain, and decide which student will present which points. The second half of the period is the actual debate.

[1] Arthur L. Campa, *Teaching Hispanic Culture Through Folklore,* ERIC Focus Report No. 2 (1968). Available from MLA/ACTFL Materials Center, 62 Fifth Avenue, New York, N.Y. 10011, for twenty-five cents.

[2] Gerhard H. Weiss, *Folktale and Folklore—Useful Cultural Tools for Teachers of German,* ERIC Focus Report No. 6 (1969). Available from MLA/ACTFL Materials Center, 62 Fifth Avenue, New York, N.Y. 10011, for twenty-five cents.

12.4.4c STUDYING CUSTOMS

Articles are selected from the foreign press which discuss table manners, dating customs, family relations, school reforms, and other customs and mores. Each group of students is given a piece of oaktag and an article to work with. The students underline salient features and prepare written comments upon them. The end result of the project is a set of posters which may be placed on the walls of the classroom.

12.5   CONTACTING REPRESENTATIVES OF THE FOREIGN CULTURE

12.5.1   *Foreign Visitors in the Classroom*

Foreign visitors in the classroom make the foreign culture seem closer, more real.

12.5.1a FINDING A VISITOR

Contact the foreign student advisor at a nearby college or university. Check the telephone directory for clubs: *L'Alliance Française, Las Buenas Vecinas, Der Männerchor*. Speak to the minister or priest of churches which have foreign language services. Write to the local radio station that sometimes has foreign language programs. Ask students if they know of members in the community who have visitors from the foreign country or if their fathers through their business know of foreign couples visiting the city. Sometimes the wife of a businessman will be happy to visit an American school and speak to the students. One or two students might take the visitor on a tour of the school when class is over.

12.5.1b INTERVIEWING THE VISITOR IN ADVANCE

Before inviting a foreign person to meet your students, talk with him to determine how well he articulates (in English or in the foreign language), how receptive he would be to answering questions about his country, and whether he meets people easily or not. If he does not meet these criteria, it may be a waste of time to invite him to class.

If he does, ask him what topic he would like to discuss with the class. Then talk with him on this topic and note his vocabulary.

12.5.1c PREPARING THE CLASS

Before the native speaker arrives, describe him to the class and teach them the vocabulary he is likely to use. Ask the students what questions they would like to ask him and help them put the questions into the foreign language.

12.5.2 *Pen Pals*

12.5.2a FINDING THEM

Addresses of agencies that arrange these exchanges are in the professional journals: *French Review, Hispania,* and others.

Write to post offices in foreign cities and ask for names of secondary schools. Then write to the English teachers in those schools asking them if their students would like to exchange letters with yours.

12.5.2b COMMUNICATING

Students can exchange letters, photos, tape recordings, movies, and so on. In the classroom letters can be put in an opaque projector and enjoyed by the entire class.

12.5.2c MEETING THEM LATER

When students travel abroad they can visit their pen pals—an added motivation for keeping up their correspondence.

12.6 TRAVEL ABROAD

Some foreign language teachers take their students abroad during the summer. The following section offers some suggestions for making the trip more profitable, from a cultural point of view.

12.6.1 *Preparing the Students*

During the semester preceding the trip, the students can begin preparing for their experience abroad.

The students meet at least once a week with a person who knows the region. Discussion includes daily life patterns of the people—what pleases them and what offends them: *formules de politesse, fórmulas de cortesía.* The students subscribe to a weekly regional newspaper or to magazines. They read in English or in the foreign language about the region: its geography, history, imports, exports, and folklore.

Each student chooses a topic that interests him. This will become his research project abroad. The teacher suggests themes: school life, recreation, family ties, industries, fashion, T.V. and radio programs, agriculture, and so on.

12.6.2 *Activities Abroad*

Once the group is in the foreign country, some time can be devoted to exploring outward signs of the pattern of daily life. Teams may be assigned to carry out the following projects:

(1) Visit a park for a few hours and keep a record of what takes place, who comes, how long they stay, what they wear, and so on. Take photos and record conversations, if possible.

(2) Keep track of events at an intersection or at another part of the city.

(3) Take a local bus to the end of the line and observe the passengers: their dress, manners, and so on. Visit a city or suburb at the end of the line and take another bus back. Report on your findings.

(4) Select a shopping area in a neighborhood and make a list of the types of stores in the area.

(5) Go to a store and make a notebook of prices of items: stationery supplies, clothes, food, and so on. Compare these with prices in your community in the United States.

(6) Go to a self-service restaurant and copy the menu along with the prices. Take a flash photo of it.

(7) Take a trip to the country on a bus or train. Keep a record of the types of farming equipment and the various crops you see from the window.

Note: Individual students going abroad with other tours may be given a summer project and asked to report on it when they return in the fall.

12.6.3 *Utilizing These Experiences back in the United States*

Students can relate their experiences to their classmates in the following ways:

(1) Make a bulletin board or showcase display of menus, ticket stubs, programs, parts of costumes, figurines, and so on.

(2) Play in the classroom or language club the tape recordings made abroad.

(3) Give a report with slides or photos of the study-tour. Find several students who have been abroad and give an entire assembly program.

APPENDIX

APPENDIX
SAMPLE LESSON
PLANS

A. ELEMENTARY GERMAN CLASS

TEXT: *A-LM German, Level One,* 2d ed. (New York: Harcourt Brace Jovanovich, Inc. 1969), Unit 3, pp. 28–30.[1]

CLASS SIZE: Twenty-five to thirty

CLASS PERIOD: Forty minutes

EQUIPMENT:

1. Overhead projector
2. Chalkboard
3. Two magnets (if chalkboard is magnetized)

MATERIALS:

1. A transparency with line drawings and an overlay with written descriptions (see Chapter 2, pp. 13–15)
2. A paper screen with four slots and four acetate strips (see Chapter 5, p. 79)

PREVIOUS LESSONS: The class has completed Units 1 and 2 and has learned the basic dialogue of Unit 3.

[1] The excerpts from this work are reprinted by permission of Harcourt Brace Jovanovich, Inc.

LESSON OBJECTIVES:

1. To answer questions orally in complete sentences using four present tense forms of *sein* correctly with eighty percent accuracy

2. To form sentences orally using a given number of German words in the proper word order with ninety percent accuracy

ACTIVITIES:

1. Warm up

2. Presentation of four forms of *sein*

   a. Third person singular

   b. Third person plural

   c. First and second persons singular

3. Songs

4. Question/answer drill on *sein*

5. Review of new material

   a. Oral

   b. Written

6. Presentation of German word order

7. Drill on German word order

PROCEDURES:

1. Warm up (five minutes)

   Using familiar vocabulary, ask questions on students' names and where they are.

   Teacher: Guten Tag.

   Wie geht's, Peter? Hans? Inge?

   Wie heißt du?

   Heißt du Karl?

   Wo ist Ilse? Helga? Benno?

2. Presentation of four forms of *sein*

   a. Third person singular

   Teach one form at a time by describing each figure and having the class repeat. Cover the rest of the transparency with a piece of paper.

Teacher: Hans ist groß.

Peter ist klein.

Karl ist traurig.

Benno ist müde.

Jochen ist schmutzig.

Fritz ist krank.

Ask questions about each boy: Wie ist Hans? Peter? Karl?

Point to each drawing and ask, Wie ist er?

Follow the same procedure for line drawings of girls on the second section of the transparency.

Describe each figure and have the class repeat.

Teacher: Helga ist groß.

Inge ist klein.

Ilse ist traurig.

Ursel ist müde.

Monika ist schmutzig.

Gisela ist krank.

Ask questions about each girl: Wie ist Helga? Wie ist sie?

b. Third person plural

Point to both sections of the transparency and describe two people.

Teacher: Hans und Helga sind groß.

Peter und Inge sind klein.

Karl und Ilse sind traurig.

Ask questions: Wie groß sind sie? Wie sind sie?

c. First and second person singular

Introduce the first and second person singular in a conversation.

Teacher: Ich bin müde.

Bist du müde, Karl?

(Antworte mit „ja!")

Karl: Ja, ich bin müde.

Teacher: Bist du groß, Hans?

Hans: Ja, ich bin groß.

Teacher: Bist du klein, Inge?

Inge: Ja, ich bin klein.

3. Songs

Rounds:

„Mein Hut, der hat drei Ecken"
(My Hat, It Has Three Corners)

Mein Hut, der hat drei Ecken,
Drei Ecken hat mein Hut,
Und hat er nicht drei Ecken,
Dann ist es nicht mein Hut!

„O wie wohl ist mir am Abend"
(Oh, How Lovely is the Evening)

O wie wohl ist mir am Abend,
Mir am Abend,
Wenn zur Ruh,
Die Glocken lauten,
Bim, bam, bim, bam.
Glocken lauten,
Bim, bam, bim, bam, bim, bam!

4. Question/answer drill on *sein*

Draw a two-story house with kitchen, livingroom, cellar, garden, and garage on the chalkboard.

Cut out paper figures of a boy and girl, Hans and Helga, and using magnets, place them singly, then together in the various rooms, the garden, and the garage. Describe them in German and have the class repeat.

Teacher: Hans ist in der Küche.

Hans und Helga sind im Garten.

Ask questions: Wo ist Hans?   Wo sind Hans und Helga?

5. Review of new material

   a. Oral

      Review the transparency with adjectives, using the overlay for each picture. Pronounce each sentence and have the class repeat.

      Er ist groß, klein, traurig, müde . . .

      Sie ist groß, klein, traurig, müde . . .

      Sie sind groß, klein, traurig, müde . . .

   b. Written

      Distribute Dittoed sheets of the new material and call on individuals to read it.

      (1) Bist du müde, Peter?
          Ja, ich bin müde.

      (2) Hans ist in der Küche.
          Helga ist im Wohnzimmer.

      (3) Hans und Helga sind im Garten.

6. Presentation of German word order

   Use strips of acetate over a paper grid (see Chapter 5, p. 79).

Position 1	Position 2	Position 3	Position 4
DIE BEIDEN	BIN	JETZT	DAS ZIMMER
ICH	PUTZEN	HEUTE	TENNIS
ER	SPIELEN	MORGEN	IM GARTEN
WIR	IST		DAS AUTO
SIE	PUTZT		IN DER STUBE
	SPIELT		FUSSBALL
	SUCHT		DAS RAD
	SPIELE		BENNO
			IN DER GARAGE

Move each slit up or down over the little windows to show one word in each position.

Ask for volunteers to read the sentences.

Example: | ICH | | SPIELE | | HEUTE | | TENNIS |

Then switch the strips so that the third position becomes the first and vice versa, but always be sure that the second position is never changed.

Example: | MORGEN | | PUTZEN | | WIR | | DAS ZIMMER |

7. Drill on German word order

Scramble the words by taking the paper grid off the transparency, leaving the four strips of acetate entirely uncovered.

Ask the class to form as many sentences orally as possible.

HOMEWORK:

Ask the class to make a drawing of each of the following German sentences and to copy the sentences beneath their pictures.

Example: Hans und Fritz sind im Boot.

1. Das Auto ist in der Garage.
2. Ich bin im Keller.
3. Ilse und Monika sind traurig.
4. Peter ist im Wohnzimmer.
5. Gisela ist in der Küche.
6. Jochen und Karl sind groß.

FOLLOW-UP FOR THE NEXT DAY

LESSON OBJECTIVE: To write complete sentences from dictation the correct present tense forms of *sein* with ninety percent accuracy.

ACTIVITIES:

1. Warm up

2. Guessing game

3. Presentation of the remaining forms of *sein*

   a. First person plural

   b. Second person plural (informal)

   c. Second person plural (formal)

4. Drill on all forms of *sein*

5. Pattern drills on tape

6. Dictation

7. Dialogue review

PROCEDURES:

1. Warm up (five minutes)

   a. Personal questions using the verb *sein*:

      Bist du müde?   klein?   groß?

   b. Questions on transparency (adjectives):

      Wie sind Hans und Helga?

   During the warm up, several students may put their homework drawings on the chalkboard.

2. Guessing game (five minutes)

   Ask the class to look at the chalkboard and guess which German sentence is illustrated by the drawings. Those who guess correctly may go to the chalkboard and write their answers.

3. Presentation of the remaining forms of *sein* (five minutes)

   a. First person plural

   b. Second person plural (informal)

   c. Second person plural (formal)

4. Drill on all forms of *sein* (three minutes)

   Use figures on flashcards (see Chapter 3).

5. Pattern drills on tape (five minutes)

   See Section 6, p. 31 in *AL-M German, Level One.*

6. Dictation (ten minutes)

   Use the overhead projector (see Chapter 7).

7. Dialogue review (seven minutes)

Use tapes and visuals. See *AL-M German, Level One*, p. 27.

HOMEWORK: Ask the class to bring in magazine cutouts illustrating each line of basic dialogue on page 27. The students will exchange them and write the lines of dialogue under each picture.

B. INTERMEDIATE SPANISH CLASS

TEXT: Brenes et al, *Learning Spanish the Modern Way, Book 2*, 2d ed. (New York: McGraw-Hill, Webster Division, 1967).[1]

CLASS SIZE: Twenty-five to thirty

CLASS PERIOD: Fifty minutes

EQUIPMENT:

1. Chalkboard

2. Overhead projector

3. Tape recorder

MATERIALS:

1. A tape recording of the narrative "El niño al que se le murió el amigo," p. 137

2. Blank transparencies

3. A set of flashcards with a pronoun on each

4. Toys or magazine cutouts of toys—marbles, a truck, a pistol, and a watch

5. Visuals to demonstrate the use of the subjunctive (Section I b)

PREVIOUS LESSONS: The teacher has presented the subjunctive and drilled the regular and irregular verbs (pp. 138–39).

LESSON OBJECTIVE: To change sentences from the present indicative to the present subjunctive, using the verbs that have been drilled in class, with ninety percent accuracy.

[1] The excerpts from this work are reprinted by permission of McGraw-Hill.

ACTIVITIES:

Use the subjunctive at all times.

1. Grammar review

    a. Warm up

    b. Pictorial stimuli

    c. Flashcards

    d. Written pattern drill

    e. Game—a relay race

2. New material

    a. Listening comprehension and word study

    b. Reading exercise

    c. Writing exercise

PROCEDURES:

1. Grammar review of Lesson 20, pp. 138–41 (twenty-five minutes)

    a. Warm up

    Students decide which actions they wish their classmates to perform.

    Teacher (looking at Pedro): Quiero que Pedro vaya a la puerta.

    (Pedro performs the action.)

    Maria, ¿qué quieres que haga Juan?

    Maria: Quiero que Juan escriba su nombre en la pizarra.

    (Juan performs the action.)

    Teacher: Carlos, ¿qué quieres que haga Teresa?

    Carlos: Quiero que Teresa salga.

    (Teresa performs the action.)

    b. Pictorial stimuli

    Show a series of visuals depicting two actions, one of a child behaving in a certain way, and the other of his mother hoping he will behave in another way.

    Teacher: ¡Miren Uds. este cuadro!

Teacher (pointing to picture on the left):

    Aquí está Felipe.

    Felipe no dice adiós.

    La mamá espera que Felipe diga adiós.

    ¿Que espera la mamá?

Student: La mamá espera que Felipe diga adiós.

Teacher (pointing to picture on the left):

    El niño no es bueno.

    ¿Qué quiere la mamá?

Student: La mamá quiere que el niño sea bueno.

Teacher (pointing to picture on the left):

Luis no va a la escuela.

¿Que manda papá?

Student: Papá manda que Luis vaya a la esuela.

c. Flashcards (with pronouns)

Give a model sentence and ask the class to change it as each pronoun appears.

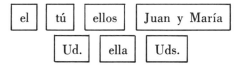

(1) Teacher: Prefiero que Ud. venga.

(Class repeats.)

Flashcard: tú

Class: Prefiero que tu vengas.

(One by one the other cards are shown.)

(2) Teacher: Insisto en que ella hable.

(Class repeats.)

Flashcard: ellos

Class: Insisto en que ellos hablen.

d. Written pattern drill

Dictate a model sentence for the class to write. Then give a one-word cue so that the class will rewrite the sentence making the necessary changes. One student writes his dictation on the overhead projector in front of the class. (The projector lamp is off.) The teacher corrects this example and then turns on the projector so that the class can see the correct answers.

Teacher dictates:	Students write:
Juan teme que tú lo sepas.	(same)
ella	Juan teme que ella lo sepa.
ellos	Juan teme que ellos lo sepan.
María	Juan teme que María lo sepa.
Ud.	Juan teme que Ud. lo sepa.
Uds.	Juan teme que Uds. lo sepan.
Yo	Juan teme que yo lo sepa.

e. Game—a relay race

Conduct the race with the boys against the girls (see Chapter 3).

Write seven pronouns on the chalkboard and ask seven boys to stand under each one.

yo   nosotros   el   tú   ellos   ella   ellas

At the signal to begin, the boys write a sentence using these pronouns in the subjunctive. As each one finishes, he moves to the next section and writes a sentence using that pronoun. The last boy to the right takes the place of the boy on the extreme left. All continue to revolve until the board is filled with sentences.

Example: yo

El quiere que yo salga.

Then the girls take their turn.

The team that has the largest number of correct sentences wins.

2. New material—the narrative "El niño al que se le murió el amigo," p. 137 (twenty-five minutes)

a. Listening comprehension and word study

Before playing the tape, ask the class two questions.

(1) ¿Quién se murió?
(2) ¿Qué dijo la madre al fin del cuento?

Before playing the tape the second time, ask the class two more questions.

(1) ¿Qué juguetes tenía el niño?
(2) ¿Qué hacía el niño toda la noche?

Continue the exercise with a word study.

(1) Give the Spanish word for each toy as you pick it up and have the class repeat.

Es un camión, un reloj, una pistola.

Then take each toy and question the class.

¿Qué es esto?

(2) Draw on the chalkboard two figures to illustrate growth.

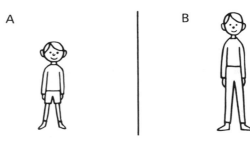

A   B

¡Miren Uds. el cuadro B!   Juan ha crecido, ¿verdad?

(3) Give the class another interpretation of *crecido*.

Otra interpretación de crecido es más viejo o más hombre.

(4) Review the parts of the body by pointing to them.

¿Qué son?

Son las manos, las rodillas, los codos, los brazos.

b. Reading exercise

Let the class read the narrative silently. Then, for today's group work, divide the class into three sections.

Group A reads fluently. Their assignment is a guided composition on the narrative.

Group B reads at a normal speed. Their assignment is to answer the textbook questions: p. 10, a; p. 160, b and c.

Group C reads slowly and with difficulty. The teacher spends the last ten minutes with them explaining sections of the story and answering questions. Their assignment is to complete a worksheet containing true/false and completion exercises.

c. Writing exercise

Worksheets

Group A (guided composition):

Write the narrative in the first person, as though it happened to you, and use the past tense.

 (1) Al levantarse, ¿adónde fue Ud.?
 (2) ¿A quien buscó Ud.?
 (3) ¿Qué le dijo su madre?
 (4) ¿Por qué volverá su amigo?
 (5) ¿Por qué no quería Ud. entrar a cenar?
 (6) ¿Comó pasó Ud. la noche?
 (7) ¿Qué hizo Ud. con los juguetes?
 (8) ¿Cuándo volvió Ud. a casa?
 (9) ¿Qué le dijo su madre?
(10) ¿Qué se le compró?

Group B (see above)

Group C

(1) Read the following sentences. Write T if the sentence is true, F if it is false. Rewrite all the false sentences and make them true.

Samples:

(a) Una mañana el niño fue a buscar al amigo.
(b) La madre le dijo, "El amigo no se murió."
(c) El amigo volverá porque los juguetes están allí.
(d) Su mamá lo llamó y el niño entró a cenar.

(2) Fill in the missing words.

Samples:

(a) El niño fue a _____ al amigo.
(b) El reloj no _____.
(c) Pasó buscándolo toda la _____.
(d) "¡Cuánto ha _____ este niño!"

FOLLOW-UP FOR THE NEXT DAY

ACTIVITIES:

1. Warm up

2. Check assignments

3. Grammar study

4. Presentation of geography and history lesson, "La Otra América," pp. 145–47

5. Group work on "La Otra América"

PROCEDURES:

1. Warm up (five minutes)

   Discuss the narrative, p. 137. Hold a question and answer period.

2. Check assignments (ten minutes)

   Group A: Sit with them and ask one or two individuals to read their compositions.

   Group B: Distribute a Dittoed sheet with the answers to the questions. Students check their papers.

   Group C: Put answers on the overhead projector. Students check their papers. When the students are finished with one transparency, they put on the second.

3. Grammar study

   a. Generalization on the subjunctive (five minutes)

   b. Dehydrated sentences, using the overhead projector, on the present progressive, p. 145 (five minutes)

   Juan está bajando.

   /niños/estar/correr/

4. Presentation of the geography and history lesson, "La Otra América," p. 145–47 (ten minutes)

   Use a map of South America.

5. Group work on "La Otra América" (fifteen minutes)

   The entire class reads the lesson, pp. 145–47.

   The teacher meets with Groups A and B to discuss the reading.

HOMEWORK:

Group A: Students are to read supplementary articles on South America from *El Sol* and do the exercises following them.

Group B: Students choose one country in South America and write about it as though they lived there. Distribute a worksheet with guided questions such as, What nation is north of your country? South? East? West? What rivers are in your country? What are the major cities in your country?

Group C: Students receive a blank map of South America and are asked to fill in the places that were mentioned in the lesson.

C. ADVANCED FRENCH CLASS

TEXT: Bauer, C., et al, *Le français, Lire, Parler et Ecrire* (New York: Holt, Rinehart and Winston, 1964, 1971). The material in this book is based on the 1964 edition, pp. 6–7.[1]

CLASS SIZE: Twenty-five to thirty

CLASS PERIOD: Fifty minutes

EQUIPMENT:

1. Overhead projector

2. Tape recorder

3. Record player

4. Slide projector

MATERIALS:

1. A transparency with the outline of the state of Texas, drawn to the same scale as a map of France, and an overlay with the outline of France in red and the following cities: Paris, Lille, Saint-Brieuc, Tarascon, Avignon, and Marseille

2. The record *Songs and Dances of France* #491 (Lorraine Music Co., 23-80 48th St., Long Island City, New York)

3. A tape recording (made by a native speaker if possible) of the paraphrases found in Section I b

4. A Dittoed sheet of the paraphrases in Section I b

[1] The excerpts from this work are reprinted by permission of Holt, Rinehart and Winston.

5. Slides of la Cannebière, le Vieux Port, Provençal costumes, la pétanque, red tile roofs, Breton costumes, Breton architecture, Saint-Brieuc (if possible)

ACTIVITIES:

1. Presentation of reading lesson

   a. Summary

   b. New vocabulary

   c. Grammar review

2. Group and individual work

PROCEDURES:

1. Presentation of reading lesson (twenty-five minutes)

   a. Summary of passage with books closed (fifteen minutes)

Teacher: La France n'est pas gigantesque comme les Etats-Unis. Voici la carte du Texas (transparency and overhead projector). Et voici la carte de la France (overlay). Lequel des deux est le plus grand, le Texas ou la France?

Student: Le Texas.

Teacher: Très bien.

(Remove map of Texas and keep map of France on the projector.)

Teacher: Aux Etats-Unis les distances sont grandes, mais les habitants se ressemblent d'une région à une autre. Il est par exemple difficile de distinguer un habitant de Baltimore d'un citoyen de Los Angeles.

En France il y a une grande différence entre l'habitant de Marseille et celui de Saint-Brieuc.

(Point to these cities.)

Marseille est situé en Provence. Saint-Brieuc se trouve en Bretagne.

Voici quelques vues de Marseille.

(Show le Vieux Port and la Cannebière.)

Qu'est-ce que vous voyez sur les diapositives?

Class: La mer, des bateaux . . .

Teacher: Bien. Maintenant, regardez ces vues de la région. Décrivez les toits.

(Show slides of Provence.)

Student 1: Ils sont rouges.

Student 2: Ce sont des toits de _____?

Teacher: De tuiles.

Use the same procedure for slides of Brittany. Show slides or dolls with Provençal or Breton costumes.

Teacher: Les français ne portent plus ces costumes tous les jours, mais on les voit quelquefois dans certains spectacles folkloriques. La musique de la Bretagne est différente de celle de la Provence.

(Play a selection from the record.)

Quels instruments entendez-vous?

Student 1: Un tambour et un fifre. (Provence)

Teacher: Bien. En Bretagne on joue de la cornemuse. Pourquoi est-ce qu'il y a de si grandes différences entre les régions françaises?

Student 1: La France est un pays ancien.

Student 2: Autrefois il n'y avait pas beaucoup de moyens de communication entre les régions.

Teacher: Oui. Au treizième siècle ces régions étaient presque des pays indépendants, avec leur propre gouvernement et leurs traditions.

Même aujourd'hui les gens qui sont nés dans le même quartier de Lille, Marseille ou Saint-Brieuc considèrent les autres français un peu comme des étrangers. On appelle cette sorte de particularisme "l'esprit de clocher." Voici un clocher.

(Draw a belfrey on the chalkboard.)

Le clocher symbolise le village ou le petit quartier où tous les gens passent leur existence. Ils sont unis par des liens étroits.

b. New vocabulary (seven minutes)

Distribute a Dittoed sheet with several difficult sentences taken from the reading. The new words and expressions are underlined.

Ask the class to read the sentences silently.

Play a tape recording with easier words, those already known by the class, that replace the more difficult new ones.

(1) Sheet: Quand on regarde la carte des Etats-Unis, on a de la peine à comprendre. . . .

    Tape: Quand on regarde la carte des Etats-Unis, on comprend difficilement. . . .

(2) Sheet: Chacun a son caractère bien tranché.

    Tape: Chacun a une personnalité bien marquée.

(3) Sheet: Cet amour des siens.

    Tape: Cet amour de sa famille.

(4) Sheet: Ce n'est pas par hasard si l'émission "Intervilles" a remporté un triomphe à la télévision.

    Tape: Ce n'est pas par hasard si le programme "Intervilles" a remporté un triomphe à la télévision.

(5) Sheet: Et par surcroît, c'était fort joyeux.

    Tape: Et de plus, c'était très joyeux.

(6) Sheet: L'esprit de clocher est détestable quand il est un esprit de morgue et de dédain.

    Tape: L'esprit de clocher est détestable quand il est un esprit de supériorité désagréable.

(7) Sheet: Les gens qui le pratiquent sont repliés sur eux-mêmes sans rien connaître du monde extérieur.

(8) Sheet: Il est fécond au contraire, et plein de ressources quand les clochers, si j'ose cette image hardie. . . .

    Tape: Il est productif au contraire, et plein de ressources quand les clochers, si j'ose utiliser cette image audacieuse. . . .

Distribute a second Dittoed sheet with the original sentences and their paraphrases. Give the class several minutes to review them.

c. Grammar review (three minutes)

Use subjunctive sentences from the text as models for pattern drills.

(1) Modèle: Le professeur dit, "Il faut que les Marseillais aient un accent." Vous allez répéter la phrase. Ensuite le professeur dit "vous." Vous dites, "Il faut que vous ayez un autre accent."

Commencez.

Le Professeur	Les Elèves
Il faut que vous ayez un autre accent.	(Repeat.)
les Lillois	Il faut que les Lillois aient un autre accent.
les Norvégiens	Il faut que les Norvégiens aient un autre accent.
nous	Il faut que nous ayons un autre accent.
tu	Il faut que tu aies un autre accent.

(2) Modèle: Le professeur dit, "Cela n'empêche pas que l'on s'aime bien." Les elèves répètent. Le professeur dit, "On s'amuse." Les elèves disent, "Cela n'empêche pas que l'on s'amuse."

Commencez.

Le Professeur	Les Elèves
On va au cinéma.	Cela n'empêche pas que l'on aille au cinéma.
On fait son travail.	Cela n'empêche pas que l'on fasse son travail.
On sort ensemble.	Cela n'empêche pas que l'on sorte ensemble.
On boit quelque chose.	Cela n'empêche pas que l'on boive quelque chose.

2. Group and individual work (twenty-five minutes)

For today's lesson, divide the class into three groups.

Group A will prepare a debate. Ask those students who are fluent and those who like to speak French to join this group.

Group B will write a composition. Ask those students who are able to write compositions and who like to write them to join this group.

Group C will answer oral and written questions on the reading selection. These students will probably have less skill in speaking and writing than those in Groups A and B.

a. Group A—Debate

See Chapter 5.

Distribute the following worksheet:

(1) Lisez les pages 6 et 7.

(2) Proposition: "L'esprit de clocher" est typiquement américain aussi. Il faut prendre un parti. Etes-vous pour ou contre? Paul Johnson va organiser les équipes. Dites-lui quelle équipe vous avez choisie. Les membres de chaque équipe vont exposer leurs arguments.

(3) Vocabulaire:

la compétition

une société industrielle

une population mobile

l'influence de la télévision

l'individualisme (individualiste)

"Chacun pour soi"

l'esprit des pionniers

nos ancêtres

le systeme d'entraide (aide mutuelle)

l'esprit civique

l'amitié

les voisins

(The teacher may supply other vocabulary when requested.)

(4) Distribute questions for both sides of the argument to guide the debators.

Est-ce que le rythme de la vie actuelle nous laisse le temps de créer des liens d'amitie?

Est-il vrai que les américains sont si sociables qu'ils se font des amis très facilement?

Est-ce que vous seriez triste de quitter vos amis si vos parents décidaient de déménager?

Est-ce que vous êtes indifférént à la ville ou au quartier que vous habitez?

b. Group B—Written composition

See Chapter 7.

Distribute the following worksheet:

(1) Lisez les pages 6 et 7.

(2) Imaginez que vous êtes en France et que vous écrivez une lettre à un de vos camarades américains. Dans votre lettre d'environ cent mots vous décrivez "l'esprit de clocher" et les différences régionales que vous avez trouvées en France. Suivez les directives en basant vos phrases sur la lecture des pages 6 et 7.

Cher/chère ———————————,

Expliquez à votre camarade la différence qu'il y a entre les distances en Amérique et en France.

Dites-lui dans quelles circonstances les français éprouvent un grand sentiment pour la patrie.

Dites-lui comment s'appelle l'autre patriotisme local et les adjectifs qu'on emploie pour le décrire.

Expliquez-lui comment l'esprit de clocher ressemble à l'attitude des membres d'une famille les uns envers les autres.

Décrivez-lui les différences qui existent entre les Marseillais et les Lillois.

Expliquez-lui l'importance d'un match de football entre l'équipe de Lille et celle de Marseille.

Dites-lui le nom d'une émission qui a remporté un triomphe à la télévision et expliquez-lui pourquoi.

Expliquez-lui dans quelles circonstances l'esprit de clocher est détestable.

Dites-lui ce qu'il y a de bon dans l'esprit de clocher (quand il est fécond).

Bien à toi,

c. Group C—Oral and written work

Spend fifteen minutes with the group and read each paragraph aloud. Explain difficult words, giving synonyms, antonyms, and definitions in French or English. Finally, ask questions on each paragraph.

Sample (the first two paragraphs)

Read:

Quand on regarde la carte des Etats-Unis, on a de la peine à comprendre ce qu'un habitant de Baltimore peut avoir de commun avec un citoyen de Los Angeles. Près de trois mille kilomètres séparent leurs deux villes. La distance est moindre de Paris à Moscou.

Pourtant, l'homme de Baltimore et celui de Los Angeles sont unis par des liens étroits. Ils appartiennent à une même nation, ils jouissent d'une même liberté, ils payent les même impôts. Si les Etats-Unis font la guerre, ils combattent sous le même uniforme.

Teacher: Regardez la première phrase. Cherchez un synonyme de citoyen.

Student: Habitant.

Teacher: Très bien.

Teacher: Combien de kilomètres séparent Baltimore et Los Angeles?

Teacher: Prononcez "des liens étroits." Cela veut dire "by close bonds." Par quoi est-ce que l'homme de Baltimore et celui de Los Angeles sont unis?

Student: Par des liens étroits.

Teacher: A quoi est-ce qu'ils appartiennent?

Qu'est-ce qu'ils payent?

Si les Etats-Unis font la guerre, qu'est-ce ces hommes portent?

Distribute the same questions, this time in written form, to be completed for homework. The students may start answering them during the last ten minutes of the hour.

Spend the last ten minutes with Group A, listening to their arguments for tomorrow's debate, supplying vocabulary, and correcting errors.

Do not work with Group B at all today. Spend fifteen minutes with them tomorrow on their compositions. Several compositions will be put in the opaque projector and read collectively.

HOMEWORK:

Group A: The students have two notebooks. They are to do the following assignment in one of the notebooks to hand in the next day.

While the teacher corrects this assignment, he can give another one to be written in the second notebook.

Exposez par écrit cinq arguments en faveur de votre position et soumettez-les moi demain. Soyez prêts à les présenter oralement en classe.

Minimum acceptable performance: Each student should present his arguments with eighty percent accuracy.

Group B: Complétz votre lettre pour demain.

Minimum acceptable performance: Each student should attain ninety-five percent accuracy in spelling and grammar.

Group C: Ecrivez des réponses aux questions.

Minimum acceptable performance: Each student should answer with ninety percent accuracy in spelling and eighty percent accuracy in grammar.

FOLLOW-UP FOR THE NEXT DAY

PROCEDURES:

1. Collect notebooks from Group A.

   Have them corrected by the following day.

2. Debate (twenty-five minutes)

   The students present their arguments. If they cannot recall a word or have difficulty finishing a sentence, the teacher may help them and members of their team.

   Do not interrupt the debaters to correct their French. Instead, take careful notes to use for discussion during the last ten minutes of the class period.

3. Correct compositions for the entire class (fifteen minutes)

   Members of Group B put their compositions on the opaque projector. Errors are corrected collectively.

4. Group work (ten minutes)

   Group A: Discuss with the students the major errors in grammar, vocabulary, and pronunciation that were made during the debate.

   Group B: Students make corrections on their compositions.

   Group C: Students check the answers to their homework assignment with the overhead projector.

INDEX

INDEX

Ability grouping, 24–25
Adjectives
  agreement of, 147, 228–29
  demonstrative, 93
  forming nouns from, 127
  in German, 127
  possessive, 92, 172, 174
Adverbs, 167
Alphabet teaching, 56
Antonyms, 116
Asher, James J., 143n.
Asterisks, 120
Audio-visual aids, 12–18

Brault, Gerard J., 260n.
Bulletin board, 252, 271

Calendar, use of, 98, 251
Chalkboard, 35, 49, 58, 70–71, 76, 87,
  100, 106, 109, 111, 118, 154, 163,
  175, 225
Charades, 142
Classroom management, 38–39
Clauses
  dependent and independent, 167–68
  infinitive, 104–06
  relative, 106–07
Clock face, 118, 144, 251

Club activities, 237, 249, 256–57
  See also Foreign visitors; Travel
  abroad
Cognates, 62, 121–26
Color coding, 91, 106, 111, 119
Colloquial speech, in listening compre-
  hension, 156–59
  See also Listening comprehension
Comic strip cutouts, 240
Comparative, 175, 230–31
Complements, 101–07
Compositions, 36, 86
  free composition, 238–41
  guided composition, 232–34
Compound words, in German, 127
  See also Word families
Conditional, 101, 167–68
Construction paper techniques, 119
Contracts, student, 10
Conversation, 25, 126, 161, 177–88, 234
Cooking, 249
Copying, 86, 217–23
Correcting papers, 88
Criterion-referenced tests, 36–37
  See also Testing
Crossword puzzle, 98, 220–22
Cue cards, 13, 69, 82, 83, 84, 91, 97,
  100, 101, 103, 104–05, 108, 109,
  118, 138, 144, 162, 165, 171, 191,
  192–93, 229–30

Culture, 204, 245–71
Culture capsules, 265–67

Dances, 188, 256–57
Dating customs, 253, 259
Debates, 185–86, 268
Deductive approach, 68–73
Definite articles, 92
Definitions, 151
Dehydrated sentences, 232
Dialogue, 46, 143, 161–62, 165, 167, 218, 234
  change to narrative, 233
  See also Directed dialogue
Dictation, 223–27
Digits. *See* Numbers
Direct objects. *See* Objects
Directed dialogue, 85, 100, 165–66
Discipline, 39
Discourse, direct and indirect, 176–77, 230
Disick, Renée S., 20n.
Dittos, 12, 35, 79, 88, 119, 149, 156, 191, 225
Double registration, 8
Drama, teaching of, 213–15
Dramatics. *See* Role playing; Games
Drawing techniques, 16, 107, 117, 119, 120, 123, 132, 163, 175, 218–19, 231

English, use of, in foreign language classroom, 117, 145, 231, 238, 264
Equipment, audio-visual, 17–18

Felt board. *See* Flannel board
Fiction, teaching of, 212–13
Fiestas, 187–88, 256
Film strips, 182
Films, 262, 263–64
Flannel board (Felt board), 15, 58, 78, 104, 107, 108, 141, 163–64, 192
Flash cards, 13, 69, 82, 83, 84, 91, 97, 100, 101, 103, 104–05, 108, 109, 118, 138, 144, 162, 165, 171, 191, 192–93, 229–30
Flexible scheduling, 6

Foreign visitors, 269
Future, immediate, 105, 123, 148–49

Games, 31, 95, 98, 100, 101, 107, 131, 142, 144, 152, 176, 181, 231, 247–48
Gender, 123, 124–25, 147
Generalizations
  cultural, 253, 259
  grammatical, 73–76
  See also Socratic method
Gestures, 116, 150, 260–61
Gilliam, B. J., 210n.
Graded readers, 203
Grading, 35–36
Grammar, 64–112
Green, Jerald, 260n.
Greetings, 258–59
Grouping, 9, 22–26, 33, 85, 119, 183–84, 205–06

Hand signals, 49, 116
  See also Gestures; Physical response
Holidays, 265–66
  See also Fiestas
Homework, 32–36, 38, 181

Ideograms, 164–65, 231
Imperative, 111–12, 174, 194
Independent activities, 26, 87, 206–07
Indirect objects. *See* Objects
Individualized instruction, 9, 10, 22–26, 61, 206–07
Inductive approach, 73–79
Inference
  in reading, 197
  in teaching vocabulary, 129–30
Infinitive clauses. *See* Clauses
Interest level, 21, 25
Interrogative sentences, 109–10, 228
Intonation practice, 50, 52

Jackson, Thomas W., 218n.

Laboratory, 28, 61, 81, 194, 215, 224–25

Learning packets, 10
Lesson planning, 19–22, 24
Letter writing, 236–38
Listening comprehension, 137–59
Listening discrimination, 51–53, 62
Lists, of vocabulary, 130
Literature, teaching of, 207–15

Magazine pictures, use of, 102, 115, 172–73, 181, 219–20, 230–31, 252
Magazines, 186–87, 250
Magnetic board, 15, 58, 104, 141
Map, 170–71, 175, 177, 229, 247–48, 251, 253–54
Mastery, teaching for, 5
Metaphrasing, 198
Minimal pairs, 51, 139
Modular scheduling, 6
Morain, Genelle, 267n.
Movies, 159
Music, 31, 54, 55, 72, 100, 103, 111, 187–88, 248, 256–57

Narratives, 233–36, 239
Negative sentences, 110–11
Norm-referenced tests, 36–37
    See also Testing
Notebooks, 33, 119
Noun markers, 146–47
Noun phrases, 90–96
Number, grammatical, 146, 147
Numbers (digits), 138

Objectives, 20
Objects, direct and indirect, 102–03, 167
Opaque projector, 220, 236, 253
Oral drills, 27, 29, 35, 80–84, 85, 177, 181–83
Overhead projector, 13–15, 35, 70, 78, 81, 87, 96, 100, 102, 111, 118, 127, 170, 173, 190–91, 224, 226, 230, 254–55

Pacing, 24
Painting (fine arts), 249

Paired sentences, 73–76
Panel discussions, 186
Paradigms, 72
Paraphrasing, 128, 157–58, 197–98
Partitive, 93–94, 223
Passé composé, versus imperfect, 99
Pattern drills, 80–84, 86, 228–29
Pen pals, 253, 270
Performance objectives, 20
Periodicals, 186–87, 202, 250
Phonetic transcription, 59
Physical response, 29, 53, 112, 116, 140, 143, 168–69, 260–61
Pocket charts, 16, 193–94
Poetry, 209–12
    pronunciation practice, 55
Politzer, Robert L., 47n.
Por versus para, 129
Posters, 13, 59, 77, 83, 88, 91, 94, 99, 100, 106, 143, 144, 175–76, 181, 251, 252–53, 269
Prefixes, 122
Prepositional phrases, 104
Preterite, 224
    versus imperfect, 99
Programmed material, 10
Projects, 34, 249, 250–52
Pronouns
    demonstrative, 95
    interrogative, 176, 228
    object, 148
    personal, 148
    possessive, 94
    relative, 230
Pronunciation, 43–63, 122
Props, 70, 83, 93, 104, 115, 174, 239
Proverbs, 267–68

Question-answer techniques, 23, 84–86, 154, 166–67, 169–72, 178–79, 194, 220
    multiple-choice, 155

Radio broadcasts, 17, 150, 151, 254
Readers, 203, 264–65
Reading aloud, 151, 194
Reading comprehension, 189–215

Reading exercises, 196–200, 204–05
  cultural, 264
Recombined narratives, 195
Recorded speech, 17, 26–30, 45, 61, 153, 156, 215, 224–25, 271
Reichmann, Eberhard, 48n.
Relative clauses. *See* Clauses
Remedial work, 60–63, 88
Reports, student, 248, 271
Retention, of vocabulary, 118–21
Role playing, 179–80, 183, 257–62

Salutations, 236
  See also Greetings
Savoir versus *connaître*, 133
Scheduling, 6–8
Scholastic series, 186
Seelye, H. Ned, 246n.
Seibert, L., 128n.
Ser versus *estar*, 131–32
Shopping, 262
Skits. *See* Role playing
Slides, 115, 182, 187, 266
Smith, Alfred N., 208n., 221n.
Socratic method, 263
Songs, 54, 55, 72, 100, 103, 111, 187–88, 256–57
Sound-symbol correspondences, 55–60
Speaking, 160–88
Speech correction, 47–49, 60–63
Spelling, 121–23
Sports, 187
Subject and object, in German, 149
Subjunctive, 100
Suffixes, 122
Supplementary materials, 11, 12–18, 65–68
Symbols, 117, 119
Synonyms, 116, 129

Table manners, 259–60
Tapes, 149, 224–25
Team teaching, 8
Testing, 36–38
  criterion-referenced tests, 36–37
  norm-referenced tests, 36–37
  recording tests, 17, 27
  standardized tests, 200–01
Textbook, use of, 65
Timing, in planning lessons, 22, 24
Tongue twisters, 54
Tracking, 7
Transcriptions, 158–59
Translation, 117, 145, 231
Transparencies, 13, 14, 58, 70, 78, 81, 87, 96, 100, 102, 111, 118, 127, 170, 173, 190–91, 224, 226, 230, 254–55
Travel abroad, 270–71
True-false statements, 154

Variety, 21
Verbs
  forms of, 96–101, 147
  tenses, 148–49
Visual aids, 12–18, 29, 115, 150
Vocabulary, teaching of, 113–33, 139, 210–11
  See also Inference; Lists; Retention
Vowels, unstressed, 63

Wall charts, 13, 59, 77, 83, 88, 91, 94, 99, 100, 106, 143, 144, 175–76, 181, 225–26, 252–53
Word families, 127–31
Word order, 107–08
Writing
  teaching of, 216–41
  paragraphs, 235–36
  See also Letter writing; Compositions
Written exercises, 86–87, 204–05, 216–41